GEORGE WASHINGTON WRITTEN UPON THE LAND

GEORGE WASHINGTON WRITTEN UPON THE LAND

Nature, Memory, Myth, & Landscape

PHILIP LEVY

WEST VIRGINIA UNIVERSITY PRESS

MORGANTOWN · 2015

Copyright 2015 West Virginia University Press
All rights reserved
First edition published 2015 by West Virginia University Press
Printed in the United States of America

23 22 21 20 19 18 17 16 15   1 2 3 4 5 6 7 8 9

ISBN:

cloth   978-1-940425-89-4
paper   978-1-940425-90-0
epub   978-1-940425-91-7
pdf   978-1-940425-92-4

Library of Congress Cataloging-in-Publication Data is available at
the Library of Congress.

Cover design by Than Saffel
Book design by Concord Editorial

For Rik
1958–2014

CONTENTS

ACKNOWLEDGMENTS

The work supporting this book has taken more than a decade and relied on the aid of many people. The list of those to whom I owe a debt of gratitude includes almost two hundred University of South Florida Ferry Farm Historical Archaeological Field School students, field interns, and volunteers who toiled at Ferry Farm over the years, whose ranks include James Trueman, Brad Jackson, Giselle Portuondo, Jean Louise Lammie, Jarred Wilson, Nunzio Carrubba, Neel Amin, Justin Castells, Jackie Barber, and Rebekah Eaton. Very special thanks also to Michelle Davison, Mechelle Morgan, and Meredith Kambic. Alena Pirok and Jill Ficarotta both have served as invaluable research assistants on this and other projects; things would grind to a halt without them, and I suspect they know that all too well. Special thanks as well to Susan Knick from the University of Mary Washington. I owe a great debt of gratitude to the staff and volunteers at Ferry Farm and the George Washington Foundation, including Kate Ruedrich Jackson, Paul Nasca, Laura Galke, Mara Kaktins, Melanie Marquis, Dale Brown, Travis Walker, Judy Jobrack, and Alma Withers. William Garner, president of the George Washington Foundation, has always been an unfailing supporter of Ferry Farm research, and he and his staff have facilitated and funded so much great work. Thanks also to Douglas Bradburn and the Fred W. Smith Library at George Washington's Mount Vernon, the Virginia Foundation for the Humanities, the National Geographic Society, the Society of the Cincinnati, the Mary Morton Parson's Foundation, and the Dominion Foundation, who have also supported my work. Thanks as well to the National Park Service and to Lucy Lawliss, Rijk Morawe, John Storke, and Logan Metesh.

A very special thanks to Derek Krissoff, who has carried a book many more miles than most editors usually do. Thanks as well to all at West Virginia University Press.

I also wish to thank a long list of people who have been of great assistance, been great friends, or been great inspirations. Thanks to William Freehling, Ann Spencer, Nancy Damon, Clint Schemmer, Holly Schemmer, Rachel Sussman, all my students, friends, and colleagues at the University of South Florida, all the faculty members of USF's Department of History, Fraser Ottanelli, Giovanna Benadusi, William Murray, Bob Ingalls, Jennifer Dukes Knight, Connie Bryan, Tami Davis, Theresa Lewis, John Lennon, Chaim Noy, Elizabeth Bird, Barbara Lewis, Gavin Benke, Drew Smith, Dwayne Smith, Anne Koenig, Judy Genshaft, and Ralph Wilcox, who has been an especially supportive advocate for and sometime visitor to Ferry Farm. Thanks as well to Daniel Ingram, Anthony DeStefanis, John C. Coombs, Elizabeth Kelly Gray, Jon Kukla, James L. Axtell, Daniel Peck, Warren Billings, Gretchen Adams, Ari Kelman, Larry Cebula, Nicola Whyte, Mark Levene, Rebecca Conard, Philip Scarpino, Carolyn Eastman, Susan Boettcher, Paula Raudenbush, Carol Underhill, Mark Wenger, Dennis Pogue, Esther White, Julia King, Barbara Little, Martha Zierden, Mary Beaudry, Marley R. Brown III, Ann Yentsch, Douglas Owsley, Eric Gable, Alan Outlaw, Greg LeMond, Robert Blair St George, Bill Dudley, Phill Solo, Sarah Anne Bachman, Rabbi Uriel Rivkin, Rabbi Lazar Rivkin, Rabbi Menachem Mendel Schneerson, Rabbi Asher Ehrenpries, Rabbi Ed Rosenthaul, Rabbi Richard J. Birnholz, Rabbi Shmuel Reich, Rebbitzen D'vorki Rivkin, Yosi Appel, Yakov Kuzmenok, Aaron Berger, and everyone at Young Israel of Tampa.

I also want to thank my parents, my siblings and their spouses, and all the members of my wife's family. Of course, I feel endless gratitude to Sarah and Rami, my ever-stalwart companions in all adventures, and to Dave and Amy, who are, simply put, the coolest.

"THE MOST STORIED GROUND IN AMERICA"

An Introduction[1]

Sometime in the early 1740s, the Washington family was living on a small, charming farm along a sleepy river. There, the family's third son, George, was able to experience nature firsthand while his loving and careful parents led him "along the paths of virtue."[2]

One day his father, Augustine, concocted a clever plan to teach a fundamental spiritual lesson to his little charge. Without George knowing it, Augustine scratched the little boy's name "in full large letters" into a patch of "finely pulverized" ground near the planting beds and the "gooseberry walk."[3] Then, he took a handful of cabbage seeds and laid them out in the pattern, and having finished that, "smoothed it all over nicely" with the garden roller. Augustine knew that the berry bushes, all "well hung with ripe fruit," would be too tempting a destination for George to avoid for long. Thus, it was only a matter of time before his little trick yielded fruit of its own.

"Not many mornings passed" before young George came running up to his father with his "eyes wild rolling" and his "little cheeks ready to burst with the *great news.*" "O Pa!" cried the boy, "come here! come here!" Feigning ignorance of his son's concern, Augustine asked what was the matter. George implored his father to accompany him so that George could show him what he claimed was "such a sight as you never saw in all your life time." The two proceeded out to the garden, with the eager child pulling at his father's hand. Once they got to the plot, they beheld there growing, "in all the freshness of newly sprung plants," green letters that spelled out G-E-O-R-G-E-W-A-S-H-I-N-G-T-O-N. George was stunned. "Did you ever see anybody's name in a plant bed before?" he asked in astonishment. Still playing it coy, Augustine suggested that perhaps such a thing could happen. But George went on—he had never seen a plant make a single letter before, let alone spell out a whole name or two—and to have his own name spelled "so exactly," and in verdant letters so even "top to bottom," was nothing short of a miracle to the young farm boy. Such a thing could not have happened by accident, George protested; "indeed, *somebody* did it" he said, beginning to fill in the gaps—"Pa, *you* did do it just to scare me, because I am your little boy."

With the cat now out of the bag, Augustine confessed his little trick and revealed the reason for the whole enterprise. "I indeed *did* it," he revealed, not to scare his little son, but rather to "introduce you to your *true* Father," God in heaven—the real author of all the wonders around them. The trick was to show George that each and every one of the "millions and millions of things" in the world was, likewise, not a result of an accident. Augustine urged his son to see the hand of the true author in all the works of creation. All the "thousands of sweet fruits" on the trees, all the "beautiful silver fishes" in the river, and all the "beautiful horses for him to ride" were all the work of one heavenly creator; moreover, they were all made for him. As the lesson sank in, the little boy fell into a "profound silence" as his "youthful soul was laboring with some idea never felt before." At that moment, "the Spirit of God ingrafted on his heart that germ of *piety*," which filled the rest of Washington's life with "so many precious fruits of *morality*."[4]

It will come as a surprise to few readers that this story came from the pen of Mason Locke "Parson" Weems, the Early National–era writer and book peddler who created the most ridiculed—and yet the most enduring—single moment in the Washington story.

In that tale, a young Washington takes an axe to his father's favorite English cherry tree and does so much damage to it that he has probably killed it. When confronted by a father angered by the vandalism, the prematurely wise little boy screws up his courage and confesses his misdeed, saying, "I can't tell a lie Pa, you know I cannot tell a lie. I did cut it with my hatchet." The result of this confession is ecstatic joy from his proud father. The story taught many lessons. It was, of course, a parable about telling the truth in all matters, but it also served as a rebuke to parents who used physical violence against their children; Augustine tells George that he need not fear the use of the rod—honesty would be its own shield.

Centuries of authors have picked up on the Cherry Tree story and gave it a life its own, and artists made it their subject as well. The image of the young boy and the hatchet worked its way into American culture, both high and kitsch, and through countless re-tellings has become an enduring and recurring piece of Americana. From February car sales to political cartoonists' handwork, Weems's most famous invention is alive and well, even if the original tree did not survive its fabled ordeal.[5]

The Cabbage Seed story, though, has been even more forgotten than the full version of the Cherry Tree story. In their day, the cabbages that spelled "Washington" were almost as well known a growth as their fruit-bearing neighbor in the Washington garden. On top of that, the spelling seeds peddled a moral lesson perhaps more profound than the value of honesty related through the Cherry Tree story. Indeed, in Weems's story Augustine set up his deception only after George had wantonly chopped at the tree. The whole trick of the Cabbage Seeds was meant as a follow-up lesson to the tree incident. Although long overshadowed by their storyline precursor, it was the cabbages that delivered the big spiritual punch—to wit, that the world itself exists for the benefit of its inhabitants, and a pious person sees God in all things. As the

Psalm says, "The earth is the Lord's, and the fullness thereof; the world, and they that dwell therein."[6] Weems used the cherry tree's vandalism as setup to teach his readers a fundamental religious environmental lesson from the Book of Deuteronomy, that if we respect God and treat the land well, the land and God will reward us. The cherry tree thus represented brash and unthinking action, whereas the cabbage seeds and the teaching moment they engendered represented the careful hand of the good steward.

I begin this book with these stories for a very specific set of reasons. They have to do with the main strands I will bring together: Washington, memory, landscape, storytelling, and human impact on the planet.

First, these are stories about George Washington—and certainly, in the case of the Cherry Tree, perhaps *the* most famous story in which he is a character. We need not devote too many words to recalling that Washington is one of the central figures in the history of the republic he helped found. His name and image are everywhere in this land, his biography is a perennial American literary genre, he is invoked in almost any discussion of civic matters, and having the man on your side in any political battle is to be on the side of the angels. To paraphrase one of his early biographers, talking about Washington is in some way talking about America. This book focuses on one small selection of the ways generations of Americans have spoken about Washington, focusing on his poorly documented and heavily mythologized childhood years. With both the Cherry Tree and the Cabbage Seed stories, Weems was helping to set in motion themes of childhood that would flow in one way or another through the entire corpus of Washington biography.

Another reason for opening with these anecdotes is that the imagined Cherry Tree and the Cabbage Seeds of Washington's childhood both grew in a specific place. Even if the tales themselves were inventions (as they most certainly were), Weems nevertheless set them in an actual place. That land, known since the nineteenth century as Ferry Farm, sits on the Rappahannock River, opposite the town of Fredericksburg, Virginia. It is a very real place with a very real history. Stories like Weems's have been at the center of how this land has taken on meaning over the centuries. Even though that place retained its actual Washington connection, much of the connection was filtered through Weems. Washington left Ferry Farm in the early 1750s and sold it off by 1774.[7] He took up permanent residence at Mount Vernon, the place that was forever after synonymous with the phrase "Washington's home." But Washington's leaving Ferry Farm as early as he did and his 1770s sale had a dramatic effect on the farm's narrative. Of Washington's three Virginia homes—his Pope's Creek birthplace, Ferry Farm, and Mount Vernon—the Rappahannock estate was the only one to have left Washington family ownership well before George became The Great Washington. This created something of a vacuum around the landscape's story, a vacuum filled primarily by Weems's Washington.

The most famous of Washington's three Virginia addresses was his beloved Mount Vernon, the home he took over after his brother Lawrence's 1752 death. Mount Vernon was the canvas on which he crafted his vision of genteel republican living; it was the place to which he retired late in life and died, and it was where he was buried in 1799.[8] His wife, Martha, lived at Mount Vernon for another three years, but after her death the estate stayed in Washington hands until John A. Washington Jr. sold it to the Mount Vernon Ladies' Association in 1858.[9] Since that time, Mount Vernon has been a shrine to the man interpreters call "The General." The transfer of ownership came complete with a fully crafted place-based narrative, the echoes of which are still audible in the house tours that are offered daily.

Washington's Pope's Creek birthplace, or Wakefield, as it was sometimes later called, has a similar story, albeit at a lower profile.

Although its Washington-era home was gone by 1810, the land stayed in the family long enough to see the beginning of its own long cycle of commemoration. Martha Washington's grandson, George Washington Parke Custis, took the lead in 1815 by erecting a small marker to commemorate where his famous step-grandfather drew his first breath. But farmers' plows eventually led to the original stone shifting over the land and finally disappearing altogether. Over time, disagreement about the exact location of the original stone (and therefore the house itself) created partisans for different locations in a dispute that never really ended.[10] A pre–Civil War attempt to buy the land and commemorate Washington on the site faltered, but by the 1880s things were back on track, leaving backers to battle over where, first, a monument, then a fancifully reconstructed house, should sit. But controversy over the rebuilt home's shape and location never really ended, and the result was that the National Park Service now oversees a complicated and contradictory commemorative landscape.[11] Wakefield's Washington home discussion may have been flawed, but it was nevertheless rooted in the actions of Washington descendants and set in motion at the height of Washington veneration.

American's interest in a unique American past emerged with increasing force with the passing of the Revolutionary generation, a shift symbolized by the deaths of Jefferson and Adams, both on July 4, 1826.[12] That Mount Vernon stayed linked to Washington and Washingtons until Americans were more ready to see such places as worthy of some special attention allowed a sort of sifting and shaping of site stories as these places moved from being private land to more national possessions. Family ownership ensured a sort of site integrity—both of stories and of the land and its features—into the years when Washington became a household name the world over and Americans were more willing to appreciate that.[13]

Not so Ferry Farm, though.[14] As Americans were discovering a Revolutionary past and planting the seeds of American history in the late 1820s, Washington's childhood home had nothing left on its fields to hark back to the days when he and his family called the place home. It was Weems and his stories of place that made the landscape's historical narrative spine.

These stories call attention to the act of writing and the acts of memory and storytelling that are all bundled together on both Ferry Farm and the Washington childhood. Augustine's cabbage seeds were fiction, but they were, in their way, heralds of future writing. Some of that writing came in the form of volumes of Washington biographies. Washington's life has proven to be a fertile seedbed for writers of all stripes; in fact, a quick search of online library catalogues lists 21,816 books with "George Washington" in their titles and 88,124 with his name as a key phrase. This is a remarkable body of writing, and much of it spins more or less the same stories, told and retold. Storytellers have been writing down their versions of Washington's life since just before it was over. Their work rests on two basic pillars, one being the surviving documentation of the man's life and the other being some mix of recycled elements of other biographies. But Weems's stories of trees and cabbages highlight something special about the childhood phase of that life: that Americans have wanted to know about it and that there was very little information from which to reconstruct it.

The lack of documentary material about Washington's childhood years—and the silences that the lack has produced—is renowned.[15] But rather than being a lamentation, this book is a celebration of the creative processes and the varied kinds of historical meaning that this lucky accident has called into being. This dilemma has made Washington's earliest years the most fiction-ridden part of his biographical writing. The gaps and silences have allowed Washington's childhood to become a wonderful area for historical invention and authorial projection. Its characters and its central location—Ferry Farm—have become canvases on which generations of meaning makers have portrayed a host of fantasies and wishful thoughts.

Here, again, Weems has had an outsized influence. His Cherry Tree is only the most famous in a long line of inventions that include one-eyed, one-legged schoolmasters; horses ridden to death; alternating weepingly pious or terrifying and illiterate mothers; relatives wealthy, poor, well meaning, and just mean; adventures taken and missed; moral lessons, ranging from abolitionism to anti–child beating; and time spent in diligent study or squandered in pointless play. Much of this invention took place on a landscape that has ranged from being a verdant idyll—a near-perfect place where the ripe fruit fairly fell from the trees and the fish all but leapt onto the plate—to being a barren, hardscrabble, worn-out make-do. The sheer range of possibilities and outcomes was itself a direct growth of the relative silence from the years between 1732 through Washington's family's 1738 move to Ferry Farm, until the time he fully took up a career in surveying at the end of 1740s and shifted from being a child to being a more documentable adult.

This book looks at those years in detail—something very few earlier works have done. But my goal is not to sort out the fiction from the fact and end debates once and for all. Nor will I offer a comprehensive narrative of an eighteenth-century childhood. Instead, through a series of thematic but nevertheless linked chapters this book weighs a variety of versions of the Washington childhood story and explores their content and their effects—particularly as they relate to Ferry Farm, a place I have spent more than a decade excavating, researching, and considering. There have been many narratives of the childhood years, and not all of them have taken the form of biography. The Cabbage Seeds inspired (or perhaps enabled) a variety of discussions that range from the historical to

the folkloric and flow through historiography, historical preservation, and other routes.

What follows is partly a memory study, in that it is very much
about how Americans have used and fought over images, narratives,
and valuations of Washington's childhood in creating their own
historical meanings.[16] Washington is a large enough character that
the study of his memory constitutes a small subfield in its own right.
Michael Kammen has produced some of the most enduring work
on the memory of the Revolution and its characters and documents,
but some scholars have extracted Washington and charted out how,
in his story and image, something unique took shape.[17] In the years
between the 1976 Bicentennial celebrations and the somewhat less
ballyhooed Constitutional Bicentennial, sociologist Barry Schwartz
referred to Washington as having been transformed into a "tribal
totem," by which he meant a sort of religious figure on whom the
hopes and aspirations of a nation could rest.[18] For Schwartz, the
various ceremonies and celebrations in the decades just before and
just after Washington's death turned the man into "an object of
emotional attachment and an exemplification of moral values."[19]
During this process, people who knew—or at least knew of—a
living Washington deified the man, in a manner not dissimilar to
the way pharaohs and kings became gods in times when the line
between religion and politics was nonexistent.

Schwartz never hid the religious nature of this transformation
and used well-chosen, freighted words—like "observances" and
"rites"—for people's practices while dividing his book into sections of "adoration" and "revelation." François Furstenberg carried
the idea of religion and state veneration somewhat further, facing
squarely the questions of race and slavery that were not central to
Kammen and Schwartz's work. Here, it was the paternalism built
into the idea of Washington the Father that nineteenth-century
artists and writers were able to exploit to make Washington both

the center of the American family and the ever-caring slave owner.[20] Schwartz and Furstenberg not only explored the working of early United States political culture but also reinforced the idea that there is something unique and special in the Washington discussion itself.

Amid the same post-1976 kitsch and mini–colonial revival, Karal Ann Marling brought her eye for material culture and imagery to the arena of Washington memory. Where Schwartz saw the effects of religion, Marling saw a twentieth-century mass consumer culture as the driving force behind Washington image making. Her study of the great colonial revival of the 1890s through the 1930s mapped out the many ways that Washington's name and image were put to use by writers, artists, home decorators, and politicians. Her work is still a tour de force about the "mythmaking" that was driven by the power of trinkets, wall hangings, and a well-crafted political moment.[21] Edward Lengel, the editor of Washington's papers, has recently picked up on the same scent as Marling and crafted a small and engaging book that challenges readers to think carefully about exactly which Washington they find so useful so often.[22] Like Schwartz and Marling, Lengel conceptualized his project at a time when popular culture was alive with images of Washington and of living men dressed in blue coats and white wigs. The late 1970s images were content and paternal versions of Washington, smiling on his children and the products of the war he fought. The current Washingtons who appear at rallies and political campaign headquarters are full of anger, fear, and revolutionary rhetoric.[23] Like a chronological inversion of Skinny Elvis and Fat Elvis, these different decades' Washingtons were not the same man—not by a long shot. Yet they all were powerful reminders that Washington as an authority is relevant enough still to be worthy of invocation, and Washington as an image is elastic enough to sustain enlistment to a host of causes, no matter how contradictory. This accounts in part for his enduring utility and his appeal. Current scholars argue that much of that ambiguity was crafted intentionally by Washington himself, a fact that makes his elasticity all the more engaging. I think that this is the central message of the Washington memory scholarship, and my book makes a small contribution to that cause while trying to stretch that elastic a bit further.[24] Parts of this book—particularly those that deal with the extensive body of Washington biography—carry on the projects of Marling and Lengel. The main difference is that my topic is not Washington's entire life but rather the creation and effects of his childhood's richly embellished story.

Missing in all this work has been specific attention to Washington's childhood. Some of this absence is a legacy of the issues this book deals with—the fact that poor documentation and persistent folklore made the childhood a troublesome topic. Some of this gap is also due to the fact that Washington mattered most as an adult, not a child. The childhood years served mostly as a mishmash of precedents and imagined foreshadowing moments and thus became a subgenre in its own right within the corpus of Washington biography. Discussing the childhood years in anything more substantive than a short article entails doing more than biography and doing more than Washington-focused history. Washington's childhood story has usually been only partly about Washington in the first place.

But even this is not my main mission. I came to this work through landscape and excavation, so what follows is, significantly, a landscape study.[25] In a masterful, transdisciplinary essay on Washington memory, Schwartz walked readers through the process that he called the democratization of George Washington, following Washington's changes of image in the years after the Civil War.[26] Although the nation began with Washington's status at stratospheric levels, his administration ended—as did his life—with his reputation having declined. Shifts in national discussions and occasional rumors of his failing mental capacity left him an iconic figure but not much more. His 1799 death saw an outpouring of warmth, but by the 1830s—and particularly during the tenure of Andrew Jackson—Americans saw Washington as not speaking to their political or cultural realities. Sectional crisis and the Civil War occasioned a rebirth of Washington as a unifying image and figure, however, and there was a huge uptick in writing about the man and his life. Schwartz was concerned about how much all this writing and art actually reflected what the American people at large thought about Washington.[27] Unlike Schwartz, though, I am not overly concerned about this matter. The writing created narratives and images in and of themselves, and my interest is to better understand not the common mind writ large but rather how Ferry Farm's landscape took meaning. From this I think we can glean larger lessons about the function of landscapes, the uses of memory, and the meanings of Washington. This book stems essentially from one question that I have been considering ever since I realized there was no escaping Weems at Ferry Farm: What does it mean for a real landscape to be defined by a fictional story? In some epochs, Ferry Farm has been given national relevance, and in other times it has wallowed in exclusively local realities. But in all those moments, it has been intimately tied to Weems's stories and the Washington and Ferry Farm he created.

Finally, all this work also relies heavily on historical archaeology, which has shown itself to be a flexible and creative way to talk about the intersection of places, the past, and the people who inhabited both.[28]

At the center of all these narratives are a few scraps of fact and well-informed conjecture about what went on in Washington's life before he stepped onto the global stage in the 1750s and pens began to bend their nibs to his story. What we have always known is slim pickings, indeed. He was born in Westmoreland County,

Virginia, on February 11, 1732 (old date), on the Potomac River estate that had been in his family since the 1650s. His father, Augustine, was a well-off member of the colonial gentry but in a part of the colony not favored with the best tobacco lands. Consequently, the Washingtons were provincial local elites living at the edges of the better locations. Augustine's first wife, Jane Butler, had given him two surviving sons, and soon after her death he married Mary Ball, then a colleague's ward. With her, he had six children, one of whom—a daughter—died in infancy. George was the first child of this union.

Augustine had a typically diversified business portfolio, with interests in land speculation, farming, and iron mines. This last project was somewhat unusual in the colony but was part of small mining boom taking place at the falls of the Rappahannock in the 1720s. Around 1736, he moved Mary and their children to a property he owned up the Potomac, a place called Little Hunting Creek, later renamed Mount Vernon. By 1738 he had moved the family once again, this time to a property he'd bought from a member of the House of Burgesses, William Strother. Here, a wood-framed home sat on a bluff and before a sloping rise of land, on the narrow upper reaches of the Rappahannock. The site was opposite the newly chartered city of Fredericksburg. Trade towns like this were thin on the ground in a colony where the solitary plantation was the main form of settlement. Nevertheless, Augustine took an active interest in Fredericksburg and owned in-town parcels. The new family home also positioned him close to the iron operation he owned with Maryland's Principio mining company at Accokeek in Stafford County.

As a boy, Washington grew up in a home that was at once rural and urban. Like any farm, it was made up of fields, fences, livestock, outbuildings, and all the common appurtenances of any elite Virginia plantation. This included a large number of enslaved

Africans, who lived in and around the home and on the outlying quarters. But at the same time, few plantations had a city on their doorstep, even one as modest as 1730s Fredericksburg. In addition, the main road down the Northern Neck peninsula ran near the home, as did the lane that led down to the ferry crossing on the floodplain. It was from this crossing that the land later took its most enduring name: Ferry Farm. This made Ferry Farm at once typical and utterly unique—given to the slow flows of farm life but also cheek by jowl with the noise and activity of city and trade life.

The 1740s began with the death of Washington's youngest sister Mildred, a fire in the family's home, and then—worst of all—Augustine's death. His estate, a large amount of property all detailed and distributed in a long and specific will, devolved to his sons. The two eldest from his first marriage, Austin and Lawrence, took possession of the Westmoreland lands and Little Hunting Creek, respectively. Next in line was George, who received Ferry Farm, the Fredericksburg lots, and some other lands, as well as nearly a dozen enslaved Africans. Because he was only eleven years old, all of this property was managed by Mary until George came to maturity. Nevertheless, ledger records show that George was actively managing some of his finances before his legal maturity.

Augustine's death was the beginning of hard times at Ferry Farm. If there was a plan to send George to England for schooling, it died with his father. On top of that, some unclear mixture of Mary's management, local economics, and the rules and division of the estates deprived the family of wealth and resources. Although they maintained their gentry lifestyle and sold off almost none of the family core holdings, they did so more with creativity than simple buying power.

During those years, George appears to have moved around between his mother's home at Ferry Farm and the homes of his older brothers, Lawrence and Austin. What schooling he received occurred here and there, and his social network would have been mostly his extended family. Of the adults in his world, Lawrence had the best connections and offered the best access to gentry circles. An active land speculator, officer in the colonial forces in the War of Jenkins's Ear, engaged in local governance, and married into the wealthy and influential Fairfax family, Lawrence was the Washington best able to stage-manage George's young adulthood. He first manifested that ability with a curious plan to send George to sea, in a man-of-war or perhaps on a commercial vessel. The plan made its rounds, but eventually Mary's opposition, bolstered by convincing arguments from her brother Joseph in London, put an end to the idea.

But the next plan took root more effectively. The Fairfaxes and Lawrence were deeply invested in Western lands. Washington took up the chain and compass and become a surveyor, a choice that made him useful to his patrons' enterprises while also positioning him to rapidly become personally wealthy. Before he was twenty, Washington had built a fortune larger than the value of the lands left him by his father. Surveying Western lands made him rich, and it also positioned him well within the gentry network surrounding the Fairfaxes. By his twenty-second birthday, Washington had become an adult with his own lands and wealth, living in the Mount Vernon estate he bought after Lawrence's 1752 death. For all intents and purposes, he was also done with Ferry Farm, which continued to be his mother's home for another twenty years.

It is a simple story as I have told it here, but most biographers do not have much more to offer. In recent years, Jack Warren stretched that story out to a full article by exploring each corner of the tale and carefully reading documents, as well as offering a few new additions—such as a new take on the house fire story—while contextualizing all along the way.[29] Jessica Brunelle padded her fine entry in the *Companion to George Washington* with as much detail as was available for all the supporting characters in the story, a frequently used and time-honored tactic in the literature. Even so, Brunelle opened with the common refrain that we "do not know much about the young George Washington."[30] The most popular of the recent Washington biographies, the one written by Ron Chernow, differs little from Brunelle's story—indeed, most of the more "serious" biographers over the past few decades have taken the same path. Chernow is more comfortable indulging in some of the more delightfully speculative questions of character and family love, but apart from that, the stories are all more or less the same.

We may not know that much about "the young George Washington," but we know a lot about "Young George," if we consider the latter a character emerging from large body of writing about the former. It is true that this character often does not bear much resemblance to the actual progenitor—or at least we don't currently think he does. But Young George's influence over the minds of so many ages of Americans is significant enough for us to not lose too much sleep over his supposed realness. Brunelle was wrong on a second score, too (although her essay is, overall, quite good), in her claim that a century of Washington historians have "ignored" Weems. Far from ignoring him, most biographers have actively and consciously fled from him—often taking a few credibility-establishing potshots at the hated minister—before moving on to embrace Weems's own project: that of showing the real Washington. The reigning consensus on Weems has been perfectly summed up by Edward Lengel, who describes the Parson has having created "some of the most beloved lies of American history," producing work notable for its "almost complete lack of evidence," and writing a book full of "fables," most of which "Weems invented," the most famous being "the cherry tree myth."[31] Lengel held off on the more personal invective. For example, he did not deride Weems for his business duplicity, lowbrow pandering, lying about his credentials, and even stealing his material—all accusations that were leveled at Weems over the last century. For most biographers, Weems was the antischolar who nevertheless still held influence over his topic and the audience. Each new author attempted to seduce readers away from Weemsian fables with the promise of trustworthy research. That project has been ongoing for more than two centuries, and yet the little boy and the hatchet is still one of the most recognizable and influential images in American culture.

It seems Weems is not that easy to shake off. His victory lies not so much in being the reigning biographer on record but in being the most enduring. And when it comes to discussing Washington's childhood, there is no escaping the Parson—indeed, even trying to escape him is a small win for his side. That is doubly true for Ferry Farm, where his shadow is at least as large as Washington's.

Understanding this landscape and how history has been made there requires not a rejection of Weems but rather an embracing of both his work and the fictive processes he unleashed there. As a landscape, Ferry Farm has its own biography.[32] The land was first surveyed and patented by Tidewater planter John Catlett in 1660. Although Catlett never made the land his home (it was never more than an investment property), by 1705 its first English resident had settled there, a recently freed servant named Maurice Clark. By the 1720s, the land was owned by William Strother, who built the wood-framed gentry home that Augustine Washington purchased in 1738. The core property stayed in the Washington family until 1773, when Washington completed moving his mother, Mary, off the land and sold it to his friend and Fredericksburg neighbor Hugh Mercer. The new owner planned to lay out a new town on the land—not too dissimilar from the one called Falmouth, nearer the Falls of the Rappahannock. But his death in the Revolutionary War ended that plan, and instead the farm became absorbed into the holdings of other families on the north side of the river.

As the decades progressed, the old home gradually lost its grandeur, as newer gentry homes went up in grander style and age took a toll on its walls, roof, and cellars. What was impressive enough in the 1720s looked smaller and older with each new fashionable home build along the river and in town. By the end of the eighteenth century it was weathered, worn, and close to abandonment. By the 1830s, when the nation was celebrating the centennial of Washington's birth, a painter rendered on canvas the last white stones of a Washington home that had melted back into the land. By that time, the acres were little more than cornfields for a pair of Northern-born landowners who were as much interested in the land's speculative value as they were in its crop capacity.

Ferry Farm might have stayed a simple, rural place with some history had it not been for the Civil War and the arrival of combatants at the opposing edges of Fredericksburg. In the summer of 1862, the land was the staging ground for the Union occupation of the city, and later that year it hosted some of the cannons that shelled the hapless town to bits. For the next two years, the armies came and went with each new campaigning season, and as they did, they gradually cut down every remaining tree and pulled down each surviving building. By the time the war ended, the land and much of the surrounding county were in ruins.

Over the years, some recalled the land's most famous son and his relationship with the place, but not many. But at the beginning of the twentieth century a new landowner began to exploit the land's historical lineage. The culmination of that exploitation was a plan to sell the farm—by then covered with contemporary buildings and one post–Civil War office, mistakenly imagined to be a Washington survival—for a princely sum, to a preservation group that would memorialize it as a shrine to the Great Washington. His plan eventually failed, but the idea of the land being historical stuck. Over the next few decades a variety of groups, both local and national, picked up the banner of preservation and made their best efforts. There were modest attempts, like the group of backers who raised funds to dedicate a plaque marking the imagined site of the original Cherry Tree. There were more ambitious plans as well; for example, a group of Seventh-Day Adventist ministers and educators purchased the land in order to remake it into a home for troubled youth. They imagined that living on the land where Washington had come of age would in and of itself have a curing and morally elevating effect. Their plan got further than many others, but in the end all that was left of it was the multiroom dormitory they had built and the vast field they had sold as a quarry to pay for it.

By the 1990s, there were well-established, competing interests for the land, which continued to change hands as ever before. On one hand, the absentee owners wanted to have it rezoned for commercial use so that it could yield its maximum price. Others still held onto the dream of it becoming a preserved site. Stafford County government had control of the area where the Washington home once stood, but funds to do more than keep the land in mothballs were always scarce. The county asked a former Republican staffer, radio disc jockey, and self-promoter named Robert Siegrist to manage the land and find the funds to cover the maintenance costs. Despite some creative fundraising efforts and his own brand of Weemsian mythmaking, Siegrist failed and historical preservation of the site hung by a slender thread. The issue came to a head in 1996, when Walmart announced plans to acquire the old "quarry" and build a vast shopping plaza there. Although the old Washington home lot was nominally not included in the area to be paved over, it was clear that the venture would so radically change the area that any sense of history would be lost amid the glow of parking lot lights and the sound and smell of trash dumpsters. The result was a locally led but nationally visible movement to save the land from development.

That effort succeeded where no other could, and soon a newly created preservation entity, now called the George Washington Foundation, had control over the land and began an ambitious project of archaeological excavation and museum building.

Visitors to Ferry Farm today can see the site (if they come during digging season), they can look into the archaeology lab, and they can use an iPad-based audiovisual tour to see the acre's sites. Soon, they will be able to walk through a rebuilt Washington home, a three-dimensional architectural presentation of the best analyses of archaeology and architectural history. Much of the tumult of Ferry Farm's history is now in its past as it settles into a comfortable distinguished life as a historical site—and a Washington site at that. But its story is still a complicated and tangled object bringing together many strands. Some have more to do with Washington than others, but all are linked in one way or another to the man whose name still overshadows the land.

This book uses Ferry Farm and its stories to look at Washington's childhood and its effect on the land itself. Less a single narrative of place or experience, the chapters that follow are rather interconnected essays that each tease out a different set of connections between Washington's childhood and how it, its memory, and its retellings have shaped Ferry Farm. My goal is to explore Washington's childhood stories to see what they have been and what they can be. As long as we revere Washington in our civic culture, we will be stuck with the uncertainties and ambiguities of his childhood story. These have produced a special species of American imagination and the least-documented section of one the nation's most told biographies, and the following chapters cast light on their meanings.

My six chapters can be divided into two parts. The first three chapters deal with ways people have understood Washington's childhood and Ferry Farm as history. Each of the many narratives in these chapters tries to dig into the past to explain Washington, his childhood, and its places. The second three look at narratives resting on what we might consider less biographical footing. Call it fabulism, memory, folklore, or what you will, but the Washington childhood narratives I explore in this second half draw on different streams than the sources that bolster the first half.

The first chapter is an exploration of the Washington biographical literature. I made an extensive study of more than one hundred fifty such biographies to tease out how the narrative of Washington's childhood took form over years of telling and retelling. As everyone who has ever taken on the topic has noted, documentation for the earliest phase of Washington's life is singularly thin. The combination of the desire to know and barriers to that knowledge turned the childhood years into a unique part of the Washington biography. Weems was only the most famous inventor in this small subgenre, and he does get credit for being the first (nevertheless, I largely pass him over in this effort and hold him in reserve for his own study). But Weems was far from alone. The chapter winds through much of the biography and organizes the results into the main themes that emerged: ancestry, the self-made-man narrative, and family relations. These themes interrelate and self-perpetuate, but they also set the stage for how we understand Washington's childhood and what are the canonical questions to ask.

The next chapter looks at how Washington himself wrote about his childhood and the place where most of it happened. As I indicated, the short answer to the question of what Washington wrote about his early life is, "not all that much." But he did produce a singularly interesting survey of Ferry Farm in 1771, on the eve of selling off the land and moving his mother, Mary, into the town across the river. I explore the circumstance surrounding this document, its slight appearance in the historiography, and the ideas it hides. I see this survey as being a personal narrative of place that Washington fashioned for himself alone. There is enormous resonance in a survey drafted by a master surveyor of the place where he spent his childhood.

The third chapter outlines the narratives of place and childhood created by a over a dozen years of excavation on the Washington home lot. This work, with its unique approach, segues with the biographies, to some extent, but is not their handmaiden. Many canonical questions arise from more than two centuries of Washington biographies, but as I argue, many of these are simply not ones that excavation will address. Instead, there are new ones it can take on. One shared theme is what I call the Hard 1740s—the longstanding premise that the years after Augustine Washington's death were a time of privation in the Washington home. Archaeology offers some distinct perspectives on the Hard 1740s, ones that disrupt other parts of the larger biographical narrative.

The next chapter centers on Mason Locke Weems and the imagined landscape his writing helped create. Weems invented the stories that most defined Ferry Farm and came to symbolize Washington's childhood, and his work is of enduring influence for both man and place. The Cherry Tree is his most famous creation, but this chapter looks not only at the tree but also at how Weems envisioned Ferry Farm as an Edenic American paradise. But just when the Cherry Tree was becoming the most resonant aspect of this landscape—eclipsing Washington, in fact—the land itself was being ravaged both by war and by the market. The place most famous for one fictional tree was in the process of losing most of its real ones.

In Chapter 5 I examine the curious story of how one of Ferry Farm's buildings became "historical," through the same processes of storytelling that made the Cherry Tree a fable. That building was an 1870s farm office that was part of the landscape's return to agricultural normality, in the years after the Civil War left Ferry Farm something of a ruin. By the beginning of the twentieth century, this building was being called George Washington's Surveying Office, a designation that gave it Washington provenance while tying it to one of the most significant events in Young Washington's life: his surveying career. That designation was a heavily freighted and singularly creative invention that brought together the impulses behind the more famous Cherry Tree story but landed on a more historically plausible subject.

The final chapter picks up on the long-overlooked, biblically informed environmental themes in Weems's tree and seeds. I look at the implication of trees, the land, historical preservation, and museums in the context of a changed global climate. Historians and other humanities scholars have begun to become aware of climate change as less of a problem to solve and more of a reality to which to adjust. In this last chapter, I look at the role of Washington memory and storytelling in confronting the reality that we live in a new climate age, the Anthropocene, the era in which human actions have become like a geological force in changing the planetary conditions for life. Historians are just beginning to understand the human-generated climate change and the challenges it presents to the humanities in reimagining life on Earth. Scholars have identified events in Washington's day as being central to bringing on the Anthropocene, and this chapter reexamines Washington's childhood story and Ferry Farm's many stories in light of this emerging concern. What does climate change mean for sites, historical stories, and how we might think of Washington and his Cherry Tree in different ways?

At Ferry Farm, the Rappahannock River met the long road that ran down the Northern Neck peninsula. On the floodplain beneath the Washington home was a ferry run that brought land travelers from one side to the other. By the 1850s, a new rail bridge just upriver from the ferry's run added the iron horse to the crossings. The meeting of roads and river brought people to the land for many reasons over the years. It brought commerce, war, industry, and tourism to what was otherwise a fairly ordinary plot of land. Travelers of river, road, and rail were the engines of the land's history. But paralleling the meeting of roads was a less tangible meeting of Washington, landscape, and storytelling. This nexus was the vehicle for crafting and recalling the many memories and histories of this place and the childhood it witnessed. What has made Ferry Farm unique is the singular meeting of place, people, and circumstances that give it voice while so many other places remain mute. It has been growing its Washington stories for some time and promises to continue into the future.

1

"SOMEWHERE THIS HAD BEGINNINGS"

Unspooling Washington's Childhood Biography

The babbling tales of old men, talking in the light
of greatness, are ever the flimsiest of legends.[1]

Worthington Chauncey Ford, 1910

There are two ways to get to Ferry Farm from the Fredericksburg side of the Rappahannock River. Both have travelers crossing modern bridges and funneling onto the state road system. In both cases, though, a driver is soon greeted by a large blue sign set up by Stafford County opposite the town. The sign proclaims that you have just entered George Washington's boyhood home, and it does so alongside an image of a colonial garment–clad youth running after a rolling hoop, the iconic image of eighteenth-century playtime.

The identification is fair enough, because this area was where Washington spent the bulk of his childhood. Ferry Farm is the centerpiece of that historical claim. In making their sign, the county chose the image of the little boy chasing the hoop to represent the Washington childhood, but in past years other images have served that role. In the 1960s, a large plywood sign with a hand-painted colonial-style child swinging an axe at a fruit-laden cherry tree advertised the site's George Washington pedigree to passersby. At other times, it was a lone building on the landscape—a holdover from the late nineteenth-century farmstead—that offered a precious link the great man who came of age here. Although the stories about this building and about cherry trees were almost always false, there has long been some sort of post facto marker on the land to signal that this is a place of national significance, the place where Washington came of age. Each of these signs, symbols, or buildings served as reference not only to Washington but to a specific phase of his life: his formative years. Throughout the large number of Washington biographies, the childhood years are the shortest and most problematic part of the story. Without a large body of documents or recorded memories to draw on, biographers found themselves relying on more fanciful stuff to fill in the years before Washington first walked onto the world stage and into the glare of documentation. But fill in they did, confident in the idea that there was something of special import in Washington's childhood.

Nineteenth-century writer, historian, and minister Jared Sparks penned his own version of Washington's life in the 1830s, so he knew the task quite well. Sparks laid out exactly what was at stake in any retelling of Washington's biography. He wrote, "To admit failings in him was therefore to attack the very fabric of America."[2]

It was perhaps Sparks's truest observation. Indeed, the role of Washington as "the embodiment of the nation" has made telling his life's story fraught with perils for those who take on the task. This deep national interest has also left the story filled with canonical moments, mandatory questions, entrenched shibboleths, received wisdoms, shoals of memory, large investments, and cherished ideas that all require careful navigation. Each new retelling of Washington's life is as much a study in how each author precariously balanced on the shoulders of previous giants (and dwarves) as it is a glimpse into Washington's time on Earth.

If Washington's story is also a sort of commentary on the nation, then retelling the childhood story is the most troublesome part of that project. If Washington is the father of his country, then his actions, choices, character, and path through life are all meaning-rich clues left for his national children, to ponder and decode for guidance, precedents, and wisdom. As one 1840s biographer cannily noted, the nation would do well "to recognize in the exalted character of its acknowledged Father, the elements of its greatness and strength."[3] In other words, in knowing what made Washington great, Americans learn what is great in themselves. To know the father is to know the child, or as one recurring phrase popular in the genre holds, "The child is the father of the man."[4]

James Flexner famously began his multivolume Washington biography by referencing Sigmund Freud's ideas of how a child's "infantile phantasies" effectively block out the truth of a father and "tolerate in him no vestige of human weakness and imperfection."[5] Flexner (with the aid of the good doctor), Sparks, and others were essentially all saying the same thing: Americans have created fake Washingtons to suit our psychological or patriotic needs; father, we have hardly known you. Yet at the same time, the need to know him has compelled every biographer who hoped to capture something real and meaningful. Indeed, as one English biographer of Washington acknowledged, "Few men are more worthy of study."[6] Or, as a rather more nationalistic American wrote when World War I began to unfold in Europe, an immigrant or native-born school child who is not familiar with Washington "clearly, is not prepared to be an American."[7] There is much at stake, then, in the *right* understanding of Washington.

So how much more vital is Washington's childhood? If he represents a nation's roots—its Moses, at least in the eyes of one writer—then his own roots gather a unique significance that often takes writers well beyond the conventional bounds of the knowable. Generations of authors have seen that Washington's background and upbringing offer a model for proper civic behavior, an understanding of the roots of the nation, and even help us locate ourselves in some great drama.

As a result, more than two centuries of biographers have transformed this short, information-poor but significance-rich section of Washington's story into a powerful national scripture.[8] A few things happened along the way that matter not only for how we understand Washington but for how his memory took shape on the land. One was that a few contrasting narratives came together in the childhood story to help set the larger biographical narrative in motion. Because Washington can be either a self-made man or a man of promise finding himself at the right place at the right time, setting the ball rolling in the right direction early on is crucial. The historical evidence for this phase of Washington's life is notoriously spotty, meaning this little body of writing has been prone to visible bouts of wishful thinking, canonical retellings, and long-lived canards. Even the best biographer becomes something of a Weemsian when it comes to the first twenty years of Washington's life.

Over time, though, a canonical version of Washington's childhood took form. It was made up of ideas and themes from many writers, but in time it became a species of subgenre. As such, it has funneled all biographers into the same channels and demanded that each weigh in on the same matters. Family background, parental and filial relationships, childhood education, physical health, and the roots of later greatness—no matter how speculative—have become the repeated central concerns, as each new volume riffs on received questions, debates, and narrative mileposts. Few—if any—books are without a mention of how Augustine's death deprived his third son of an English education or how George's use of the much beloved and fetishized manners manual, *Rules of Civility,* served as the root of his self-attained gentry graces. Likewise, certain exalted moments, such as the story of Washington nearly going to sea on a merchantman or frigate (versions vary) and the beginning of his surveying career, become staged set pieces. The influential people of his early life parade by in familiar succession, from father to mother to brother (almost always clearly marked as being a "half" brother), although the emphasis differed somewhat over time as biographers shifted from a maternal emphasis to the influence (real and imagined) of his brother Lawrence. Additionally, each of the three Washington Virginia homes became a symbol for one of three respective attributes of what the biographers assume to have been the core of Washington's makeup. Mount Vernon and Lawrence's influence signify gentility, Pope's Creek and the "Chotank" Washingtons signify education and deep family ties, and Ferry Farm has become a symbol of physicality and rustic hardiness, although it later became a physical surrogate for Mary Washington. The going assumption in the writing has been that Washington existed at the meeting point of all three places and their contributions.

My goal, therefore, is to dismantle this construction so that we can move on to narratives of Washington's childhood that are less in the thrall of these received forms. My objection to these tales is not that they are untrue—there is more than enough debunking in the Washington literature. Rather, even though the childhood biography carries much truth—or, at least, offers many reasonable readings of existing documents—the childhood narratives are often less about Washington than they are about locating him within a set of emerging middle-class values and virtues that were crystallizing in and around the writing of the first wave of biographies. Once that was done, the elements of that narrative solidified and became *the* childhood story, seemingly freed from the early biographers' motivations. The pieces of the childhood story became more and more entrenched, through retelling after retelling, until they became the only way to tell the story. As one early twentieth-century scribe confessed, "it is natural for the biographer to write his own character into the characterization of his subject." He meant it as an attack on Weems, who, being a "small prig," made Washington into one as well.[9] Really, though, he reminded us that biographies often are mirrors as much as they are windows.

In 1792 Washington received a letter from Sir Isaac Heard, then the "Garter Principal King of Arms"—essentially, the official genealogist serving the British peerage system. Sir Isaac was after information about Washington's ancestors; specifically, he wanted to know what he could learn about the president's lineage so that he could more effectively determine from which line of that family this most famous of (former) Britons descended.

Washington had to have been at least a little bit interested in the request, because he indulged the inquiry and even reached out to gain more information. But Washington biographers have long loved one line in what survives of the brief—and admittedly, quite odd and ironic—correspondence between this representative of the very core of British privilege and the man who humiliated it on the battlefield.

Washington wrote that his family background was "a subject to which I confess I have paid very little attention."[10] And if that wonderfully unpretentious, dutifully republican demure was not enough, the hero of the Revolution went on to lay it on a bit thicker. His life, "from an early period," had been far too "busy and active" to have allowed the leisure for "researches of this nature, even if my inclination or particular circumstances should have prompted the inquiry."[11] But there was more. The new United States (Washington informed Heard) had "no Office of Record" to preserve such "exact genealogical" information because there were "very few cases" in which a "recurrence to pedigree for any considerable distance back" has been needed "to establish such points as may frequently arise in older Countries."[12] In a comic book version of Washington's life, the artist would no doubt draw a big "Pow!" or "Biff!" at this point in the story.

But despite his admirable revolutionary sentiments, Washington was only half right. True, titles may not have been an issue in the new nation, but descent certainly was—and as the day dawned on a new nineteenth century, questions of descent and their racial implications would take on more and more weight, especially in Washington's native South. On top of that, the topic for which he had professed little interest would become crucial for writers trying to tell his story.[13]

The earliest biographers looked at the Washington family background much as Heard would have, to assess the line's connection to British history and to locate Washington in a stream of derring-do. Many also wanted to assure readers that the Washingtons' roots were deep in American soil. John Marshall, whose multivolume biography devoted a miniscule proportion of its bulk to the childhood, noted only that the English Washingtons had been a "very respectable family in the north of England" and that George was the great grandson of John Washington, whose station in the world Marshall elevated by mistakenly calling him a "gentleman."[14] Years later, David Ramsay wrote that Washington's ancestors "were among the first settlers of the oldest British colony in America" and repeated the elevation of John Washington's status to that of gentleman. Aaron Bancroft offered nothing more, writing only that the Washingtons were "a family of some distinction in north of England."[15] Even the inventive Weems kept his powder dry when it came to ancestry, noting only that Augustine Washington was "a Virginian" and that Augustine's grandfather "was an Englishman."[16] In Weems's hands, though, this sounded more like an apology than a claim to fame.

Jared Sparks devoted somewhat more page space to the English Washingtons than the other earlier major biographers. But even though he offered more detail, Sparks's concerns were no different from those of his predecessors. Sparks took an otherwise ordinary northern middling family and highlighted their line's highest risers as having been "scholars, divines, and lawyers, well known to their contemporaries," and some had received "the honors of knighthood."[17] He claimed Washingtons had been "persons of consideration, wealth, and influence," as well as being soldiers, such as Cavalier Sir Henry Washington, who was "renowned for his bravery."[18] This inclination toward influence and bravery made the ocean voyage in the family mettle and settled in Virginia as well. John Washington took "military command against the Indians" but also made himself a "successful" planter, a description that carried into the next two generations of biographies.[19] Sparks's genealogical work set the standard for the rest of the century as others cited his efforts in volume after volume.

A few years later, Washington Irving went even further than had Sparks and charted out a lineage of "ancient English stock" that extended back to the centuries before the Norman Conquest.[20] Irving walked readers though epochs of English history to show that at major turns, Washington's people were there, playing their roles. For much the rest of nineteenth century, this basic storyline made up the opening pages of biography upon biography.

For more than half a century, biographers emphasized that Washington came from a lineage that was accustomed to wealth, education, military service, and social influence. The family was free from the rather un-republican taint of title but instead produced ideal men of substance, and these traits made the trip over the Atlantic and took root in American soil. This was a vision of ancestry that was not far removed from the questions that initiated Sir Isaac Heard's inquires. As this generation of writers understood it, valor had roots, and those roots should be visible in the actions of ancestors. This was a question of lineage—of being in the right descent to receive the best family traits. All of this was its own challenge to the democratic logic taking fire in the republic from the 1830s on. Biographers used Washington's quiet greatness and background as a counterpoint to boatloads of new migrants and lines of new voters and in so doing helped establish Washington as something of a conservative icon.

But as the century moved on, the ancestry discussion moved from one of lineage toward a broader racial basis for Washington's inherited traits. The peerage approach to ancestry was a tool in the unequal distribution of wealth and power between people with essentially similar backgrounds. Past family deeds explained the privilege of some families and the denial of it to others. The early nineteenth-century biographers were satisfied with this approach. Going back a few limbs on the family tree was enough to establish that there was a family tradition of achievement. But increasingly, writers enlisted Washington's background in the broader project of explaining the successes and superiority of the white race as a whole as a basis for a different unequal distribution of power, privilege, and preferment. This shift also, ironically perhaps, made Washington's greatness rather more democratic, or at least a greatness that white readers could share more fully than they could with the older model.[21] The peerage approach established the basis for gratitude to a great man from a great family. The new racialized Washington was "one of us," making the roots of his greatness not a singular family possession but instead a source of pride and point of investment for all white people.

Racializing Washington's ancestry was emerging by the 1850s. Washington Irving wrote that Washington ancestor William de Hertburn's name "would seem to point out" his Norman descent— a claim that went somewhat beyond the sort of good-family claims that had preceded it. Caroline Matilda Kirkland, a dreadful writer and something of a social reform crusader, moved well beyond the established parameters of descended greatness to connect the extended Washington genealogy to somewhat higher-stakes issues. In her 1857 biography, Kirkland argued that George was "the ideal

American man," possessing all the "component points of the true American character," statements so packed with meaning that they tipped the scales.[22] Her list of traits included self-control, economy, courage, enterprise, public spirit, and religiousness as the defining characteristics of the man. "It follows," argued Kirkland, that by emulating Washington "the American rises toward a higher point of virtue," but "in departing from such a model he sinks to a lower grade." This ranking mirrors nothing so much as discussions of race, but Kirkland revealed that this was just what was in her mind. She claimed that Washington was neither "the slow dogged Saxon" nor "the mercurial and chivalric Norman" but rather "a product of both," yet perfected by American experience.[23] Kirkland connected Washington with all things that made the Anglo-Saxon the ideal human. Ancestry was the key. In his 1860 biography, Edward Everett retraced the Sparks genealogical path but added a detail that at least hinted at race. He claimed that the Washingtons hailed from the same part England as did the ancestors of Benjamin Franklin. Both families were "established for several generations in the same county of Northamptonshire" and, on top of that, "within a few miles of each other."[24] Everett allowed his readers to infer that there was something meaningfully revolutionary in this coincidence—at least something more resonant than simple ancestry.

Bradley T. Johnson, though, took exception to this sort of mixed ancestry. In his 1894 biography, he claimed the Washingtons had been "strong, hardy, manly people," and in words almost exactly like those soon to be said about Teddy Roosevelt, the Washington family were "hard riders, hard fighters, men of action, meeting and dealing with the responsibilities of life in a straightforward, positive, and clear-headed way, without the least sentiment of any kind about the hardships of life."[25] The historical evidence for this sort of romantic gushing is as thin as that supporting the much-maligned Cherry Tree, except in one specific arena: racial theory.

English success in Virginia was due to "the highest hereditary traits," which had been "transplanted" into American soil and there "subdued" both wild man and nature.[26] But Johnson bemoaned that many mistakenly "designate the race" that achieved all this "as the Anglo-Saxon." This "curious error" was easily corrected. All one needed to do was look over "the portraits in Lodge's Gallery of British Worthies" to see "long-headed, lean-faced, strong cheek-boned men" who were clearly of "Norman blood." These men were all the "leaders of thought and action" that carved an English world from the woods. And indeed, "the same gravity" and "the same contour of face and head" seen in those days was still visible in any portrait of Washington. In fact, Johnson was confident that "six generations" of time made no difference—the "same grave deportment, the same reserved carriage, the courteous intercourse" were on display at Mount Vernon as would have been in the court of Henry the Fifth. Race obliterated time, and Washington was a perfect specimen of his racially pure Norman ancestry.

True, few authors went as far into the rabbit hole as did Johnson, but even though the norm was to pass lightly over ancestry, most would have nevertheless agreed with the underlying premise of Johnson's now amusing prose. It was easy for Edward Taylor, a few years after Johnson, and many others to pen lines like "the Washington family in England were a race of thrifty people."[27]

The twin approaches to Washington's genealogy assured readers, on one hand, that Washington was a genuine creature of America from a family of great "doers." The language of race, though, assured readers that Washington—and therefore the roots of the nation—were above racial suspicion. This increased in importance as an ever more mixed nation looked to its father to be its exemplar and shining light. Biographers took on the task because they believed in that premise and wanted to offer a relevant Washington to their readers. If flaws in Washington were flaws in the nation itself, as Sparks wrote, let no one imagine that family mediocrity or race mixing were possible flaws.

Although Washington's ancestry was important, his own personal experience and development were of far greater weight for those chronicling his life. David Humphreys was Washington's first biographer, even though his work never really reached fruition. A stocky, Connecticut-born soldier with literary pretensions and unique access to his commanding officer and his papers, Humphreys foreshadowed today's celebrity biographers.[28] That is especially true because Humphreys had his subject almost literally whispering in his ear. Humphreys's biography offered a short handling of the childhood period, but it noted a few crucial elements that would become a core theme of all future work. Washington had come from a family of some wealth, but his father's death meant he was denied the English education of his older brothers, and he was "rather unsure and reserved in his appearance."[29] But what he lacked in advantage he made up for with an "active, indefatigable, persevering" nature and a "remarkably robust and athletic" build.[30] This gave him the strength for long days in the saddle and even longer days in the backcountry—the vital skills of his young adulthood. His mind was keen enough to make the best of domestic tutelage, and his character strong enough to avoid the "indolent repose" so common to many bred to a life of "commanding slaves." In short, Washington was born on a fulcrum that could have tossed him one way or the other. That he became the man he did was primarily because he made it so. Washington was what James Flexner later labeled a "self-made man."

This idea is perhaps the most deeply rooted idea of all of those running through the biographical literature. Indeed, as Scott Casper has shown, American biographers of the early nineteenth century commonly used the device of the self-made man. From presidents to candidates, the idea that the subject was "the architect of his own fortunes" was essential to the larger republican project of self-governance and a central part of the creation of manly identity.[31] Self-made-ness also was an essential building block in the emerging logic of a liberal market-based economy; each new self-made man provided another exemplar and served, as well, to naturalize the entire model. Humphreys's and Weems's Washingtons were perhaps a bit ahead of the curve in this trend, but not by much, and both are best understood as part of a large and enduring theme in the written creation of ideal Americans. In discussing Washington, though, high-stakes issues emerge, and invariably the motif of self-making appeared in one form or another in book after book, because on one hand, it is self-flattery for the nation he founded, and on the other, it provides the main reason for looking at the poorly documented childhood in the first place.

The creation of Washington's self-creation took text form in a few related discussions dealing with the quality of the homes the family inhabited, the nature of Washington's education, and the young man's physical abilities. Family station and poor schooling presented unique obstacles that the young Washington would have to overcome, whereas physical prowess and its assumed parallel of strength of character carried him through hard times and placed him in the right place at the right time.

Biographers have differed over whether Washington was "well born" or not. It would have been folly for a contemporary such as Humphreys to have played down Augustine Washington's finances; a man who held ten thousand acres at his death was well off by any rural measure. But despite this seeming advantage, Humphreys argued Washington was lucky to have avoided all the scars and flaws that came with privilege and slave owning. Jared Sparks later noted that Augustine had "possessed a large and valuable property in lands," but these "had been acquired chiefly by his own industry and enterprise," meaning that whatever wealth George was born to was fairly earned.[32] Being born to a family of some standing was no guarantee of success—Washington could still claim that prize on his merits.

But Mason Locke Weems went in the opposite direction. Washington, he claimed, "was not born with a silver spoon in his mouth."[33] Far from it—Weems gave Washington a singularly rustic childhood, set amid verdant country fields, childish games, homespun characters, and a humble, simple household. This view held sway well into the twentieth century, with most biographers emphasizing rusticity over elegance for much of Washington's childhood (and specifically for Ferry Farm). There has long been tension between a Washington who made more of much and one who made much of little. In both cases, though, biographers were clear that the conditions of his upbringing did not by themselves set him on the path to greatness. He would have had to do that himself.

Many biographers used subtle language to insinuate Washington's humble upbringing. He was born in an "old Virginia farm-house" or in a "plain, wooden farm-house" that some thought burned to the ground soon after it played its main role in history.[34] Others suggested that the birthplace, and Ferry Farm, were both "dilapidated" homes that had long since "crumbed into ruin." In any case, no matter in which of the three childhood homes the family resided, "the same plain style of living continued."[35] Even Washington Irving, who offered the first popular sustained and impressive family genealogy, still found a need to hint at rusticity by placing these decedents of titled grandees and Oxford dons in "primitive farm-houses of Virginia."[36] All that served as an elaborate setup while also removing any taint of aristocracy, fashioning a democratic Washington to whom rank and file American readers could relate.

There were some dissenters, of course. William Thayer, for example, saw Ferry Farm's house as having been a "low-pitched, single story building," rustic seeming, perhaps, but nevertheless "the style of the better sort of houses in those days."[37] Some went farther, particularly around the dawn of the twentieth century, when biographers desired their Washington to have more than humble origins. Others swung the pendulum too far in the opposite direction of rusticity. Take, for example, C. M. Stevens's mysterious claim that Washington was born into "one of the wealthiest and most cultured homes in America" and that his father "Augustus" (sic) was "estimated to have been at his death the wealthiest man in Virginia."[38] Witness also the work of Charles Arthur Hoppin, who in the 1920s seems to have taken as a personal affront the idea that Washington could have lived in a "small cottage of one story with a low attic," as had been claimed by Washington Irving and later by Benson Lossing.[39] Even Thayer's blame-the-conditions-of-the-day sleight of hand was not good enough for Hoppin. Washington had to have been born in a home befitting whom he would eventually become. Despite concerns such as these, the overall trend was to emphasize charm and rusticity over wealth and power, or at least find the perfect balance, as one 1901 biographer did in claiming that Washington "grew up like an aristocrat, and like a pioneer."[40]

Washington's education makes up the largest single portion of the childhood literature. Some of this stems from the fact that it was one of the few areas of his childhood that Washington addressed later in life. That Washington was self-conscious about the effects of his lack of a proper formal schooling is well established. His lack of formal learning was even a source of comment for others; for example, John Adams declared Washington to have been virtually illiterate and certainly ill-lettered and ill-read.[41] Jefferson noted that Washington preferred "action" to reading, and what reading he did was largely restricted to "agriculture and English history,"[42] although recent scholarship suggests a more varied bookshelf. As if to offer a post facto repost to naysayers such as Adams, biographers (themselves all keen on the written arts) rushed into the breach to defend Fortress Washington.

Another factor fortifying this section of the biography is that this part of Washington's upbringing produced some actual written material, a real rarity in this subfield of a subfield. Classroom-style exercises, mathematics problems, and some scribbles and doodles provide the earliest written material from Washington's own hand. Adding to the volume of material is the much (some might say overly) fussed-over collection of antique manners aphorisms, now famous as *Rules of Civility and Decent Behavior,* a popular manners guide made up of one hundred ten maxims that Washington famously copied by hand—to perfect either his penmanship or his character, depending on which biographer handled the topic.

All biographers agree that Augustine's 1743 death, among other effects, brought the curtain down on any chance George might have had at a formal British education in Latin, Greek, and the classics at the Appleby School, Augustine's and his two eldest sons' alma mater. The earlier biographers were content to see Washington's schooling as having been merely elemental. John Marshall noted only that Washington had what he called an "English education," by which he meant a local curriculum that "excludes the acquisition of languages other than our own."[43] Other early nineteenth-century writers claimed George had a "private education," meaning in-house tutors, or "a plain English education," or "a mere English course of study."[44]

Later writers tried to shoehorn in the traditional elements of schooling. James Trumbull, for example, averred (wrongly) that Washington "acquired the Latin language" with help of a private tutor.[45] Frederick Trevor Hill hedged his bets a bit in his 1921 biography by claiming that Washington had learned "a little Latin," and a few others averred even more cautiously that if he had learned any Latin or French, he never had occasion to demonstrate it.[46]

Most writers, though, could not kick against the obvious evidence that Washington never mastered another tongue to any meaningful degree. With more confidence than the evidence warrants, Wayne Whipple was probably more or less on target in 1911, claiming that Washington "never attempted to learn languages, nor manifested any inclination for rhetoric or belle lettres."[47] This was no great loss, though, as "no one expected him to be a scholar."[48]

Most writers made the necessity of an education "of the plainest kind" a positive virtue.[49] Sparks speculated that Washington's "slender" education must have been a worthy one, at least judging from its results.[50] Others argued that Washington's "education was decidedly utilitarian" but was "immediately capitalized" upon.[51] The utilitarian nature of Washington's schooling is, in fact, an area of broad consensus. Most biographers made much of the surviving exercises of "book-keeping, copying, drawing, and arithmetic and mensuration," concluding that these were the main skills needed for a career in surveying and to develop a military engineer's eye.[52] S. G. Arnold, in 1840, wrote of Washington's studies in "geometry, trigonometry, and surveying, for which he manifested a decided preference," making these endeavors as much a matter of young George's choice as one of divine providence.[53]

In the 1850s, one J. T. Headly went further, arguing that it was a good thing that Washington was denied an education "in the universities of Europe," for had he had one, he could not have avoided "coming under influences" there that would have rendered him "unfit . . . for the place assigned him by heaven."[54] This theme took on a renewed energy around the turn of the twentieth century, as social theorists such as G. Stanley Hall began to see a wild period as a necessary developmental stage in a young, middle-class American boy's life. Biographers of the early twentieth century showed their indebtedness to this line of thought, first, by beginning the practice of deriding Weems's truth-telling little George as a "prig"—a descriptor that quickly became ubiquitous for those trying to escape Weems's shadow. Others went further. Frederick Trevor Hill imagined a little George "allowed to run free, without schooling of any kind."[55] Still others echoed that view, and thus spared the potentially deleterious influence of "goody-goody" Latin grammar books, Washington was free to indulge in outdoor activities and benefit from a simple education of "readin', 'riting, and 'rithmatic."[56]

Even for those who saw the Cherry Tree and its ilk as "sheer nonsense," little George still learned "obedience, manliness, courage, and honor" through a schooling that taught much "that is not taught in books."[57] Rupert Hughes added a racial element to this wildness by having his Washington grow up like a "young Indian prince with a slave to wait upon him," in a setting of "almost primeval savagery."[58] Hughes tempered that remarkable view by allowing his George "no other education than reading, writing, and accounts."[59] Beginning in the 1930s, though, scholars such as John Fitzpatrick, Marcus Cunliffe, and, influentially, Douglas Southall Freeman all stepped back from this sort of hyperbole. Working more closely with the Washington papers (the first set of which Fitzpatrick had edited and thus standardized the documents available to most writers) than had most of their predecessors, they shifted the trend to a more honest acknowledgment that the "school exercises are the only authentic source of our meager knowledge."[60] There were still those eager to share the old stories, but these increasingly had to be tempered with hedging phrases such as "tradition says."[61]

This tension between what the documents say and what has been said played itself out as well in the story of Master Hobby. There was a man named John Hobby living near Ferry Farm in the mid-eighteenth century, but that is all documents allow. Weems had introduced Hobby as the man who provided Washington with the rudiments of literacy and ethics in what he called a simple "field school" in the neighborhood of Ferry Farm, although some authors placed him at Little Hunting Creek. The earliest biographers ignored Hobby, leaving schooling to have taken place under Lawrence's or Austin's guidance. But by the mid-nineteenth century, Hobby—often paired with a Mr. Williams, who was alleged to have run a similar school at Pope's Creek—had become a fixture of the story. Washington Irving included Hobby in his popular biography and helped propel the story into two more generations of writing. Lacking any ability to discuss curriculum at the Field School, biographers turned instead to exactly who Hobby was alleged to have been. George Washington Parke Custis also boosted Hobby, echoing Weems's claim that he had been "one of Mr. Washington's tenants" and that he had boasted of his young charge's achievements later in life.[62] Stories varied. Some claimed "Old Hobby" to have been actually a convict "transported from England as a punishment for some minor offence against the law" and hired by Augustine to teach local children; others claimed him to be "sexton of the parish" or a "poor sexton," or in one case, "a slave to Mr. Washington," probably meaning "servant."[63] In 1864, William Thayer wrote that he had "his own reasons" to believe that Hobby was a "broken-down old soldier" who walked around with a "big cocked hat that shaded a kindly and weather-beaten face," and if that was not colorful enough, "a wooden leg," in which he took more pride "than if it had been a sound one of flesh and bone."[64] Bradley Johnson went so far as to suggest, in 1897, that Hobby had been a gentleman and probably also "a university man," despite his keeping a small rural schoolhouse.[65] The invented Hobby was indeed a fitting vehicle for any number of fantasies.

Hobby also benefited immensely from a small collection of self-identified fictional Washington biographies, some written as first-person memoirs complete with imagined dialogues, freshly conjured characters, and situations invented out of whole cloth. The best known of these was Silas Wier Mitchell's *The Youth of Washington*. In it we meet Hobby as a short, good-humored, one-eyed convict who "resembled the grave digger in the play of 'Hamlet.'"[66] He would scare the children with his tales of London and was prone to believe the "negro superstitions," many of which he learned from his friend and faithful slave, Peter.[67] Absurd as it seems, this profile of Old One-Eyed Hobby nevertheless made it into a few otherwise serious biographies. No less an influential writer that W. E. Woodward wrote that Washington received "whatever sluggish pothook instruction" he could get from a man whose "business was not to teach people, but to bury them."[68] Frederick Trevor Hill recycled Mitchell's story that Hobby used to boast of having taught the Great Washington, and Joseph Dillway Sawyer repeated Mitchell's claim that Hobby "taught with a birch rod in hand."[69] By the end of World War II, Hobby was all but gone from most biographies, his entire story—not just his one-eyedness—having been an invention. Likewise, Mr. Williams of Westmoreland, who never received the same level of energy and invention as his colleague, also faded from the genre, even though his existence was slightly more plausible. Rev. James Marye's Fredericksburg school lasted a bit longer in the writing, and has had some recent advocates, but as with Williams, Marye was rarely more than a mentioned name.[70] Freeman, Flexner, and the rest of the more contemporary biographers contented themselves with the materials in the copybooks and Washington's later surveying certificate at the College of William and Mary. Hobby only appeared alongside the Cherry Tree—both as objects of sniggering dismissal.

The Hobby story, and the other details of the education story, blossomed for a while in response to the profound silence Washington's early years produced. Because Washington and others addressed his education in later life, the topic was fair game and factual as well—there had indeed been an education. But at the same time, generations of biographers were guilty of reading later achievement backwards and imagining the rest. Figures such as Hobby, Williams, and Marye also played the useful role of becoming stand-ins for male authority in a story that otherwise was lacking such (seemingly vital) character influences. Just as moving young George away from Ferry Farm as soon as was possible reestablished male influence, the education was a theme in which men could be made prominent.

Most of all, though, the near-universal agreement that Washington had a simple homespun education was a central tenet in the self-made-man narrative. As a child, Washington could not control the circumstances of his education, but that which he could control—his diligence and the care he brought to his work—he did masterfully. It was a rare biographer who did not lavish praise on Washington's penmanship (even if his spelling was poor) and the tidiness of his schoolwork. His note books were "models of neatness and accuracy," all written in a "neat, precise, and clear manner."[71] Latching on to the eighteenth-century convention of tidy writing exercises to show the roots of greatness and ordered habit reveals less about Washington than it does of the biographers' desire to fill the foundational years with meaningful precedents.

The other area with a deep historical rooting, and resonances to match, was the Washington family itself. Whereas questions of ancestry touched on the obscure, distant Washingtons, the im-mediate family was more influential in young George's life and enabled a larger and richer discussion. The main characters here were father Augustine, whose main role was in dying while George was young; brothers Lawrence (almost always called "half-brother") and, to a somewhat lesser extent, Augustine Jr. (called Austin), both of whom served as surrogate fathers; and mother Mary, who played the most complicated role, vacillating between nurturer and hinderer through the generations of writers. Each of these people appeared in repeated anecdotes, even though perspectives varied somewhat over the retellings.

Augustine's narration was perhaps the most unchanging of all the family members. Weems, of course, used Augustine as a surrogate for his own voice and made him the wise and pious teacher of moral lessons. For most early writers, it was enough to call him "an excellent father" and note, as did Jared Sparks, that the property he amassed "was chiefly by his own industry and enterprise."[72] One turn-of-the-century biographer called Augustine a "well-to-do farmer," and Woodrow Wilson, perhaps building on Augustine's several trips to England, declared him to have been "a man of the world" who was generous, hardy, and independent.[73] was "estimated" to have been "the wealthiest man in Virginia"—Augustine's treatment had generally been well-rooted in the evidence of his will, his mining activities, and his involvement with the Appleby School.[74] However, the simple fact that Augustine passed away and out of the story early made his treatment scant. He was notable less for his life than for the effects of his death.

Washington's older brothers also served singular stylized purposes in the biographies. Authors devoted much more time to Lawrence than to Austin, about whom almost no details emerge in most biographies. Some of that attention resulted from the reality that their relationship was well documented, and some of it stemmed from Washington's later association with Lawrence's home, Mount Vernon. Humphreys noted that Lawrence played an active role in colonial military affairs and was an eager volunteer during the War of Jenkins's Ear. Interestingly, Washington himself toned down Humphreys's fawning praise of Lawrence, playing down the scale of his military achievements. But all biographers credited Lawrence's influence on the young George as a significant source of his military ambition and personal refinement. The intensity of that influence grew over the course of the biographies. The earliest works were content to note that George frequented his brother's home and benefited from that connection.

Aaron Bancroft's 1808 biography noted that the conflict of 1747 "kindled" in Washington's "young breast that spark which at a subsequent period burst into a flame" but left Lawrence's role as the lighter of that spark only implied.[75] Sparks also credited Lawrence with serving as an exemplar and "having observed the military turn of his younger brother."[76] These treatments focused on what Lawrence *did*, such as provide an example and offer connections to the important Fairfax family—the patronage link that would set Washington on the road to wealth through surveying Western lands.

It was not until the mid-nineteenth century that Lawrence's actual character and possible motivations became a part of the story. Washington Irving claimed that Lawrence "looked down" on his brother "with a protecting eye," and others went further, noting Lawrence's "affection" for George and claiming that Lawrence's influence "was always good."[77] What was at issue here was the desire to construct Lawrence as a second father after Augustine's death—a positive male influence like Williams and Hobby, but in this case one cut more from the same cloth. Writers did not disguise this concern. With almost no evidence to support him, Irving imbued Lawrence with a "paternal interest in his concerns," Edward Everett wrote that Lawrence stood for George "in many respects in the place of a parent," and others saw Lawrence as "adopting" George or serving as a surrogate "after the death of his father."[78] From there, Lawrence "lived"—in the words of Woodward—"in George's dreams as a shining hero."[79] Flexner had Lawrence, "the dark, sallow man with a narrow intellectual face," even eclipse Augustine, and there was wide agreement that through time with Lawrence at Mount Vernon, "young George Washington blossomed."[80]

The centerpiece of Lawrence's role in young George's life, though, is the story of his arranging for his younger brother to pursue a life at sea. The event certainly happened—or, more accurately, there certainly was a discussion of sending George to sea. We know this thanks to a letter from Joseph Ball, Mary's London-based brother, roundly condemning the idea as little better than a death sentence.[81] Nevertheless, the idea of Washington narrowly missing going to sea—perhaps in his majesty's service—was too good to pass up, and evolving variations of the story became a set piece in every biography. As with other themes, the earliest biographers were content to just briefly note it, whereas Weems added yards of colorful detail and dialogue. Ball's letter denounced George's going to sea on either a military or commercial vessel, but most writers focused on the military side. The details varied, with some writers asserting that "the place of midshipman was obtained" or that Lawrence's former commander, Admiral Vernon, offered the posting, and that the waiting frigate was "riding at anchor in the Potomac," although some claimed it was in the Rappahannock.[82] Some biographers saw the whole plan as having been devised by Lawrence and his father-in-law, Fairfax, whereas others credited the initiative to an adventure-hungry George. Some even imagined his youthful excitement at the plan and his "disappointment at the frustration of his hopes" when the plan died on the vine.[83]

All have agreed, though, that it was Mary who for better or worse killed the plan. The actual letter from her brother provides a window into what her reasoning may have been. Ball claimed that, should George go to sea, cruel masters would "Cut and Slash him and use him like a negro, or rather a dog."[84] Biographers varied in their assessments of Mary's reasoning, with some crediting her being an "affectionate mother," whereas others credited her "strong objections" to little more than selfishness.[85] The story was useful, however—first in casting Lawrence as the caring sibling who looked (however ill-advisedly) to move George ahead in the world and, second, as a foreshadowing of Washington's military career and even a glimpse of some innate martial spirit imbuing the Washingtons.

That Lawrence was the conduit for George's first successes in the world is beyond doubt, but he served biographers most readily as a useful stand-in for a masculine influence otherwise lost to the young boy facing the death of a father. In the biographies, the Washington men were rather like the portrait of Lawrence, which to this day hangs in Washington's Mount Vernon office and which is often treated as prima facie evidence of his affection for his elder brother. Like the painting, they are straightforward, two-dimensional figures most notable for their gaze.

Mary is quite a different story. Augustine's death famously left her in charge of her children's upbringing, and thus her character and choices became significant factors for those trying to understand Washington's formative period. Every aspect of her life has been subject to some measure of scrutiny, and she plays some role in all the major themes; in fact, it is not an exaggeration to say that most retellings of Washington's childhood are really veiled tales of Mary. From her Ball family ancestry to the noticeable tension between her and her celebrated son late in life, biographers pored over the same information and connected the dots in different ways.

In his writing, Weems largely overlooked Mary, preferring instead to land his tales on Augustine, but few followed that lead, even though most of the early biographers gave her little more mention than did Aaron Bancroft, who in 1808 called Mary "a solicitous mother." It was not until that noted fifty-year mark of the 1830s, when living memory of the Revolution was yielding to a collective one, that Mary emerged as a significant figure.[86] And when she did, it was as a sort of patron saint of American motherhood. Confronted with the challenge of inventing a national culture that would secure the gains of the Revolution and ensure the health of the republican experiment, Americans artists and writers turned more and more to figures such as Washington, and particularly Mary, as iconic exemplars. Mary's tributes, though almost always written by men, also tapped into a growing maternalist language that was an early step toward female suffrage. While Elizabeth Cady Stanton and Lucretia Mott laid the groundwork for Seneca Falls, artists created images of a sainted Washington mother and son, and memorializers sought to commemorate Mary with the first monument to an American woman, and biographers lavished an increasing amount of praise on the first mother. Behind this was the confidence that the grounding of each "great man" can "be traced to the original characteristics or early influences of his mother."[87] And if Washington was canonized the nation's father, then the maternal source of his own personal greatness became a national matter.

Biographers portrayed Mary as an "affectionate mother" possessing "good sense, assiduity, tenderness, and vigilance."[88] She was "assiduous," and "tender," blessed with "good sense, conscientiousness, and excellent qualities"; she was "all that a mother ought to be"; she had a "love of order, prized "active industry," and sought nothing more than the title of "good wife and mother."[89] Biographers also commented on her piety, noting her love of scripture and devotion to religion. Many also claimed that she was a great beauty in her youth, and the tale of her having been the "Belle of the Northern Neck" quickly became an unsupportable commonplace.

All of this was generic filiopietistic boilerplate, so much so that it was of little real relevance to who Mary may or may not have been. A careful hedging criticism did enter the early literature—usually appearing right alongside the mushier stuff—and tapped a bit more into the realities of the eighteenth century. Around the mid-nineteenth century, George Washington Parke Custis, Benson

Lossing, and few others provided a major counterpoint in Mary's story by describing her as a woman of "reserved manners and rather stern character."[90] This Mary was certainly pious and affectionate, but her manner was not "adorned feminine sweetness." Instead she was "firm," marked by "a vigorous character," and a woman who demanded from her children "the strictest obedience."[91]

Parke Custis introduced the story of Lawrence of Chotank (a real kinsman of Washington's, even though the most famous anecdote about him may not be as real), who recalled from his visits to Ferry Farm that "of the mother I was more afraid than of my own parents" and that he could not "behold that majestic woman without feelings it is impossible to describe."[92] The intention here was as much religious as earthly, since the fear of which Lawrence spoke was more akin to awe or fear of heaven than a domestic terror. But the effect was to create a dichotomy in the way biographers handled Mary from then on. On one hand, there was the sweet and doting former Belle of the Northern Neck with her Bible and copy of Sir Mathew Hale's *Contemplations Moral and Divine,* and on the other, there was a more fearsome creature with her "deficient education," from whom Washington inherited both his "warm temper" (meaning quickness to anger) and the ability to govern and direct it.[93]

These twin strands were entwined for the next few decades of biographies. They worked because they helped explain what was perhaps the central role Mary played in the larger story: her management of her and her children's estates after Augustine's death. There has long been wide consensus that Mary found herself in an unenviable position when Augustine's death left her with a set of scattered properties, confused obligations to the sons of his first marriage, and five underage children in her charge. Hard finances, legal obstacles, and perhaps even outside meddling made the 1740s and early 1750s hard times at Ferry Farm, the home where she had lived longer than any other. The Janus-faced view of Mary provided the perfect explanation for how she managed her task and produced a son like George.

But the balance did not last long. By the end of 1800s, biographers—and often writers more often calling themselves "historians"—found a powerful need to renounce Weems, his stylistic successor, Benson Lossing, and anything that smacked of what they saw as evidence-free fabulism. Henry Cabot Lodge offered an early battle cry in this fight, writing that Weems was "simply a man destitute of historical sense, training, or morals" who had one goal in mind, and that was to "take the slenderest fact and work it up for the purposes of the market." Indeed, Cabot Lodge claimed that "until Weems is weighed and disposed of, we cannot even begin an attempt to get at the real Washington."[94] Mary's reputation suffered collateral damage in this struggle for a new authenticity and what would later crystallize into the idea of objectivity and the methods of professional scientific discipline.

Paul Leicester Ford's Washington biography was an early indicator of where things were headed. An editor of Jefferson's papers, Ford was one of a new breed of scholars working more fully from the documents and not simply reprocessing a distillation of the previous work (errors and all), as had been common practice. All this was part of a larger process of professionalizing the historical discipline; Weems was a casualty in that process.[95] Ford's work represents a turning point in many ways, but his handling of Mary was particularly striking. He began by dismissing her story as damningly as Cabot Lodge had denounced Weems. He claimed that the previous assessment of Mary's influence on George "partakes of fiction rather than of truth." Indeed, rather than being the Belle of Northern Neck, Mary was "illiterate and untidy, and moreover, if tradition is to be believed, smoked a pipe."[96] On top of that, Ford set in motion a narrative that pulled George away from Ferry Farm as soon as possible, thus removing both Mary and the landscape from the story posthaste. "After his father's death," wrote Ford, "the boy passed most of his time at the houses of his two elder brothers." Ford also was the first writer to list all the problems between mother and son later in life, a task that took up nearly four pages. The effect was to enumerate all of George's concerns and stresses about his mother and create the impression that this was, in fact, the real assessment of her character throughout her life. Ford drew a line in the sand that subsequent biographers came to respect: The old tales of sweetness and beauty could be included, but only under the dubious rubric of "tradition." And because so much of the "tradition" praised Mary, the new face of "truth" rebuked her.

Over the next few decades, this turn in the literature was quite useful. New ideas of human development, changes in frameworks of manliness as manifested in public figures such as Theodore Roosevelt, and Progressive Era ideas such as what scholars have called Muscular Christianity—the turn-of-the-twentieth-century middle-class embracing of a heretofore more working-class vision of rugged manliness—all reimagined the shape of ideal home life.[97] The doting, pious mother of Victorian ideals became not so much a wellspring of strength for young men as a sapper of male energies.

The longstanding interest in Washington's physical strength took on renewed meaning as biographers worked to assure readers of his vigor, despite nearly a century of his having had a dew-eyed, doting mother and—perhaps even more dangerously—no father to temper that engulfing femininity. In 1853, Washington Irving had claimed for George a "large and powerful frame" even in infancy, and many of his contemporaries reveled in remarking on Washington's strength and love of riding, wrestling, throwing stones, and, especially, horseshoes.[98] Physical mastery was the outward expression of spiritual and moral mastery, and so they went hand in hand in defining Washington's character. But by the end of the century, such praise took on a defensive tone. Washington now had a "pleasing" appearance "yet sufficiently severe to dispel from the mind of the beholder any idea of undue softness."[99] He had been a "natural and normal lad," and Joseph Dillaway Sawyer gave voice to the underlying concern more clearly than anyone else in his 1927 biography, writing that the "staunchly religious" Mary had "no opportunity to effeminize" her son's "stalwart nature."[100]

But the remaking of Mary did not stop at minimizing her potentially deleterious influence on her charge or removing him to other places. It also entailed coloring her character with different brushes. Lawrence of Chotank played a central evidentiary role here as Mary became "something of a terrifying woman," a "domestic tyrant" possessed of a "violent temper," and capable of "very severe measures" when needed.[101] Whereas words such as "tender" and "affectionate" had been the most common currency, a new word with a new overtone dominated the discussion. It seems to have been first used by William Woodward in his 1926 biography, when he claimed for Mary a "hard querulous" manner.[102] Shelby Little picked up the new framing in his 1929 biography, in which he labeled Mary "illiterate, untidy, and querulous."[103]

Samuel Eliot Morison, in an essay published in 1932 amid the Washington's birth bicentennial celebrations, picked up on this word and its subtext and brought derision of Mary to new levels. In his inimitable swaggering prose, Morison told the nation that the first mother had been "grasping, querulous, and vulgar." This "sainted mother," he wrote, with an irony-dripping pen, "opposed almost everything that he [Washington] did for the public good" and would have had this most indispensable of men spend less time at war or in government and instead be more devoted to his "duty to her." Mary added to Washington's stresses with her "strident complaints" and her "complaining letters," she was "selfish" and "exacting," her own children avoided her as soon as they were old enough to flee, and although she had been the subject of much "sentimental writing," the reality was that the level of "false sentiment, misrepresentation, and mendacity" written about her was second only to the same level of lies told about Washington's personal Christian piety (of which, Morison claimed, he had virtually none).[104]

As the century progressed, this version of Mary's character became entrenched, even though usually stated with less colorful vitriol. Douglas Southall Freeman picked up and built on this critique. He eschewed Morison's fondness for the adjectival slight, but the vision was there in outline. Instead, Freeman's extensive, heavily sourced study killed Mary with a thousand small cuts. Mary was parochial, homespun, and a "poor manager." Even in the 1740s, she was in the "early stages of what later became a fixed state of mind," to wit, that her family was obligated to make her every concern and worry their own—an attitude that defined her relationship with her kin and especially her increasingly cold but long-suffering first son.[105] Indeed, this reading of the First Mother was innovative enough to make it into popular reviews of the biography.[106]

Two decades later, James Flexner held the same view and granted that Mary had been a "powerful woman."[107] The problem was that "all of her power was centered on herself," and anything George tried to do that "was not to her immediate service, she attempted to stop."[108]

Mary's crankiness has since become a commonplace in the literature's mainstream. It sits so confidently as an unquestioned reality that some writers have begun to drift back into more Morisonian waters in order to spice up their prose. Witness this litany of scorn from only a small portion of Ron Chernow's popular Washington biography: She was "strong-willed," "unbending," "shrewish," "disciplinarian," "trying," "hypocritical," "querulous," "crude," "illiterate," "self-centered," "slovenly," and a "veteran com-plainer"; there was "nothing especially gentle" about her and "little that savored maternal warmth."[109] It seems George was lucky to get out alive—or, as Alan Nevins put it in 1948, "George had reason to keep his distance."[110]

Even as the biographical tide turned against Mary, there were still those who found good words for her. Rupert Hughes so-licitously suggested that "the picturesque little old woman" who struggled against "unusual hardships and even her own traits" deserved "all the sympathy in the world."[111] After all, "it cannot be comfortable to be the mother of an arch-rebel."[112] Even the of-ficial publications of the 1932 Washington birth bicentennial—the same moment that unleashed Morison's attack—found praise for a woman "who should be enshrined in the hearts of the people of the United States."[113]

Mary had maternalist champions who saw in attacks on her a broader attack on American values. The effort to dedicate a new monument to Mary at her supposed Fredericksburg grave site was a significant driving force behind this view, and like many similar commemorative and preservation efforts of its day, it was an elite, white female activity. The coalition of women who raised the funds and the obelisk were fired by the vision of Mary as a virtu-ous paragon—surely the "women of this republic" would rally to ensure that "the memory of the mother of the Great Washington" should be fittingly honored.[114] Their appeal clearly spoke to some, because they collected the needed funds and achieved their aim in 1902.[115] In crafting her 1903 biography of Mary, Mrs. Roger Pryor, herself one of the founding "Hereditary Life Members" of the Mary Washington Association that raised the monument, relied on a mix of made-up dialogue, recycled anecdotes, and some biography cherry-picking. Pryor concluded that Mary was a "strong, self-reliant woman, with executive ability and a supreme power of awing and governing others," sentiments that not only were thinly veiled calls for women's suffrage but also were the exact values enshrined in Mary's monument.[116] Fredericksburg has long celebrated its connection to Mary, with her home becoming a preserved site in the 1930s. The town even saw the last gasp of maternalist Mary veneration in the writing of a local historian who, as late as the early 2000s, was penning essays that could have been at home in an 1880s Mary Washington Association fundraising appeal letter.[117]

Mary has been a canvas on which generations of writers played out competing ideas of motherhood, family, and the Washingtons—great or otherwise. But somewhere, hidden by all this writing, was a real woman, and one who probably possessed some combination of the elements ascribed to her. There is every reason to believe that she loved and cared for her children and that she showed them both kindness and harshness. In a time and place where female formal education was limited, she no doubt had a limited education, the effects of which would have been familiar and visible to all who cared to look. She was a lifelong slaveholder and was accustomed to the sense of privilege that came with her class in a world where human bondage was common.

Washington's papers suggest that he certainly could be irritated by his mother, especially later in her life. He was not always confident in how she managed her enterprises, but it is hard to tell how much of that was Mary and how much was her son's unflagging confidence in his own rectitude. Trying to fish out her actual character from the few scraps of evidence we have is more an exercise in historical imagination than anything else. Gleaning her influence on her most famous son only runs the risk of perpetuating the flaws already built into the discussion. In a later chapter, we will see how archaeology has shed light on one aspect of the story and given her choices some voice through material remains. But that is not the same thing as siding with those who revered

Mary or those who reviled her. Neither position really makes that much sense, removed from the context of its iteration. Mary is as much a creature of historiography as of history, and her changing treatment tells us more about the writers themselves and their own times than about her.

In that way, she is no different from any other continually evolving element of the childhood story. The poor documentation of this period of Washington's life left only a few key events and people on which to hang the narrative. Washington's ancestry, the fortunes and death of his father, that he was locally schooled, that he was under his mother's care, that he moved between homes, and that there was a un-enacted plan for him to go to sea make up the bulk of our reliable document-based knowledge. The rest is inflection. The story changed, of course, once Washington became involved in Western land surveying, and, predictably, there is a convergence in that part of the story across the biographies no matter how much they differed in their handling of the childhood years. As Washington left childhood and became a surveyor and landowner, his biographers moved from one form of speculation to another.

Joseph Ellis played it safe when he wrote that "history first noticed George Washington in 1753," the year in which he turned twenty-one.[118] He avoided the whole tangled mess of lore, half-reads, and invention that made Washington's childhood the most varied and creative portion of the larger life story. But ultimately Ellis was wrong: History has been fussing over Washington's childhood ever since the day he passed away as an old man.

2

COMPLETING THE CIRCUIT OF MEMORY

Washington and His Parting Survey

109th: Let your recreations be manful not sinful.
Rules of Civility and Decent Behavior

The focus of this chapter is a three-page handwritten survey that George Washington composed in the fall of 1771. The yellowed original sits in a private library in Philadelphia, the Library of Congress holds a high-quality photostatic copy, and I use a digital photograph of the original that the George Washington Foundation in Fredericksburg keeps on its computer server. The survey's multiple forms and locations, and the tensions between its security and its accessibility, mirror the core purpose of a survey: to turn land into a reference-ready document available for all to see while simultaneously covering the land with a veil of private ownership—theoretically accessible papers proving the land's theoretical inaccessibility.

Almost all the writing about Washington's childhood has been done by others, Washington himself having never formally put pen to paper on this topic. His host of biographers over the centuries have created a set of canonical concerns that mark out—like a surveyor's stumps, stones, and chop marks—the various turns and highlights of his earliest days. The man himself remained mute on the topic. His letters are a carefully shaped record through which he sought to create the future's memory. Without some magic find, we'll never know what Washington intentionally hid from our prying contemporary eyes. The resulting silence has been a productive field for invention.

Nevertheless, Washington did produce a few texts that speak in odd ways to his understanding of his childhood, his relationship to Ferry Farm, and some of the themes formulated by the biographers. I see the 1771 survey as having been one of these. Rather than being a business activity like his early work, this was a personal and private act by a man already rich from farming and landownership and now saying a special farewell to the place he knew for much of his life. Therefore, Washington's wording and choices of objects on the land are all a hidden text about how he understood the place he came of age. In addition to opening a rare window into how Washington may have understood his personal past, this exercise in reading against the grain also makes for an important step in connecting Washington to place.

The survey is a fine example of the eighteenth-century surveyor's craft. It is a set of short statements punctuated by measurements and directional indicators. The hand is strong and clear, and the lines are almost ruler straight, even though the ledger pages are unlined. It looks as if it could have been a post facto copy transcribed from field notes, except for one line on the third page. There, what appear to be about ten letters are carefully crossed out with a gently looping and very effective line. Washington may have written in this ledger on the day of the survey, or he may not have. In either case, the text's clarity, efficiency, even—perhaps—artistry all reflect the fact that the drafter was a master of his craft.

By September 1771, Washington was long past making a living with his chains and pen. That phase of his life ended in 1754, when he formally took over his brother Lawrence's estate and began profiting from its acres. But even before that sad but opportunity laden passing, Washington's skills and connections had made him a rich man.

The "professional surveyor" phase of Washington's life is well known and is a well-documented section of any of his many biographies.[1] Douglas Southall Freemen wrote that Washington took to surveying in 1746, perhaps under the tutelage of one George Byrne, a man then in the employ of Washington's future employer, Colonel William Fairfax. There is some stylistic resemblance between Byrne's and Washington's work, but the surveys of another possible early mentor, George Hume, bear "GW" initials. No matter who first taught Washington, Freeman writes, "the work entranced him," and "he could not do enough of it."[2] The image is of a man both bedazzled and obsessed. Joseph Ellis treated surveying in rather more modern terms, calling it Washington's "first job."[3] In Ellis's work, Washington's surveying sits alongside a love of outdoor adventure and the promise of amorous adventures. The trade was part of a suite of manliness-building exercises. Although Ellis notes how the profession made Washington rich, that is almost secondary to a larger concern about how the surveying phase made little George a "well-muscled and coordinated" epitome of a "man's man."[4] For Paul Longmore, surveying was part of Washington's long effort at self-fashioning. The trade, Longmore wrote, was a gentry art "of some social standing," reckoned on par with that of "doctors, attorneys, and clergymen." For Longmore, Washington's surveying met his gentry styling while making him as much as 400 pounds in just three years and familiarizing him with the Western lands where his next great adventure would unfold.[5] Surveying was one part of a process that made the Rappahannock farm boy into a gentry man of standing and influence.[6]

In that way, surveying was a crucial moment in Washington's upbringing and career development. It was also a defining moment in his relationship with Ferry Farm. After the collapse of the plan to send him to sea, there appears to have developed a consensus that George needed some activity that would open doors and make him some money. The Western land boom and the Fairfaxes' deep involvement made surveying the natural choice and—as some scholars suggested—one that Mary would not oppose.

Surveying entered the documentary record early. One of the best windows surviving from those teen years is a rough and incomplete ledger into which the young George entered in his own hand his transactions with his neighbors and relatives. The entries date from 1747 and 1748 and show Washington working with a sort of double-entry bookkeeping that listed on the left side the ways he was getting poorer by goods bought, money loaned, or work done and listed on the right side the ways he got richer though goods acquired or debts paid him. Overall, though, the ledger is incomplete—the sums never quite add up, and it is impossible to tell how full a reckoning it really is. Washington seems to have dropped the whole project at some point and he, or perhaps someone else, picked the book back up in 1763 for a few new entries.

The 1740s lines show him lending money to several people and winning considerable sums from his intimates. He purchased a number of imported consumer goods such as shoes, ribbon, shirt buttons, "knee bands," limes, and silk stockings, and he paid the wine and punch bills at a few local taverns. His exchanges with Mary are notable because they appear to have involved an unusual amount of coin. Whereas most of the other exchanges were for goods against debt, his mother seemed to be providing him with cash in the form of "dubloons" and "pistoles" in addition to the "cash" that fleshed out the incoming side of the ledger.[7]

Two purchases stand out from all the others because they shed light on the mind and interests of the young man monitoring his spending. The first is a cryptic entry for three books he acquired from his cousin Baily Washington, a slightly older peer from the

Chotank branch of the family. Two of the books were unnamed, but the third was listed only as "Scomberg." This was a copy of *A Panegyrick to the Memory of His Grace Frederick Late Duke of Schonberg* [sic], originally published in 1690 but reprinted a few decades later.[8] The much misspelled Duke of Schomberg was something of a military superhero in his day—or at least he was to the readers of his printed dispatches from the front lines of King William's wars in Ireland and to those eager to read tales of martial adventure. As befits one of the principal soldiers in the service of a Dutch king of England, Schomberg was a German-born nation hopper who over the course his career fought in Protestant causes for most of Northern Europe's monarchs and satraps. His long ride came to an end in 1690 at the Battle of the Boyne, where he became a martyr to an Orange Protestant Ireland. He rests still in Dublin beside a commemorative inscription by Jonathan Swift carved the year before Washington's birth.

Though little remembered today, Schomberg was the very image of martial valor to young Britons such as George and Baily Washington. Biographers like to draft Lawrence into the role of the main military model of George's youth, but if indeed the fifteen-year-old was reading of the deeds of Schomberg, then perhaps he had his sights set somewhat higher than the failed Siege of Cartagena. Add to that the fact that Ferry Farm excavations have turned up a cufflink celebrating King William, and it seems that the late king and his causes still resonated on the banks of the Rappahannock.[9]

The other notable 1747 entry was for an item also acquired from Baily Washington. This was a "two foot Gunter" scale. This was a wooden ruler inscribed with measurements and conversions that allowed the user to scale down drawings. That it was 2 feet long suggests that it was two pieces of wood joined with a central hinge. The tool was an essential part of any surveyor's kit and is the first documented moment linking Washington and his youthful career. The year after that purchase, he received the only formal degree of his life: a surveying certification from the College of William and Mary.[10] Heading west made Washington very wealthy, very quickly—wealthy enough that whatever value his inherited estates held was rapidly eclipsed. With each new line of chains, Washington's future veered away from Ferry Farm. In addition to setting Washington up for the military career that was his next stepping stone, surveying was also the path that ensured that Ferry Farm would not be his home for long.

For the bulk of Washington biographers, surveying hit some combination of these three bells: It made George tough, it made George rich, and it made George Western. It is easy to see in surveying the roots of the Washington that most mattered to the nation. As a result, the trade has become deeply connected to Washington's life and legend. It also is, reciprocally, a singularly important part of Ferry Farm's stories, as we shall see.

As Freeman noted, even though surveying was a youthful métier, it was one Washington stayed with for his entire life. In the words of Charles Henry Ambler, Washington made "frequent use of the chain and compass."[11] He conducted more than 100 surveys of Mount Vernon for his own purposes and took the measure of numerous other lands he owned or to which he had easy access.[12] His eye for land also aided him immensely in the most significant act of his life: his leadership of the Continental Army during the Revolution.[13] Just over a month before his 1799 death, he was out on a distant property marking its bounds with the same skill and care he had shown as a youth.[14] But although his post-1752 surveys were often more for enjoyment than for practical purposes, they nevertheless have come to constitute important records of his holdings and activities.

The Ferry Farm survey was one of these. It was a survey made for private reasons, an activity chosen by a wealthy and influential man practicing the arts of his youth, and a document drafted more out of desire than demand. Most importantly, though, my contention is that it is a singularly revealing and significant text. It was Washington's most sustained literary effort devoted to Ferry Farm or to his childhood, and although it takes the form of a terse prose of numbers, directions, and locations, it is nevertheless a memoir that Washington created specifically for his own purposes.

This view holds that the survey is two distinct things within American historical writing. First, it serves as a window into Washington's memories of his childhood. That project matters to a reader in direct proportion to how much that reader cares about Washington and the corpus of his biographical literature (a genre and library section unto itself). Nevertheless, Washington's upbringing is a famed silence in the literature, and there is a respectable argument to be mounted that all insights are valuable—especially given how vital Washington is to the national story, how useful he has been as a symbol, and how the desire to fill the silences has spawned its own literature—Weems being only the most famous purveyor.[15]

Additionally, though, the survey becomes a crucial part of a small written record in which Washington reflected on the place of his upbringing. The survey is the longest written narrative of any kind linking Washington and the landscape of Ferry Farm, a pairing at the core of Weems's and others' stories of the place. It was a pairing that made this specific tract of land "historical," that is, it could claim a relationship between place and a personage that enabled discussions, texts, memories, and meanings to attach here in a way that did not occur on neighboring tracts in most respects no different from these acres. Biographers might say that Ferry Farm made Washington. In truth, Washington made Ferry Farm. The survey becomes the first meaningful step in that process. It becomes thus a document that is at once a personal revelation—a set of cryptic clues to the Washington experience of Ferry Farm—and the beginning of Ferry Farm's memory and storytelling.

On September 10, 1771, Washington took a break from monitoring his affairs to ride down to Fredericksburg from his Mount Vernon home. He spent the night with Colonel Harry Lee near Dumfries and then set off again the next morning. He took a break along the way, probably at the home of Stafford County justice Valentine Peyton, before finally reaching his destination—his mother's house at Ferry Farm—sometime late on the 11th.[16] Mother and son dined together that evening, probably in one of the home's front rooms with views of the lights of town across the river. After that repast, Washington bedded down somewhere in the old home of his childhood, a home he still officially owned but that had long since become his mother's place. The next morning, he saddled his horse again and "rid all over the plantation" to look over the acres surrounding what he called either "the Ho[me] House" or, more often, "my mother's."[17] After that reconnaissance, he traveled off to look over other family lands. With that done, he returned to Ferry Farm, crossed the Rappahannock, and repaired to the home of his sister Betty and her husband, Fielding Lewis. That home sat on a rise of ground above the river, much like the one at Ferry Farm, except this was closer to the falls and on the town side of the river. He dined with his brother-in-law, presumably with his sister as well and their children, joined by their brother Charles, who had come over from his home a short walk away.[18] Washington then spent the night there in the company of his family. The next morning, the 13th, he mounted his horse once again, recrossed the Rappahannock to Ferry Farm, and breakfasted there with his mother. With autumn daylight wasting, Washington got to work and "surveyd the fields," a task that took up most of the day. When that was done, he returned to Fredericksburg and spent another night there.[19] On the 14th, he and his brother-in-law rode out to

Lewis's mill, after which he returned one more time to dine with his mother and spend what was probably his last night at Ferry Farm. On the morning of the 15th, Washington said his goodbyes and headed back to the place he had called home since the early 1750s, stopping once more at Dumfries and then heading home the next day.[20]

All that information comes from the sparse entries in Washington's diaries, entries that serve as a supplement to the survey itself. This story is augmented a small bit with scholars' sleuthing and some rudimentary geographic knowledge. It is worth noting that in the total of seventy-eight words he devoted to this trip, the only people Washington mentioned were Colonel Harry Lee and Peyton, with whom he rested or spent a night on the way; his brother-in-law Colonel Fielding Lewis, with whom he stayed; and his brother Charles, with whom he dined. The entries offer a small glimpse of the social landscape that made up his time in town. Even though Washington no doubt saw his sister Betty, she received no mention. He mentioned his mother Mary thrice but each time only as a possessive noun: "my Mother's."[21] Mary was a character in the diary not by her action but rather via her presence on, and seeming control over, the land. Even in that that little act of written possession, Ferry Farm and Mary were fused.

The diary casts the trip as a singularly male affair—appropriate enough, given the gentry manliness for the trip's central act of surveying. On top of that, Washington made no mention of those who presumably helped him with the surveying itself—the other men who would have run the chains or helped with measurements. Thus, not only did he present the trip as male, its main event is cast as a solitary act.[22]

Yet the extant scholarship (such as it is on such a small matter) places Mary, filial love, and the quality of Ferry Farm at the center of the trip. Donald Jackson and Dorothy Twohig, who edited the

Washington diaries, augmented Washington's text with their own well-informed observations and contextualizations.[23] They saw the trip as being designed to make the "final arrangements" for settling Mary (then sixty-three years of age) in a new "commodious white frame residence." Washington's goal, they further argued, was to allow Mary to "spend her latter years in comfort, free from the cares of the plantation."[24] Their notes make clear that concern for Mary was foremost; in fact, their notes encourage us to imagine Mary's future and the various financial arrangements attending it being the main topic of conversation, as the two Washington brothers and Mary's son-in-law sat at the table those evenings.

Freeman also discussed the trip in two pages of his Washington biography, the study that is still the most thorough treatment of the subject. Freeman noted, pointedly, that Washington preferred to stay with the Lewises during his "longer halts" in town, as opposed to staying with his mother in the home he still officially owned. On top of that, Freeman contended that Washington would have had "no intimate knowledge" of the state of Ferry Farm, which Freeman saw as dire.[25] Only one field was viable, although the rest was "poor and worn," and even in its best days that one was never all that great. On top of that, most of the land had not yet been cleared. In Freeman's handling, it is easy to see Ferry Farm as what John Ferling would later call it: "a worn out tract."[26]

But Freeman went on. Mary had asked her eldest son repeatedly for funds—requests he invariably honored. And yet barely any of the earnings from the land or any filial largesse had gone into the farm's upkeep. Freeman argued things had gotten so bad that the September trip was essentially a conference between local interested parties about how to solve a problem like Mary. The end result was that Mary would move to a new home on the Fredericksburg side, overseers would manage her properties, and Washington would set about selling off Ferry Farm. Freeman wrote that it was "doubtless a relief" to have set matters to rights as he rode back home to Mount Vernon on the 15th.[27]

These two versions of Washington's September trip use the diary to narrate Ferry Farm, through the language and concerns of two distinct larger Washington biography story lines. The first is Ferry Farm as property, a story that goes back at least as far the seventeenth century. The second is the more complicated story of the relationship between Mary and her eldest son, a story that has roots in the documentation but really is a creature of historiography.

John Catlett surveyed and patented around two thousand acres, including what would be Ferry Farm, in 1666. His papers were the land's first definitive appearance in writing. But Catlett was a lowland tobacco planter of some wealth and status—upriver lands were speculative ventures—so it would be some time before an English resident came to settle.[28] That man was a freed servant named Maurice Clark, who lived for a few months on the land around 1710. We have his land deed, and archaeology has made him one of the site's major players, thanks to the discovery of his small, heavily repaired two-room, Virginia-style, earth-fast home.[29]

The narrative of Ferry Farm as property that began with Catlett was one of monetary values and surveyed measurements. It was one that cast the land as a bit player in the drama of Virginia colonization. In treating Washington's September trip as being about assessing, ascribing value, and making financial arrangements and setting prices, Jackson and Twohig and others folded Ferry Farm into the long story of how these Virginia acres became English property.

The Mary side of the narration is a bit subtler. The issue rests on questions about the relationship between Mary and her celebrated son, and about Mary's own character. This places the relationship between Mary and her son front and center in the discussion of the survey. The biographers working with poor documentation and the lingering shadows of Mary's various castings and recastings have created a general consensus. The current view shows Mary Ball Washington as something of a difficult and occasionally obstructionist personality. As we have seen, the most recent work on the topic uses some of the harshest anti-Mary language in making its case. As in the years around the Washington bicentennial, much of this stems from writers' desires (secret or acknowledged) to mark the differences between their own efforts and those of filiopietistic antecedents. Nevertheless, the harshest animosities to Mary are as received as was the mindless veneration of her.

The simple truth is that there is very little material to build on, either one way or another. What little there is in the Washington papers and other writings (such as her role in thwarting Lawrence's plan to send Washington to sea) has usually been read in light of later sources. Only a few basic facts gleaned from Washington's writings are clear. The first one is central to the 1771 survey, and that is that Washington was not satisfied that his mother was able to manage her lands or her finances. The reason for that lack of faith remains unclear; it may have been concerns as much over age as over acumen. In other words, we have evidence that Washington was concerned but not much to suggest whether he was right to have those concerns. That someone—perhaps George or Lawrence—asked the King George County Court to redistribute Mary's enslaved property at Ferry Farm in 1750 may also indicate some dissatisfaction with her management. It may also have been something far more mundane, though—we just can't tell. Scholars have danced around this question, either by suggesting flaws in Ferry Farm itself or by accepting that Mary was to blame.

The other issue touches on her character and the nature of their relationship. The surviving letters show a tension between them later in life, hanging on what appears to be her perception that she was being left in difficult straits. It is indisputable that

Washington was less than pleased with some things his mother was doing or some of what she was saying about him and about her conditions. In 1781, Washington wrote to Benjamin Harrison that he had gone to great lengths to ensure her well-being during the war. Indeed, he told Harrison, "she has not a child that would not divide the last sixpence to relieve her from *real* distress. This she has been repeatedly assured of by me: and all of us, I am certain."[30] He was also bothered by Mary's attempt to gain a state pension on the strength of her son's service. Washington wrote that he and his siblings "would feel much hurt, at having our mother a pensioner while we had the means of supporting her," and additionally, at least in his eyes, "she has an ample income of her own."[31]

Washington stopped the pension plan, but Mary's worries did not end, regardless of his assurances and assistance. Washington told his brother John Augustine, in 1783, that, "like every other matter of private concern," he had "totally neglected" the many land management concerns Mary had brought to his attention. But he also made clear, again, that from his vantage point she was in no actual distress and wanted for nothing substantive. Nevertheless, she was making it a point "upon all occasions, and in all companies" to complain "of the hardness of the times, of her wants, and distresses."[32] Washington asked his brother to check in on her when could and also to "represent to her in delicate terms the impropriety of her complaints and acceptances of favors" from anyone other than family members.[33] In 1787, two years before her death, Washington was again assuring her that he had her care and well-being in mind, writing to her that, "whilst I have a shilling left you shall have part, if it is wanted, whatever my own distresses may be."[34] Washington bristled a bit that she had been leveling complaints to friends and neighbors and that, despite his attention, he was nevertheless "viewed as a delinquent, and considered perhaps by the world as unjust and undutiful Son."[35]

These concerns for his local reputation may have been the backdrop for his most quoted statement about Mary, which he wrote to her Fredericksburg neighbors in 1784, saying that it was "the maternal hand" of his "revered mother" that had led him from childhood.[36]

These tensions over money in the last ten years of Mary's life offer a glimmer of insight, but biographers have been all too willing to make the Mary we see at the edges of these letters a singular timeless person—one constant annoyance over a period of four decades. This is the main evidence for casting Mary as the selfish, grasping woman who fumed at everything her son did that took him away from her. In reality, though, it is only the lens through which all of her previous actions have been read, ever since historians of the 1880s felt a need to distance themselves from earlier writing and wanted to remove from Washington too much doting female influence that risked feminizing him. Nevertheless, every writer's review of the relationship has been colored by this discussion.

I would not want to cast Jackson and Twohig as having been being partisans in this enduring fight over Mary.[37] But the fact remains that their notes read as something of a defense against the allegation that relations between mother and son Washington were less than loving. The diary notes call specific attention, in telling language, to Washington's filial duty—perhaps even love? It is not enough that Washington moved Mary closer to her daughter and son-in-law, to the home Washington purchased for her—a home the editors called "commodious," when "middling" would have been a fairer description of the small house. On top of that, the trip that Freeman saw as an attempt to problem solve at Ferry Farm was, in the diary's notes, rooted in a desire to secure Mary's dowager comfort and ease her twilight years by sparing her plantation life.[38] For Freeman, Mary's flaws were the source of her worries; for Jackson and Twohig, alleviating maternal need was the son's mission.

Thus, beginning with Washington's calling the land his mother's and continuing through the biographies, the scant existing discussion of the September 1771 trip places Ferry Farm within a parent–child relationship, a role it played more fully, at least, since Weems. Freeman, Chernow, Jackson, and Twohig connected the trip to different strains already at work in a larger narrative about Washington and his family—and Mary, especially. There is a logic to this. Ferry Farm was Washington's old home. By 1771, he was still its nominal owner, but it had long been his "mother's home." He needn't have had a strained relationship with her for the place to be alive with maternal echoes, all the more so because Mary was still alive and kicking and—perhaps more irksome—was still working to control her own affairs, regardless of what contemporaries or later critics might think of her management.

Ferry Farm's archaeology has somewhat disrupted the vision Freeman set in motion and others had carried on. Augustine Washington's death made the 1740s undoubtedly tough times on the home farm. The evidence for that is plentiful in both documents and finds. In one 1749 letter, a young Washington lamented that he could not visit his brother Lawrence, then at Williamsburg, because he could not scare up the corn "sufficient to support" a horse already "in very poor order."[39] The standard read of this letter is that Ferry Farm could not even provide good horse fodder. Later on, in hard times, Washington recalled almost this exact moment and wrote to his friend James Craik that "I never felt the want of money so sensibly since I was a boy of 15 years old."[40] The challenges of life at Ferry Farm loomed large in Washington's memory, even though some may have been enlarged over time.

The site's archaeological evidence fleshes out the story. A house fire damaged part of one room and would have caused considerable mess and expense in the repairs.[41] The family's tablewares and domestic goods show attempts to retain and reuse items while also buying things that displayed gentility, but doing so on the cheap.[42] Excavations also show that the combination of Washington's increasing wealth, his sister Betty's marriage to Fielding Lewis, and Charles Washington's growing stature all combined to make the 1760s and 1770s something of a renaissance on the Rappahannock. The quality of material goods increased in and around the home, and there is considerable evidence of comfortable—if not lavish—living on the site. In fact, the worst days, for the home at least, were in future years, after Washington's sale of the property and its use by tenant farmers or enslaved labor hastened its deterioration. The argument that Washington sold Ferry Farm because it was poor land, or in disarray, or because his mother was troublesome or unable to manage the land, all rest in one way or another on assumptions about his relationship with Mary—indeed, they rest on little else. But there is nevertheless something curious about the sale that warrants investigation.

In describing Washington's career as a surveyor and landowner, historian Philander Chase noted that even though Washington had begun plans to sell off most of his western holdings in the early 1790s, the deal never went through. Instead, he sold off only two small holdings in what is now West Virginia.[43] Jack Warren went further in his work on Washington's childhood. He saw Ferry Farm as "remarkable" for being the "only substantial tract of cultivated land in the northern part of Virginia that Washington ever sold."[44] Qualified as this statement is, it is nevertheless meaningful.

Indeed, the sale is remarkable; that is part of the reason scholars have gone to such lengths to create reasons that tied in with other concerns they saw in Washington's biography. What both Warren and Chase help us see is that Washington was far more often the endpoint for land deeds than a passer-on. Given that reality, the fact that he sold a large plot of viable farm land—land he even called "pretty good"—that was along a major road, had deep river access, bordered a ferry landing, was partly well timbered, and was across from a town should not be passed over. That the same piece of land was the one where he had spent his childhood, where he saw life's first challenges, and where his mother had lived longer than any other home she had occupied only makes the sale more interesting. That he took the time to personally survey the land before its sale, and in so doing created one of the site's first real acts of memory and narration, makes this place and this sale remarkably rich in meaning.

And so we return to the September 1771 survey. As we have seen, scholars have treated Washington's Fredericksburg trip as a small chapter in the story of mother and son's relationship. But few, if any, have given the survey itself more than a passing glance, viewing it as functional, technical text covering a matter that was either settled already or better understood through the diaries. Because my main focus is on landscape, memory, and narrative—and not on Mary herself, or even the Washington biography—I want to treat the survey as the closest thing we have to a memoir of George's time at Ferry Farm.

The first thing to establish, then, is that this was indeed a unique survey—not unique in its execution but rather unique because it was never meant to be seen. Or, at least, Washington saw this as a personal act, as opposed to being part of creating an official record. The survey was certainly part of his developing plan to sell the land. It was the way he knew best to look over land and see what it had and where—to best grasp what was of value and how it all sat in relation to the land's advantages and improvements. Some landowners might have been satisfied with a day's ride over the acres for old-time's sake. For Washington, though, his craft was his best pair of eyes. The craft also provided him a comfortable and familiar language through which to speak about the land.

The evidence of the survey's privacy comes in a few forms. One small bit comes from the way his diary entries cast the survey as a solitary act by not mentioning anyone else who helped. That is curious but not the most telling bit of evidence. It also may matter that Washington never actually drew out the measurements he recorded on September 13. That task had to wait until more than a century and half later, when Washington bicentennial commemorators created a map of the site for inclusion in *The George Washington Atlas.*[45] But even the fact that the survey stayed as notes and did not produce a map does not in and of itself mean secrecy; there are many possible explanations for why a very prominent man, active in the affairs of a colony on the verge of a sustained international crisis, might not have platted a small survey.

Another curious detail is the fact that the survey itself is somewhat incomplete. The two documented attempts, by later experts, to create a map from the notes have yielded odd results, the main one being that Washington's circuit was not quite circular. There are gaps; areas do not quite match up. In 1771, these errors were probably not a failure of Washington's skills of method. Rather, it seems that the project itself was only partly completed. This may in part account for why he never mapped out his work. It also may account for the fact that Washington's notes made no mention of any assistants, the helpers needed to do the more-than-one-man task of making a good survey. This hints that the mission was about something other than creating a perfect record.

Most telling, though, is an odd omission in Washington's letters about the actual sale of the land a few years later to friend and Fredericksburg neighbor Hugh Mercer. No doubt, the two had a chance to discuss Ferry Farm and its future once Mary was well settled near the Lewises' home. It also might be that Lewis acted as Washington's agent in this matter, as he had in others. On March 21, 1774, Mercer informed Washington that he "had an inclination to purchase" Ferry Farm for the three pounds an acre that Washington had been seeking. This made the actual size of the land itself fundamental to arriving at a complete cost.[46] Mercer wrote that he had "heard that the tract contains about 600 acres," a figure that reflected not only the land Washington had inherited on his father's death but also additional parcels, mostly to the east, that he had acquired over the years.[47]

Washington quickly agreed on the per-acre price and terms, but he was vague on the actual acreage of the land. He noted that the old surveys tended to be a bit "over measure," and so they were not that reliable—especially by the more scrupulous standards of the 1770s.[48] On March 28, Washington wrote to Mercer that, in fact, he was not at all sure whether the farm "measures more or less" a full 600 acres, because, as he curiously added, "I really know not, as it never was survey'd to my knowledge."[49]

Weems soon made Ferry Farm famous for being the place where Washington could not tell a lie, and yet here he was right in the middle of one in the process of selling off the land. What did he mean by that apparent lie?

Of course, he may have meant simply that the land's total metes and bounds had not been recorded since Catlett's day, and those records were not to be trusted in the first place. Washington may have meant to say "never fully surveyed" and left that incompleteness implied in what was, after all, a deal between friends. Likewise, he may have meant "never officially surveyed," meaning that no good and current record was sitting in the King George County courthouse.[50]

Nevertheless, the fact is there: Washington had surveyed the land three years earlier, and it is quite unlikely that he had simply forgotten. And even though the work seems to be incomplete, it is nevertheless unlikely that there was some flaw, some embarrassment in the survey notes themselves, that made Washington unwilling to mention it at all as he discussed the acreage of the property.

Instead, his omission is the single best piece of evidence that Washington, in fact, saw the 1771 survey as having been a private act—one he conducted for his own reasons and thus, in the long run, not germane to the sale of that same parcel. Overlooked and unmentioned, the survey was nevertheless partial and, most importantly, personal.

One key to a good survey is the selection of landmarks. Lacking the repeatable precision of the Global Positioning System, eighteenth-century surveyors had to locate parts of the land that were remarkable and permanent enough that they could serve as reliable future references. There was no point in resting measurements on the fleeting ephemera of field and forest or leaving future artisans left to stand wondering to exactly which tree or rock the old survey referred. A good document thus had to land on things that would be there later when others came back. In eastern Virginia, with its lack of impressive rock outcroppings or huge standing boulders, those things tended most often to be trees. They could be singularly enduring hardwoods or any easily identifiable species cut down to make a good stump or hacked at so that the scars would stand the test of time. Borders of rivers and creeks, edges of swamps, and microclimatic vegetative changes also made their appearances in surveys, but the standing, easily noticed marker was always best.

When Washington set out on the 13th to mark out what he called "the fields" near "my mother's" house, he took in a landscape dotted with good markers that promised to be there for some time. Roads, bounding fences, field fences, and various structures were all the dots he could connect length by chain length. But the best marker of all he specifically excluded from the survey: the house itself. He hinted at its general location and even noted the location of a bordering garden. But actually placing it on the land? He chose not to.

By 1771, the house was showing its nearly fifty years of age.

It had been appropriately grand when William Strother had it built in the 1720s, and it was a worthy enough gentry seat when Augustine Washington bought it in 1738. But its trajectory was always downward.

At the same time, prominent local families built grander and bigger in such a way as to leave the old family home looking small, antique, and perhaps even a bit ramshackle. Despite its family history, by 1771 Ferry Farm had long been overshadowed by the other homes of his life. Mount Vernon, the Fairfaxes' Belvoir, his father's and his own birthplace at Pope's Creek, and even Lord Fairfax's hunting lodge, Greenway Court—all were places of more current personal meaning. In so many ways, the old home was yesterday's news. The fields, though, were different. Although they also carried memories, their value made for a happier assessment than the dwindling value of an aging and old-fashioned home. Thus, on the 13th Washington edited the home itself out of his narrative. Instead, he created a place of growth and commerce, but he left it almost entirely free of domesticity. Is that to say that he left it free of femininity or maternal impulses as well? Mary haters might happily say he did. Whether by intent or not, that was one effect of the survey: Its narrative highlighted the agrarian and commercial over the domestic.

Even so, the survey started with a reference to one of the Washington family's most intimate moments of its Ferry Farm years. Washington began his circuit at "the little gate by the tombstone."[51] It is difficult to place this exact site, but the 1932 platting of the notes showed it sitting a small distance to the south of the home. When John Gadsby Chapman painted the ruins of the Washington home, around 1832 he showed a small toppled-over gravestone in the foreground of his view. That would place the graveyard a bit even farther south and deeper inland than the 1932 mapmakers imagined. In the early 2000s, a team of ground resistivity researchers used ground-penetrating radar to seek out the grave shafts. Their work located a number of graves sitting a few dozen yards east of the Washington home. Although that find does answer the general question about graves in the area, it does not shed much light on which of those might have been within the specific enclosure Washington identified.[52] Nevertheless, it is fairly certain that a small cemetery sat a bit inland and south of the home. It is certainly upon this cemetery that Washington anchored his survey.

But who was in the cemetery? That is a more intriguing, perhaps more telling question.

I can count only two of Ferry Farm's dead—that is to say, I can name with some certainty only two people of the many buried at Ferry Farm. One was Maurice Clark, the man who was the first recorded Englishman living on the land. John Catlett may have done the first, albeit unreliable survey, but he never moved from his downriver address to the falls. That honor went to Clark, who had served a tidewater master for some years before he signed a Northern Neck Proprietary deed and set into clearing and farming.

In 1710, Clark and a servant named Dennis Lindsey were living in a small two-room post-in-ground home not too far from where the Washington home would later stand. By 1711, Clark had passed away and left the land, and his few possessions and livestock, to Lindsey and some neighbors. No record survives stating just where Clark was finally buried, but given that this was his land—land he worked for years to own—it is a pretty safe bet that he was laid to rest not too far from his house.

That grave would have been as humble as the life Clark lived. The next owner to build a home near the site was William Strother. Although he also died at Ferry Farm, he was more prominent than Clark, serving as a member of the House of Burgesses and owning many other properties. Upon his 1738 death, Strother may have been buried near his home, but he also may have been buried further down the Northern Neck in another family plot. We know nothing of his family or children who may have died and been buried there as well. However, it is reasonable to expect that Strother's burial at the site would have had more enduring markers than that of Clark—but then again, it may not have.

By 1739, Ferry Farm was a Washington possession, and in that year they suffered the first of the family's deaths there. Mildred, an infant named for Augustine's sister, was the only one of her children Mary outlived. Given common practice, Mildred was almost certainly laid to rest near the house, perhaps in the same sequestered area that held Clark and even others. This would make the "little gate," and perhaps even the tombstone itself, the last marker of the only Washington buried at Ferry Farm. This is certainly the view that has prevailed for centuries.

The "little gate" is a simple testament to a cared-for and maintained plot—a place set apart from the rest of the farm. The Washingtons may have overseen the building of the gate and the fence or wall it implied, or it may have been a holdover from Strother's day. Likewise, the tombstone may or may not have been Mildred's. But Washington's pairing of the two at the outset of an essentially private survey of his childhood landscape is telling. As he set about parting with the land, he began his narration not with a place of life (the home) but with the most visible reminder of death and loss. At Ferry Farm, Washington lost his father and his brother Lawrence—family losses that began with the death of Mildred and were most visibly recalled on the landscape by the "little gate" and tombstone.

The next two places to make the survey were those associated with the domestic yard—evidence perhaps that the graveyard and the home yard boundary sat in alignment. Washington noted the "henyard" and the "garden poles" before following the line of the garden fence along to the "gulley leading to the ferry landing."[53]

These ordinary farm markers would be unremarkable except for two echoes. One is in the word *hen*. Rural people have long used animal attributes to describe people. "Messy as a pig" and "stubborn as a mule" resonate best with people familiar with those creatures' habits, and only county folk would see it as high masculinity to have soldiers march in line raising their straightened legs as does a prize strutting rooster (of course, we best remember this stride as the goosestep). Amid the many animal analogies, the hen has a special place. The birds' inbred domesticity and their daily role as valued egg layers made the words *hen* and *biddies* common low, marginally insulting terms for women. Might it be that he was coyly winking when he neglected to locate his "mother's house" but nevertheless included the residences of many of the site's old biddies?

The second standout is the reference to the garden poles. When it came time for Weems to create Ferry Farm's best-known narrative—that of the boy who could not tell a lie—the poles made a second appearance. In that story, before George chopped at the cherry tree he tried his hand at the pea poles in his mother's garden. Thus, the two narratives converge on this single ordinary farm element. The point is not that there is some causal relationship in Washington's and Weems's invocations, nor that Weems may have reviewed the survey notes before writing. Rather, what matters is that both writers used this farmyard element in connecting the landscape to Mary. On top of that, Washington's pairing of garden poles and hens carries hints of sexuality. Although it is probably not an intentional double entendre, it is worth remembering that this was the place where Washington reached sexual awareness. In some small way that fact is hinted at, however inadvertently, in the survey.

After passing along the line of the home lot and reaching the ferry lane and the ravine it passed, Washington then turned northward and inland. What followed in his narrative were primarily listings of the fences marking the borders between his and his neighbors' land, a "corn field" here and there, and some wooded lots. He noted a small "drain" sitting in some "flat land" and the edge of "sawpit branch." All of these are exactly the sorts of places one would expect to see in such a survey—references to a place valued for what it could produce and how well watered was its soil.

Washington's measurements all anchor on equally typical landmarks, such as a "box oak," or "the oaks," or the "large white oak stump," or the "hedge row," all signs of a familiar cultivated landscape—reminders that the hardwoods survived at the edges of fields that were otherwise cleared for cultivation. Here and there, particularly near the back of the land where the woods were thicker, Washington noted the "marked trees."[54] These markings were cuttings chopped into the bark for the next surveyor. There is no way to know whether these were preexisting chops from earlier surveys or new ones cut in by Washington and his unnamed assistants. If they were, in fact, new markers, what a delight to imagine Washington chopping away at trees in creating his text of the land that would soon enough be remembered primarily for just that act—albeit on one specific tree.

But the complicated crossing of roads made this survey different from others. Washington mentioned three roads cutting through the fields. One was the Ferry Lane on the northwestern edge. The others were the larger, more traveled public roads, fenced in and gated—arteries of public activity hovering annoyingly close to the otherwise private world of the "plantation." Washington referred to the roads with a confusing jumble of names: "the Road to Stafford Court," or "the County Road," or the "Stafford Road," or even "the Great Road." Reconstructing this web is no easy feat, and in the absence of other maps it relies on the same survey notes and what seems to have survived of this network into later days.

What is clear, though, is that major roads cut through Ferry

Farm's fields. The main one, Washington's "Great Road," was King's Highway, the main path down the Northern Neck peninsula.[55] At some point near the house it forked, one spur heading down to the Ferry Landing, and the other turning back and heading up toward the Stafford County Courthouse. It was this three-way junction that Washington kept on crossing and recrossing as he measured Mary's fields. This hub and meeting of road and ferry landing ensured that Ferry Farm would be a singularly busy place in a Virginia more accustomed to riverfront quietude. Back in May of 1749, Washington had complained to Lawrence about the noise and bother from the road and ferry, claiming, "I think we suffer enough" from having so much activity near the home.[56] That letter constitutes perhaps the single most referenced document of the busy comings and goings surrounding Ferry Farm.

In describing the crisscross of roads and fences, though, the survey echoed concerns Washington had outlined in 1749. He had complained about the comings and goings of the ferry just below the family home, its loud calling bell being a regular part of life on the farm. He also noted, with some concern, that plans for other ferries then in the works would only make things worse and even have an effect on some of Mary's land downriver. The busyness he complained of was manifested in the survey as well.

Although the noise and activity may be been annoyances at the time, the meeting of road and river was probably Ferry Farm's most important attribute, one that singularly shaped the young Washington's horizons, as more than a few biographers have noted.[57] This confluence meant that he was literally raised on a crossroads of empire and eventually became wealthy and powerful through his connections to that empire. Thus, it seems fitting that the roads away from Ferry Farm play such a large role in the 1771 survey— larger even than the home site—because it was these exits that made him the global figure he became.

Washington's circuit next took him along the land's southeastern border and down to where the floodplain meets the river, and from there back onto the "hill which is above the low grounds" and on back to "the beginning at the little gate by the tomb stone."[58] The survey notes left the actual acre totals blank, although Washington wrote the notes in such a way as to fill them in later. He then concluded his narrative by noting the presence of "some pretty good land" near the Sawpit Branch and where his line crossed the Stafford Road. That was it.

Changes in the land and its vegetation have made identifying the exact spots noted in the survey quite a challenge. The name *Sawpit Branch* seems to have been gone by the early 1800s, making the stream hard to definitely identify, and the actual runs of the roads are also very tricky to pin down. Subsequent activity widened and straightened King's Highway, and the Stafford County Road all but vanished. Post–Civil War rail lines and later road leveling terraced what was in Washington's time a wide, gentle slope. In 1932, a team of cartographers working with the federal Washington Bicentennial Commission created their imperfect and incomplete map based on Washington's original notes and published it in their commemorative collection of Washington maps. They peppered their work with extracts from the survey itself, printed in Washington's hand; mostly it seems to have given the very new map a feel of the authentic and to have kept it from standing out too much amid maps actually penned by Washington with which it shared covers.

Nevertheless, the map was not particularly accurate—at least, crucial parts of it do not jibe well with what one can see of the land. The Ferry Lane goes off at an odd angle that makes no sense, and the gully is in the wrong place entirely. The roads are curious, and much of the rest is informed guesswork.

But in making the map, the unnamed draftspeople and the Library of Congress map supremo Lawrence Martin situated the 1771 survey within discussions of their own choice. For unclear reasons, Martin claimed that his team's drafting project "fully confirms the general evidence that Washington was a good surveyor." He also saw the map as being proof positive that this was indeed the land where Washington came of age, an issue of some concern in the late 1920s.[59] Martin included the map in his collection because it gave breadth to the collection but also because it spoke to Washington's skill and its origins.

Noting, but not being particularly interested in, the absence of the home in the original document, the drafters went ahead and obligingly placed it on their map. They represented it with a small reprinting of a mid-nineteenth-century imaging of the old home. It first appeared accompanying the writing of Benson Lossing but was made famous by Currier and Ives, who offered a chromolithograph for patriotic customers. This home was a low-roofed, rustic ramshackle with large chimneys; the viewer is led to imagine low ceilings, small cozy rooms, and hearty farm living. In short, the nineteenth-century drawn Washington home was a graphic version of the one Weems described, in 1807, as being a "low front of faded red." Thus, in rendering Washington's farewell survey, the bicentennial drafters shoehorned in a later text and blended Washington's own words about Ferry Farm with elements of the later—invented—version of Ferry Farm. Two narratives entwined in this new bicentennial text.

But even so, Washington never created his own map from his own notes; he left the acre totals as uncalculated blanks and stashed the document away. He overlooked it, and even silenced it, when he sold the land to Hugh Mercer and his heirs. In time, the document itself became separated from the rest of Washington's papers just as Ferry Farm itself became separated from the rest of Washington's properties, a fact that left its story an orphan to be told principally by others.

The 1771 survey, paired with his 1749 letter complaining about the ferry and his *Virginia Gazette* ad for his sale of the farm (with a few slight and passing notices later in life), make up the full corpus of Washington's writing about this place. However, his narrative emphasizes a few aspects of the land and his time there that not only speak to his own family experience there but also foreshadow later discussions that, overtly at least, take no notice of Washington's own writing about Ferry Farm.

The September diary entries blended Mary and Ferry Farm, a pairing that is both understandable and enduring. But, at the same time, Washington's survey erased Mary by bypassing the home she had lived in longer than any other. Instead, his survey landed on parts of the landscape that echoed his own experiences in ways that are quite revealing. The gate by the tombstone recalled losses the young man Washington had endured at Ferry Farm—losses that we must assume were emotionally difficult and we know shaped the direction of his life.

Washington made ample note of Ferry Farm's unique intersecting network of regional and local roads. Those paths were an irritation for Washington in one moment, but in other moments they were his main avenues away from a place that must have felt small and contained compared with the larger houses and estates he had seen close up. That joining of these roads and the Rappahannock riverfront just below the home made the place distinctive, in a Virginia more commonly settled in a less compressed fashion. Washington may not have liked the bustle so close to his doorstep, but he well appreciated the value of networks (social as well as transportation), and some of that was learned at Ferry Farm.

All was compiled, recorded, measured, and then tucked away— a seemingly inconsequential fragment of a large record of great deeds. But even so, Washington set in motion elements of the narrative that would come to define the place of his youth, even though he chose not to tell us much, and hid what little he did write.

What he did not hide was the sales advertisement he took out in the *Virginia Gazette* soon after making his survey. In many respects, it was the same as the one his father had seen in 1738. In the ad, he called attention to the site's "clear and distinct view of almost every house" in Fredericksburg and the ability to watch "every vessel that passes to and from it."[60] The ad made no mention of the home, the same omission he made in his survey the year before. In fact, the "most agreeable" vista Washington was selling was probably not from the old home's front step but rather the one from higher up the hillside. Even in selling the land, Washington hid the more domestic side of the land and his family's imprint there, describing instead the westward views the land afforded.

Washington's own writing about Ferry Farm was all views, local concerns, and land focus—all of which makes sense for a surveyor. Whatever other memories he had, he chose not to share; thus, all we have of his own mind comes from these few texts about the land and its value. He left a picture of the place that emphasized it as a landscape—a place of roads, views, fencelines, boundaries, and trees, his written Ferry Farm. But that is nevertheless a narrative in its own right. The biographers wove together their themes, all with an eye toward understanding Washington's character. Thus, their gaze landed most often on questions of schooling, nurturing, and background. In that project, places were surrogates or attributes—grace, learning, or boyhood. Ferry Farm became little more than reference to hard times and wild conditions—attributes that set the land's story for generations. In the mainstream of the biographies or Weems's invention, Ferry Farm was given over to the forces of nature and markets. It would be some time before it became something more historical.

The narrative of childhood and place Washington left in the edges of his own writing provided a glimpse into his values, both moral and fiscal. Washington's writing recalled Ferry Farm mostly as property and a place with a view, and his time at the place was recalled through images of neighborhood irritation and poverty. These, too, helped set the land's course: For more than a century after Washington, the land was little more than property changing hands and commercial visions. Washington ultimately treated it as little more, and so it was for a very long time. But at the same time, his letter to Lawrence became a vital link in casting Ferry Farm as a poor place—the "blown out tract" some later scholars describes.[61] In that way, Washington covered both bases. On one hand, he described a place of bustle and prosperous potential and, on the other, he penned a single detail—the lack of corn—that would mark the land as poor, or at least poorly managed. Local people and subsequent landowners attached to the former—the observations in the survey and the land's potential—whereas scholars seized the lack of corn and its implications for both the land and the effectiveness of the woman then running its operations.

The survey hinted at many aspects of Washington's childhood and the place most associated with that part of his life. In a rough, half-formed way it created—with the aid of few other short texts—a hidden narrative of Washington's formative years. It did so through the plain language of surveying, but each mark was a choice, and each choice was actively made by a man who knew very well the land he recorded.

As Washington sealed the deal to sell Ferry Farm, he also had his eye on the future of Mount Vernon, a home he had owned by then for nearly a decade. When he took up residence there, it was not too unlike the other homes of his childhood. Augustine's home at Pope's Creek, and the home he left to Lawrence, like Ferry Farm, were all basic rectangles of one and a half stories. In each, rooms on the first floor flanked a central passage, and sleeping and storage rooms filled the dormer-lit loft spaces above. Chimneys stood on each the far walls, giving the whole presentation a pleasing uniformity very much in the style of the day. It was a convenient arrangement, really: Each home the Washingtons owned looked the same and so functioned the same way. This style home also was common for the better sort of Virginians: not too extravagant or ornate but substantive, comfortable, and powerfully suggestive of the early-eighteenth-century's elite families. Its like was visible all along the colony's riverbanks and inlets.

But just as Washington ended his family's time at Ferry Farm, he was laying plans to transform *his* Mount Vernon into something new. Until then, the grandest homes he knew were those of others. But now, as a wealthy man, he set into expanding his mansion into something bigger, unique, more his own. He had begun that transformation in 1757 when he had a second story added to the home.[62] This made the loft space into a full second floor. Although this added room, it left the basic footprint and profile largely intact. It was undoubtedly larger than either of his other childhood residences, but it was still only a larger *version* of them, not something wholly new.

Wholly new was exactly what Washington had in mind in 1773. There would be new wings on either of Mount Vernon's ends. These would surround the outside chimneys with new rooms and quiet their previously dominant visual effect. The new wings would have sloped roofs, which would transform the old straight ridgeline into a new one of hips and angles. A new façade with a shallow but tall and pointed gable would frame the inland entry, and most distinctive off all, a glass-windowed cupola would cap off the whole thing. These changes would utterly remake the old home into some entirely new and distinctive—a true standalone residence.

Washington built for himself a seat befitting his wealth and prominence in the colony and even the empire. But his drafts and plans did more. They silenced the old home that still hid somewhere in the core of Mount Vernon's frames and siding. He wrapped the old Washington floor plan in a new skin of his own devising—in short, he enacted in architecture the kind of self-fashioning he did in life. All this happened right as he said his goodbyes to Ferry Farm—right as he sold off another one of those old-style Washington family homes. Washington ensured that his present and his future would not be lived in places or structures that spoke too loudly of his past. Through rebuilding, surveying, and sales Washington broke with some of the most enduring remnants of his childhood—and all at the same time.

As a member of the House of Burgesses, Washington had played a small role in confronting the tax policies that helped unleash the imperial crisis that would sunder the empire. But by the 1770s, those matters seemed somewhat remote from day-to-day life at Mount Vernon. His foremost concern there was making a good life even better. Even though he may have understood that British policy was sowing the seeds of conflict, there was no way he could have foreseen the scale of the violence only a few years away or imagined the role he would play.[63] Yet as the wheels of conflict picked up speed in distant ports and on far-away streets, Washington was providentially breaking ties with parts of his personal past. In some small way, therefore, Washington's private survey of Ferry Farm in 1771 helped set the stage for a far larger and riskier break with his past that would emerge as the decade progressed.

3

THE SUBTERRANEAN YOUNG WASHINGTON

Crafting a Material Narrative for the Childhood Years

It's an amazing time; It's a very important site that was thought to have been lost; This now gives us one more part of the story to tell; We are a nation now where people want to have heroes.

Virginia governor Timothy Kaine at Ferry Farm, 2008[1]

In 1996, Walmart announced its plans to develop Ferry Farm as a new shopping plaza. They had purchased the land after years of failed private preservation efforts and lobbying by landowners to have the tract rezoned as commercial property. The response to the news was quick and dramatic. Locally and across the nation, concerned citizens banded together to insist that there be "No Walmart, by George." Arrayed against them were a powerful—but at that time still rather naive—corporation, a county government eager to boost tax revenues, and the ever-resonant argument of jobs and amenities. Recent successes at stopping similar development projects in nearby counties and the shutting down of Disney's planned theme park near the Manassas Civil War battlefield put wind in preservationists' sails. The biggest gust propelling the cause, though, was the simple power of the name George Washington, one of the best rallying cries any group could have.[2] Once the issue moved beyond local media venues and became national news, the mounting pressure stalled the county's review of Walmart's plans, and the retail giant was forced to face the reality that public sentiment meant it would never be able to build on the historical land it owned. Before long, it sold the property off to a quickly assembled mix of backers that in time became the George Washington Foundation, the not-for-profit organization that still owns and curates the land.

Some of what motivated Walmart's opponents was a desire to maintain the historical feel of the town across the river. For others it was a then-growing worry about suburban sprawl. But the unifying concern was a powerful sense that there was something simply inappropriate about a shopping plaza covering the land where Washington had come of age. Some of that feeling was rooted in two hundred years of memory and sentimental association, but much of it also stemmed from the sense that Ferry Farm had something unique to say about Washington. The fact that the land still held the physical remains of the old Washington farmstead hidden on it meant that somewhere there were objects George had touched as a child, remains of buildings he had inhabited, and hints about the place he once owned. More than serving as a shrine, this patch of land may well have been a pile of secrets waiting to be decoded and an irreplaceable source of new information about Washington. As the editor of Fredericksburg's *Free Lance Star* put it in the midst of the Walmart debate, "What treasures will be destroyed forever" should development move ahead? "What else lies buried at Ferry Farm?"[3]

What indeed. From the beginning of its life as a preserved historical site, the promise of archaeological findings has been at the center of the land's nonmonetary value. From the very beginning, project planners knew archaeology would play a central role in how the site would make its contributions and the type of story it would present to the world. Even before 1996, there had been some work on the site by contractors, volunteers, and early staff. But it was all small-scale and not part of long-term commitment to understanding the site. Once the land became a preserved site, excavation could begin in earnest. For the next few years, a small team of professionals and a dedicated group of volunteers tested out a few different parts of the site and got the first glimpse of features that would turn out to be of considerable significance.

By 2001, the foundation intensified the focus on its archaeological mission and committed to what promised to be at least a twelve-year project to excavate, interpret, curate, and ultimately recreate the site, its artifacts, and its lost structures. This ramped-up version of the project expanded the professional staff, students, and volunteers from all across the nation and brought a well-developed and nuanced research agenda to what had been a somewhat piecemeal program beforehand. Several seasons of excavation explored each part of the site's core in great detail and located a wide array of features. By the summer of 2008, the George Washington Foundation was able to announce that it had found the remains of the Washington home and had recovered more than a half a million artifacts from the site's prehistorical and historical occupations.

In the attending press coverage, one idea came through loud and clear: This land and its archaeological study were creating what I called at the time "a new text" about the Washingtons and George's childhood at the site. *Smithsonian Magazine* captured this sentiment perfectly in an article quoting me and Ferry Farm's director of archaeology David Muraca. The site was our best chance to look into the world that produced Washington. As Muraca summed it up, "If we do our job right, the Washington biographies will change."[4] This chapter is, in essence, a follow-up to the expectations that I, Muraca, and others set for Ferry Farm's excavation. Archaeology is slow work and excavations are ongoing, so I offer it as a manner of "interim report," a state of the field as opposed to a final statement.

Nevertheless, as we will see, the site reveals its own narrative, distinct from the ones that Washington and his biographers created. Crucially, it differs not only in the conclusions it draws but even more in the elements and characters it brings into focus and how it recasts elements of the narrative. The corpus of the biographical literature is text filled with names and events—the residue of correspondences, court records, and memoir. It is a deeply human text, rooted in the words people chose to capture emotion, opinion, and desires of all kinds. The material record is an entirely different animal. Whereas the former relies on words, the latter interprets things, their proximity to one another, and the marks they bear from use. Gone are the days when scholars argued that the material provided in some way a superior, "truer" record of the past. Whereas once scholars were quick to assign bias to the written and objectivity to the material, the entire field of historical archaeology is much more at peace with the idea that the discipline's unique charge is, in fact, to move back and forth between records in order to create new, otherwise impossible narratives of sites and their people.

A central part of the archaeological charge at Ferry Farm has long been to "understand George." The challenge is that archaeology has, at best, a mixed relationship with the individual as a concept and unit of study. On one hand, the excavation of human remains cannot be any more individual. Data gleaned from the bones and teeth of people themselves is one of the most intimate and personal forms of information possible.[5] But more commonly, sites are made up of features—meaning the in-ground remains of structures, fence posts, trash pits, and so on—and artifact assemblages that, though created by individual people, do not so easily credit their authors. Nevertheless, ascribing individual agency to a given feature or spread of artifacts has been central to the discipline's interpretive mission. Over the years, archaeologists have used an array of frameworks to understand the motivations, social structures, ideologies, and gender systems of the past peoples who created a given site or feature. Arguably, the material residue of past action is as intimate a glimpse of people as can be afforded by any diary or correspondence.[6]

But there is a unique element to this notion of individuality: The individuals themselves often remain anonymous. Who dug a specific set of postholes? Who broke this cup or that plate? Who dropped this shoe down this well? The answer is usually lost to time: It may have been a servant, coal miner, an enslaved African, or any other of countless possible agents. Rarely—and almost always only in conjunction with a fortuitous set of documents—will an individual's name emerge from the residue of his or her actions. The ground may produce a rich text showing individual action, but the individuals usually remain nameless. This is not a problem, and in some cases it is an advantage. On most sites, though, a name is not all that crucial. It is enough to know that these bottles were dumped by the workers at Lowell Massachusetts Boott Mills, that the resident of this home owned these cufflinks, or that these enslaved people cooked in this fireplace. This is usually enough to enable a new view of life at a site and connect people to the remains of their actions and, from that, glean the thought processes behind those actions.

At a site where George Washington lived, though, the stakes for individual identity take on the added weight of national discourse. This adds a challenging dimension. Sites associated with celebrated people have long confronted this matter. For great homes such as Mount Vernon and Jefferson's Monticello, the guiding hand and plan of a famous homeowner are easily read in the ground, especially when supporting documents double the streams of data. But isolating specific individuals within the material record is no easy task.

Ferry Farm and its inherited narratives of Washington's childhood present a unique problem: How do we find the actions of a single child on a site that was home to an entire family and several extended families it enslaved? There is a constant tension between the very powerful desire, for a project like this one, to locate George proper—to uncover some special, significant object that can tie the site to the man-as-a-boy and reveal some hitherto unknown personal moment. But that desire runs against the unyielding reality that a site is still a site, no matter how famous the people it once housed. On top of that, two hundred years of biography have created—as we have seen—a set of canonical concerns and silences. Thus, "looking for George" was a venture made more challenging both by the nature of the record itself and by the inherent mismatch between that record and the kinds of questions for which centuries of scholars and devotees have sought answers.[7]

The first question to answer is the one about the depth of Washington's association with Ferry Farm: How much time did he spend on this land, and how much did he connect with it? This issue has proven to be both more difficult to answer than one might expect and more contentious. Different scholars have read the same materials and arrived at different conclusions. That the family moved to Ferry Farm in 1738 is easily established by Augustine Washington's purchase of William Strother's home and the resulting paperwork. But questions about how much time Washington spent at the farm are a different matter. It became a commonplace in the biography to move George to Mount Vernon and Lawrence's care soon after Augustine's death while also having him spend much time with Austin at Pope's Creek. Without disputing the probability that Washington moved around quite a bit, it is also true that this emphasis served rhetorically to place the young George under male guidance while leaving Ferry Farm, feminized by its association with Mary, to the side of the discussion. Just as biographers saw Mount Vernon as refinement and opportunity and Ferry Farm as rustic and wild, they also cast the two places as being essentially male and female. Yet the evidence for an early-leaving thesis has been little more than an assumption of Ferry Farm's inadequacy, the conflation of Mary and the land, and the awareness that, in the end, Mount Vernon would become Washington's main home.

A quick survey of some major works show how thin and dismissive Ferry Farm's treatment has been. John Ferling called it "a worn out tract," but also claimed, probably correctly, that Lawrence's Mount Vernon "must have been more elegantly furnished" than the more threadbare Rappahannock estate.[8] Joseph Ellis reduced Ferry Farm's dwelling—impressive in its day—to a "six room farm house" in his narrative, which focused on Ferry Farm's poor educational prospects and emphasized Lawrence as the defining influence over the young Washington.[9] In Paul Johnson's biography, Ferry Farm appeared only as Washington's "father's own residential farm on the Rappahannock," left to George in 1743.[10] Douglas Southall Freeman imagined a young George excited to move to the Rappahannock, to see his first town, and to explore the farm's acres. Nevertheless, Freeman argued that life at Ferry Farm "had not been stinted or meager, but neither was it opulent or gracious," in a narrative that stressed George's connections to his older brothers and their homes.[11] Samuel Eliot Morison saw Washington as having been "parked" at Ferry Farm, trapped there by the death of a "land poor" father and thwarted by a shrew of a mother.[12] For Morrison, Ferry Farm's limited opportunities and association with the hated Mary Washington made it a place to leave as soon as possible. James Flexner, on the other hand, saw Ferry Farm as a place of "modest comfort" and also noted that this was "for rural Virginia a lively place" because of the meeting of the river with King's Highway, which ran down the Northern Neck and ended at the ferry landing almost at the Washington doorstep.[13]

One can almost feel the pens of many authors pushing young George out of Ferry Farm's front door! Biographers conspired to remove George as soon after his father's death as possible—for some writers perhaps as little as eight years. Advocates of the "early leaving thesis" have had a place in the literature from the beginning of the genre. The guiding assumption has been that George rushed off to Lawrence's Mount Vernon once the brothers became fatherless. Certainly, George ended up there, but the actual date of that move and its concomitant leaving behind of Ferry Farm has been an odd area of speculation. Paul Longmore, for example, saw Washington as moving completely to Mount Vernon just as soon as Augustine breathed his last—a common assumption in the biographies.[14] Others have stretched the interval out a bit to 1747, or even to 1749. Jack Warren argued that the Washingtons returned to the Mount Vernon area (then still called Little Hunting Creek) in 1741 and then came back again to Ferry Farm.[15]

In the lead-up to the 1932 bicentennial of Washington's birth , the issue of Washington's location was something of a hot potato as different groups competed to have their own projects recognized and funded. Not content with the arguments of other early-leavers, Charles Arthur Hoppin—the 1920s historian of the Wakefield Foundation in Westmoreland County, Virginia—crafted a self-serving case that Ferry Farm had never even been Washington land. He was then promoting a rival Washington commemoration project at the birthplace site and had no interest in seeing his own efforts compete for funds with a similar project across the river from Fredericksburg. In referring to an imaginative nineteenth-century drawing of Ferry Farm, Hoppin wrote that Augustine Washington had never "owned this cottage, never lived in it" and, rather astonishingly, "never owned the land around it."[16] Instead, Hoppin claimed that the Washingtons lived more than a mile inland and downriver—a conclusion he based on a creative reading of land records, a selective overlooking of Washington's own writing, and land sales advertisements. The 1920s promoters in Fredericksburg fought back against Hoppin's dramatic but erroneous claims, to some good effect. Nevertheless, Hoppin's writing became part of the written record, available for anyone looking to find useful heretical tidbits. As late as 1996, a Washington biographer named Harrison Clark picked up on the idea, making himself one of the last of the Ferry Farm deniers.[17]

Whether through early leaving or outright denial, all this debate silenced Ferry Farm in the historical version of the Washington childhood story. Its longstanding association with Mason Locke Weems's body of stories was one motivation of this forced omission. For those wanting a "real" Washington, freed from cherry trees and performed priggish morality, cleaning up the story often meant throwing the landscape out with the Parson. Furthermore, for twentieth-century Mary haters, conflating the woman with her home-of-longest-residence made Ferry Farm a topic best passed over. The undeniable documentary silence that surrounded Washington's childhood years created space for this sort of writing. Biographers either passed over the early years or creatively filled the gaps as we have seen.

But that silencing had an effect on the land and, ultimately, on the site's archaeology. By passing it over, writers crafting the Washington narrative denied Ferry Farm the very historicity it might otherwise have had. Whereas the Westmoreland County birthplace began a long and interesting process of commemoration in the 1820s and Mount Vernon became the first historically preserved American home in the 1850s, Ferry Farm's historical memory hung from a slender thread for nearly two centuries. The excavation of Ferry Farm was far more than the search for the remains of a 1740s home. It entailed working through the remains of no less than five successive homesteads, all occupying the same parcel of land. Each new building and reuse of the old place grew from the economic imperatives of individual landowners seeking to make a living. Washington's shadow never fully left the place, but most often it was his image on the dollar that mattered most. Had Ferry Farm been an accepted and acknowledged Washington shrine from its earliest days, then the site itself would have been entirely different. The point here is that excavation is a place where memory meets the material in very real ways. The silence around Washington's childhood years created the conditions under which the site of the Washington home would be repeatedly mauled by subsequent land use. All that use and reuse increasingly limited the scale and quality of the archaeological record. At Ferry Farm, silence in one discussion imposed a silence on others.

A root cause of the silence has been the enduring questions about exactly where Washington passed his time between 1743 and 1752. There is every reason to believe that Washington spent the years after his father's death moving between Ferry Farm, Pope's Creek, and Mount Vernon. The documentation for this question of specific movements, though, is singularly thin—no one was keeping a recording eye on the young George's comings and goings. As a consequence, this has long been an arena for all sorts of motivated speculation. The question of location is, at the same time, a curious one. Biographers made each of the three childhood homes symbolic of different aspects of Washington's character: Mount Vernon was style, aspiration, and connections; Pope's Creek was family and lineage; and Ferry Farm was the West, ruggedness, and physical ability. For early biographers, that made them all equal players in a larger project. But with the professionalization of history, precise eyes sought precise answers to questions not because they mattered in and of themselves but simply because they were unknown. By the 1920s as well, the increasing pace and scope of Washington commemoration added a new monetizable value to claiming a portion of the Washington childhood.

But strong as the will may have been for some concrete answers to emerge, the data simply have never been there to definitively bring down the curtain on the "where was George?" question. What we can say is this: Washington spent enough time at Ferry Farm that he could write his 1749 complaints to Lawrence and that he was still signing documents as a man from King George County until at least 1752, a year in which he deepened his commitment to Free Masonry at Fredericksburg's lodge.[18]

The "where was George?" question mattered for reasons of local pride and politics, but it is not a question that the site's archaeology can take on in any definitive way. Artifacts found in the 1930s excavations at the Pope's Creek birthplace site help locate the Washington family on the land. Early- to mid-eighteenth-century wine bottle seals marked with "AW" indicate either Augustine or Austin Washington. Sadly, no similar personal artifacts are in the Ferry Farm collections, and no single object emerged that could be said to have belonged to George exclusively. Excavators found a remarkably well-preserved white ball clay pipe, marked with an elaborate masonic emblem on its inward facing curve. The pipe dates to late in the eighteenth century—after George, and even the other Washingtons, were gone. Additionally, large numbers of white salt-glazed stoneware table setting fragments came from layers and features in and around the Washington home. This would almost certainly have been the table service in use in the 1740s, but again, connecting a given plate fragment to Washington is a stretch.

But despite the work of Ferry Farm deniers such as Charles Arthur Hoppin and the occasional more modern nonbeliever, the documentary chain of title linking the Washingtons to the land is just too strong to break. In the 1990s, local historian Thena Jones conducted a study of the Ferry Farm titles as the property was securing its historical designation. More recently, George Washington Foundation researcher Travis Walker reviewed the same record set and arrived at many of the conclusions as had Jones.[19]

Both studies tell very similar stories of parcels of land changing hands through sales and inheritances, or large holdings breaking into smaller ones and then smaller ones reconsolidating into larger ones. "Running" (as the lingo holds) a chain of title is a famously complicated and error-prone exercise, given the vicissitudes of older land records and the endless permutations possible in past land deals. At the same time, the records can be very authoritative—and in Ferry Farm's case, they are. What the records make clear is that the parcel of land excavated beginning in 2001 was, without a doubt, the Washington family homestead. And even though no smoking-gun object linked George personally to the land, this was indeed his childhood home. However, none of this can show us how many actual weeks of that childhood he spent at this homestead.

Likewise, the material record is fairly silent on the specific questions of the content of Washington's education that have so fascinated biographers. Evidence of Washington learning to be an elite Virginian is certainly part of the site's record, however. The creation and maintenance of regimes of capital, property acquisition, and racial slavery that defined colonial life all were crucial parts of Washington's education and are manifested in the site's record. The particularities of a single child's schooling (perhaps a better word here) are less visible. All that discussion about Washington's mathematical skills, his lack of Latin learning, and homespun diligence as a student does not carry over well to the site's archaeology. The larger landscape does carry some references to the extent of this concern, though. About a mile upriver from Ferry Farm, in the vicinity of Falmouth, there is a small restored log cabin known locally as the Hobby School House, in reference to the largely mythical teacher. Nevertheless, a specific material or artifactual tie to Washington's schooling has not emerged on either site. The particulars of reading, writing, and arithmetic belong to an arena prioritized by the childhood genre literature but one not fully resonating in the material record.

These concerns intersect over questions about the quality of life at Ferry Farm during the 1740s. These were the lean years, highlighted by Washington himself and staple in the biographies. Indeed, excavations revealed evidence of the exact contours and scale of the hard times in 1740s. But rather than working to confirm or deny the assumptions of the written record, the site's archaeology allows us to refocus the discussion.[20] The biographies see the issue as being one of wealth or want—a case of Washington being born into one material reality and set of opportunities and then having all that change dramatically with the loss of his father. That dichotomy fed the self-made man narrative that has been so much a part of the Washington story; seeing Ferry Farm as having been a rough start worked well with that theme. Yet that is the problem: It has been a dichotomy.

The archaeology opens a window onto the material experience of the 1740s, a time of great influence and consequence to Washington, as almost all authors agree. The challenge is to use that record to determine as well as possible the sets of choices the Washingtons made during those years and read outward from there to questions of motivations and outcomes.

What we see this way is less a story of rapid collapse than one of adaptation and stretching. Ceramic assemblages, for example, show that the family plate was very much in keeping with then-current trends. Numerous fragments of white salt-glazed stoneware with delicate press-molded edging attest to early 1740s purchases that were right in line with metropolitan tastes. These acquisitions happened while the family still had Augustine's connections and buying power, of course. But that fashionably current table setting was made to last longer than it might have needed to had things gone differently for the family. It was not until the early 1760s that highly fashionable ceramics appear again in the assemblages, but even then there is evidence of care and repair of more expensive purchases. This and similar evidence points to a suspension of buying during the years between Augustine's death and George's wealth and an ethic of frugality in place afterwards.

This is more than a mere index of family spending. It is evidence of conscious choices being made in and around the Washington home—family economies that a young George would have experienced firsthand. Mary Washington becomes a singular focus in this discussion. Her not remarrying (be it by choice or lack of suitable suitors), the limitations she faced as a woman in a society and legal regime that enshrined male authority and ensured female subordination, her management of her own and her children's properties, and her positioning of them for successful gentry marriages and careers have been themes in the Washington childhood literature from the beginning of the genre. Likewise, the question of Washington's maternal affections has also cropped up over the years. Love is a hard to thing gauge in the archaeological record, but the other matters raise questions that resonate within the site's archaeological record.[21]

There can be no doubt that Mary was not as well connected as her late husband had been and so was not as able to secure for George solid gentry connections and opportunities. But Mary became masterful at doing much with little, and it is less in George than in the younger sister, Betty, that we see Mary's greatest success, as Ferry Farm archaeologist Laura Galke has argued. Betty's early marriage into the locally prominent Lewis family was a triumph of Mary's ability to teach her daughter the gentry arts. Supporting this conclusion are a few singular finds that point to Betty's training at Ferry Farm. A bone handle from a rare needlepoint tool, a fragment of an ornamental ceramic figurine, and remnants of tea sets all speak volumes about what was going on in the family rooms at Ferry Farm.[22]

Colonial Britons adopted metropolitan style and trends as readily as did residents of the home islands.[23] Scholars have seen this as a process of refinement that unfolded over the course of the eighteenth century, whereby colonists shed a rough-hewn material world in favor of something more refined. The development of manners, the rise of consumerism, and the consolidation of colonial purchasing by British Isles manufacturers and marketers reshaped colonial life and helped sow the seeds of Revolution. Recent work—specifically on Virginia—has suggested that the dichotomy between a rough seventeenth century and a genteel eighteenth may be somewhat overplayed.[24] Nevertheless, there were real changes in how material life was lived in American British homes, especially in the first few decades of Washington's life. He came of age at time when the contours of gentry life were changing, and while still retaining the core values of his immediate ancestors—principally the quest for land, titles, and social prestige—Washington quickly developed an affinity for, and skills with, newly fashionable styles, trends, and habits.

The bulk of the biographical literature saw Mount Vernon as the wellspring of Washington's gentry manners. But some of what Ferry Farm has revealed suggests that the old place may have played more of a role in that process than previously allowed. In light of finds from the site, Mary becomes the main agent in ensuring that newly fashionable trends were part of the home even as family finances were assumed to be under stress.[25] One rare find—a tambour hook, used for high-style needlework—was a sign that Mary was teaching Betty the most current of gentry women's pastimes. A set of ceramic figurines showed visitors that Mary was able to buy fashionable objects, even if they were no more than trinkets. A small pewter spoon marked with a "B" (presumably for "Betty") pointed to mother and daughter serving tea in the then-fashionable manner. Significantly, though, each of these items was in its way the cheapest high-end purchase possible: A bone handle was nowhere near as costly as a horn, gem, or metal one, the figures were clear-glazed but not hand painted, and the spoon was not silver. This points to a careful home economy, one that was in touch with metropolitan trends yet at the same time very much concerned with keeping an eye on costs.

All this brings a close focus on the Washington family's finances in the 1740s and Mary's management of them in particular. Although Augustine's death certainly disrupted the family's financial course by breaking his single estate into three, the 1730s and 1740s were already not the best times on the Northern Neck. Never prime tobacco land, the region suffered from newly instituted tobacco inspection regimes that stemmed falling crop prices for some planters but at the expense of forcing others to see their crops destroyed because they were of low quality. Northern Neck soils were never ideal for tobacco, and Northern Neck settlers had to be pretty clever to make a good living.[26] For a while, it seemed that mining was a possible boom, as Augustine well knew through his Principio Company venture. But the boom proved to be more of a bust, and most planters turned to provisioning crops to get by. Washington's own survey of Ferry Farm, for example, showed that corn, not tobacco, was in the main fields. Augustine's will made clear that he ran a fairly diversified operation on his three main holdings, and he left to his children cattle, hogs, a mill, large numbers of enslaved Africans, speculative land holdings, and lots in Fredericksburg.[27] Tobacco would have been a part of the project but not the core of it, as it was on so many Tidewater plantations. What marked the Washingtons' economy as perhaps not as well-positioned as that of wealthy neighbors, such as the Lewises, was the latter's extensive involvement in the shipping trade (an absence Lawrence may have sought to correct by sending his brother to sea). Fredericksburg's best opportunities rested in exploiting its resources as a port, and here the Washingtons were not in the fore.

The combination of local realities, Augustine's economic plan, and ultimately his death all collided to make Washington's teen years hard ones by gentry standards. At the time of his death, Augustine had more than ten thousand acres to his name and stakes in enterprises such as the Accokeek Iron Furnace and properties in Fredericksburg. As most of the biographers have noted, his will divided these properties so that Austin became the master of Pope's Creek and Lawrence received Little Hunting Creek, which he soon named Mount Vernon, as well as control over the Accokeek and parts of Ferry Farm. At his maturity, George received the bulk of Ferry Farm and some other undeveloped lands and lots in town, and his young brothers had similar bequests.

Augustine's human property was similarly distributed, with most people staying at the places where they then lived. But crucially, Mary received almost no direct control over any of her husband's lands, retaining only the land she owned herself, the habitation rights that came with her stewardship of her children's holdings, and a few years of annuity from Austin. The will also left Lawrence as the guiding hand at Accokeek, as that capital-intensive business gradually fell apart. Although Augustine's will was a model of planning, its controlling nature also set the terms for the rest of decade and thus was itself a contributing factor in the hardships of the 1740s. Therefore, Mary's choices, as seen in the material record, reflect the area's economic challenges and the legal requirements that she operate within the terms of a will unable to change as conditions changed.

These material insights enable alternative perspectives on the written record so often used by the biographers. The written records document Mary's ongoing concern about her ability to manage her properties and her charges. She turned at times to her brother

Joseph in London to seek his council, and she also had some local friends and allies. But not all the men around her were as support-ive.[28] Augustine's will gave her only the slightest authority, leaving her to receive an annuity from Austin to help with costs and leaving Lawrence as the master of mine operations and formal owner of a portion of the land she oversaw. Lawrence's move to send George to sea shows that the Mount Vernon side of the family and its allies believed that all was not going perfectly at Ferry Farm. Whereas Joseph Ball argued for time and patience in handling George's future, Lawrence and his allies clearly saw in George's situation either a problem to solve or an opportunity to seize.

On top of that, in 1750 one of Mary's enslaved Africans named Harry murdered another named Tame, leading first to a trial and execution, and then to a rearranging of all of her enslaved prop-erty.[29] It is impossible to tell exactly who were the agents behind this court-overseen human redistribution (might it have been Lawrence, or even George?) or even exactly what discussion led to it. Neverthe-less, the arrival at Ferry Farm of three county officials armed with the papers and authority to reshape Mary's world (albeit perhaps the least defensible part of it) shows what she was up against both in her life and in the documents of that life. Finally, when Wash-ington prepared to sell the land in 1771, his meetings at the Lewis home were rooted in his documented worries about his mother's ability to run the farm. Whatever economic hindrances Mary had to navigate in the 1740s, she was also still subject to second-guessing, and even outright interference, from her male relations. Some of that legendary crustiness may have stemmed from the possibility that she was being undermined by some of her own extended family even as she tried to enact the plans she thought would work best.

In so many discussions, Mary has been a vehicle for other con-cerns. Washington biographers—both supportive and derisive of Mary—have enlisted her to fight battles that often had little to do with her. Rather than adjudicating these conflicts or weighing in on one side or another, Ferry Farm's archaeology looks at a conflicted material record reflecting both wealth and hard times and tries to explain behavior, choices, and agency from their remains. Mary ends up in focus simply because she was the site's longest free white resident (or at least she is the most readily identifiable person to associate with the record), and portions of the record reflect her thinking and the resources available through her extended network. Even though biographers still revel in casting Mary one way or another, that back and forth is not relevant to the site's material record, nor does it provide any substantive help to either side. For those who read in the remains of Mary's careful purchasing and training a special love of her children, the fact remains that it was entirely in her own interest, as an aging woman, to place her children as well as possible. Acts so obviously self-motivated make for a curious altruism. But those who would read in the Hard 1740s some core failing of Mary's simply do not see how much the odds were stacked against her. Instead, what the record does best is provide a window into how material goods were part of strategy to maintain gentry status within a slaveholding family facing numerous challenges.

The nature of the Washington home as a physical object has been the subject of nearly as much back and forth as has Mary's character. Here, though, is a question archaeology can address with more authority than any other means of inquiry.

Washington having been raised in a homespun setting was central to the self-made man narrative, and more than a few biographers have projected that discussion onto the Ferry Farm home. Although Weems certainly had seen the home firsthand when he described it as "weatherbeaten" in 1806, others lacked the benefit of a visit in forming their opinions.[30] Instead, later images of the Washington home were repetitions of others' descriptions, shadows created more by needs in the biographies than architecture itself. But amid all the invented details was still the correct assumption that there was something to be learned about Washington and his family from the home they shared.

Before excavation, the best clues about the home came from Augustine's will and probate inventory. Those documents make no mention of dimensions or total number of stories. However, they do provide a baseline number of rooms, suggesting a one-and-a-half-story home with two pairs of rooms on the first floor separated by a central passage hall. Above these were three rooms, presumably serving as children's sleeping quarters. A conjectural image of the full home was in circulation perhaps as early as the 1830s and was popular in the 1860s, but that image seems more folkloric than those based on the probate record. During the lead-up to the 1932 Washington birth bicentennial, drafters created a best-guess floor plan of the home, based on the probate and nineteenth-century art. This sketch was as useful to colonial revival architects as it was to historical commemorators.[31]

With this floor plan as a basis and references to the earlier art to fill in details, a canonical vision of the home was in place by the time excavation began in earnest in 2001. In the end, this floor plan was not terribly far off, even though it ignored a substantial cellar not mentioned in the probate records and imposed a neatness and symmetry the actual home lacked. Nor could the plan and drawings address how the home itself changed over time—something the excavations made very clear. In art or writing, though, the images of the home were ways to personalize Washington by insinuating family and domesticity. Likewise, showing the home to be comfortably ramshackle made it familiar and relatable and thus brought Americans closer to Washington himself.

Here again, archaeology (working in conjunction with architectural history) forces a change in the Washington home discussion.

On one level, excavation brought the physical to the emotional—all that concern manifested in art and writing represented a manner of longing and reverence. Unearthing what survived of the original home was not only an attempt to understand the past as phrased in the carefully dispassionate language of a science; it was also the making of shrines and relics. That dualism was always at the core of Ferry Farm's excavations. Washington has long had a transitive power, as witnessed by the many homes that bear the "GW Slept Here" tag and the way his name has been used again and again in naming American places. He was special; thus, the things and places of his life were special as well, and to invoke him has a special power. Media interest, visitors, and fundraising kept the weight of the Washington name in mind at all times. For example, there was some concern to make sure that no script writer or reporter casually labeled a ceramic monk figurine Mary owned as being a specifically Catholic object and giving a wrong impression. Likewise, we were cautious to not claim that any specific artifact actually belonged to George himself, no matter how much reporters wanted us to make just that claim.

But at the same time, ours was one of many mid-eighteenth-century Virginia sites speaking to regional concerns such as those of domesticity, consumerism, local building styles, and the rise of slavery. If biographers have looked at the childhood to locate the roots of greatness, archaeology has looked at the childhood as a window into the world that produced Washington. This reverses the whole flow of concern. For biographers, Washington matters, and therefore his childhood matters because it helps explain how he came to matter. For archaeology, the fact that Washington matters facilitated the excavation of a uniquely well-documented site (many projects can only guess at the names of the people who lived at a particular site), and that promised a deeper understanding of the shape and meaning of the material world of the 1740s.

The biographies saw the childhood as a way to contextualize later greatness; archaeology sought to contextualize a famous childhood within its larger world in order to understand both a bit better.

So, whereas biographers and memorialists have focused on the home, a building and resonant symbol of domestic tranquility, the archaeology focuses instead on units such as home lots and households—things very different from (but including) a home and also having a different cast of characters.[32] The home is certainly a major part of this matrix, but so are outbuildings, work yard, fencelines, trash pits, gardens, and so on. Home lot and household scales also call attention to the spatial relations of social dynamics within a landscape that was both a dwelling place and a work place. This moves beyond a narrow definition of family and encompasses the full range of those living and working on the site, freeborn white Washingtons or otherwise.[33] In focusing on the household, we are able to begin to recreate the physical elements of the day-to-day reality that would have surrounded young George at all times. The archaeology may not speak to mathematics and Latin, but it has revealed for us perhaps the most significant educational text Washington studied in his youth: the social dynamics within the home lot. It may not speak directly to his day-to-day location, but it reveals nuances in the dynamics of the world he inhabited. The archaeological narrative of Washington's childhood sees him as only one player of many.

The Washingtons' home lot was made up of a set of structures and structured spaces extending back from the main home and nearly reaching the fence that bounded King's Highway, which ran at a slight angle across the land. It would have been nearly impossible to see the larger home lot from any forward-viewing angle, but from the neighboring parcels or from behind and up the rise of Stafford Heights, the effect was reversed. The Washingtons put some effort into maintaining the home lot's façade, which let the brick-colored home block the view of the yard behind it. The front of the home sat so close to the where the land dropped off to the floodplain that very little activity was even possible in the front space. That may indeed have been by design—a good little trick that maximized the natural effect the land's sharp rise. The area was kept clean—so clean, in fact, that very little trash made it down to the floodplain, a sure sign that the home lot's front face was kept presentable and work was carefully segregated in the rear.

There was a set of buildings running roughly on an east–west line, just north of the home. The largest of these was a frame-built kitchen with a large stone-lined cellar. The little that survived of this stonework suggests that it was well and substantively built. The remains of this cellar had been identified in the 1990s and were mistakenly thought to be those of the home itself, despite the large quantities of utilitarian ceramics in the fill. Other yard buildings were more poorly built, leaving only a few footer-supporting stones and earth-fast pits to show their locations. These, too, were wood framed and contained small brick chimneys. Evidence of fires suggests, as well, that the relationship between wooden framing members and fireplaces was not always a happy one.

There was a remarkable uniformity in the home lot's material culture. The enslaved side of the Washington household was using largely the same plate as were the free Washingtons in the main house. Most of these items would have been hand-me-downs of cracked or outmoded plates and cups, but this shows the degree to which the Washington Africans were integrated into a British material world. One notable exception is in the form of a single carnelian gemstone bead. These stones were popular in Africa and, although rare in the Americas, have been found in burials of enslaved people in the Caribbean.[34] David Muraca saw in the rare bead hints of a larger African worldview playing out at Ferry Farm.[35] The site has yielded many objects that speak of belief and identity; buttons with royal images, a Masonic tobacco pipe, and cufflinks saying "tallyho!" make sense only within a larger English identity. Likewise, finds such as the bead and cowry shells that were common African hair adornments may just as simply speak of African identity. Southern excavations often turn up mysterious little sets of finds that once baffled archaeologists. Beginning in the 1990s, though, the field began to realize that little bundles of coins, polished stones, arrowheads, oyster shells, and other small items were, in fact, material survivals of ritual practices. The Washington home's main cellar had closed oyster shells carefully set or buried in corners, an indication that people in the household may have been using charms to address some problem in their lives. Muraca saw these—and, specifically, the carnelian bead—as relating to the stress-filled period of Augustine Washington's death, the 1750 killing of one of the Washingtons' enslaved Africans by another, and the alleged killer's eventual execution. This would be a trauma for any community but all the worse for an enslaved one unable to formally handle its own crises. Spiritual practices may have been one way for enslaved people to maintain order in a world not of their making.

Another insight into the lives of the enslaved people living in the Washington home lot came from a pair of cellars—one in the Washington home itself, the other associated with a dwelling for enslaved Africans in the yard. Both of them were subfloor, earth-fast pits, little more than carefully carved holes beneath the flooring that served as storage areas. These are common features in the region and are often the only indication that a building once stood on a location. This was a unique pair of cellars, however, because both were open in the 1740s and filled in soon thereafter. Because both of these cellars were associated with the storage and preparation of food, both contained the often small remains of the bones from the animals people in both households were cooking and eating. The lens into these food ways is a clouded one. There are many ways that food remains make it into a hole in the ground that is being filled, and it is a bit too simplistic to argue that each bone is a sign of a meal right nearby. Nevertheless, the remains are an interesting indicator of the kinds of animals the Washingtons and their enslaved Africans were bringing in and cooking.[36]

On top of that, the two cellars showed noticeable differences in the kinds of animals they held, a good indicator that the diets were very different between these two households. Both cellars contained large quantities of rat and mouse bones—creatures that probably were there as scavengers and not food. Both cellars also contained large amounts of freshwater fish bones, such as catfish, long-nose gars, bass, and perch—all finds that make sense next to a river. But it also appears the Washingtons ate a range of large mammals in addition to their fish, although that range was more limited than that found on other similar regional sites.[37] Beef and pork were represented in good quantity, with beef eclipsing pork, as was the normal regional pattern. But the Washingtons ate a large amount of deer meat as well; in fact, venison made up nearly a quarter of all of the meat volume, the bones suggested. By contrast, that is a higher percentage of the represented animals than either beef or pork, which together made up about a third. This means that wild, hunted animals were almost as central to the Washington diet as were the animals the family kept—and that includes chickens and goats, which were a surprisingly low percentage of the overall bone assemblage, although ducks, pigeons, and other small birds were there in abundance. Add to that smatterings of turkeys, turtles, rabbits, and wild geese, and the picture that emerges is one of the Washington boys using their time and energy to catch fish and hunt animals for the family table. The biographers loved to imagine Washington passing his time in running and fishing. Their images invariably were ones of a childhood nirvana, though few saw these activities as actually being more for subsistence than a pastime.

One of the central themes though in the Washington biography has long been that of the frontier. Ferry Farm sat right at a busy juncture of river and road that helped set Washington's eyes westward. He famously made his first fortune in Western land investments and stayed involved with Western projects until his death. Scholars have long tied Washington's surveyor and early military career to the idea of the frontier; his activities have been crucial chapters in all Washington biographies and served as an enduring metaphor for westward expansion and belief in manifest destiny. The idea of the frontier itself has been used to sanitize American continental colonization and render natural the displacement of native peoples over three centuries. We already know that Washington's increasing wealth from Western land ventures benefited his mother and siblings back at Ferry Farm. But the faunal data from these cellars add another dimension of meaning to this issue.

Despite the fact that Ferry Farm sat in what was for Virginia a densely populated area, the Washingtons' diet was unusually high in a limited selection of wild game. Rather than being responses to hard times or catches of opportunity, these were intentional choices reflecting a very active set of practices by the Washingtons. Because many of these animals were not simply local but rather were hunted and killed only with some effort and travel away from the immediate area, this sort of diet constituted an active engagement with the West, a dietary model of the idea of the frontier.

The picture that emerges from the cellar in the enslaved dwelling is rather different. The percentages of large mammals are essentially the same as in the big house, including the large amount of venison. The big differences were in the small animals with which the enslaved fleshed out their diets and the percentages of their food these composed. The range of animals was much smaller than in the main home: Gone were the ducks, turkeys, pigeons, and rabbits that the Washingtons enjoyed, the range of river fishes was smaller, and the quantities were smaller as well. Instead, there was somewhat more turtle, as well as possums and even a fox. The enslaved had far less access to the smaller caught animals and lived more on the domestic animals and some local catches.

Most of the area's artifacts recovered from the yard areas were run-of-the-mill British domestic material culture. Utilitarian ceramics, wine bottle fragments, pipe stems, bits of broken table settings, and rusted iron objects were the main elements. One category of artifacts stood out, though, and that was the usually high number of wig curlers, all of which clustered around the site of small building and in the area of one trash pit. A few were complete and located within the home, but large numbers were broken and concentrated in one part of the lot. Scholars usually see the making and care of wigs as a specialized artisanal task, not one usually associated with domestic activity, so the Washington home lot's more than 200 white clay curlers were a singular find.[38]

Wigs were expensive and maintenance-heavy, high-fashion purchases in the early eighteenth century, but they were very much a part of the battalion of material goods the British gentry used to distinguish themselves from the lower orders. Cary Carson has shown how anxieties of class and differentiation were heightened by the fact of being colonial in a time when overall material culture was homogenizing.[39] Presented with the challenge of class differentiation in a new-world setting where the old trappings of wealth and power were rarely at hand, British Americans latched onto the portable fashionability of practices such as fancy table manners and staying current in clothes and dinnerware in order self-present in the best light possible. This view reversed the older view of increasing industrial production wherein makers seeking markets were the driving force. Instead, after Carson, we are more likely to see demand as the drive pushing makers to make more and sell more widely.[40]

A combination of colonial anxiety and an increasing flow of British manufactured goods and styles helped shaped the Washington household. In a world in which marriage proposals from well-off Virginian William Byrd II to elite young English women were casually brushed off because his estates were in Virginia and not in England, it easy to understand the zeal with which colonists, and Virginians in particular, adopted metropolitan trends.[41] Williamsburg may not have had a year-round population of more than two thousand, but by the 1730s it had a well-appointed (though economically decorated) London or Bristol-style coffeehouse, and by the 1750s it had its own theater.[42] Even before homeowners had filled out all of Fredericksburg's lots, the young town already had its own wigmaker.

From when they first entered English fashion in the 1660s court of Charles II, wigs, perukes, and periwigs played an interesting and unique role in the tension surrounding material goods. Like all fashion accessories, they were about image making and were, to an extent, deceptive. Wigs, in particular, touched a nerve on this last score, and pamphlet writers found much to dislike in the "falsehood of perukes."[43] Male wig wearing challenged biblically established gender norms, especially if men wore wigs made of women's hair, as sometimes happened. They undid "one noble distinction of age" by allowing the hoary to appear young again and the young to appear venerable.[44] Wigs could also be a deliberate act of deception whereby rogues or the lower orders might cover up their true selves and purposes. But most of all, it was said that wig wearing "marreth the Workmanship of God, and so defaceth his image."[45] The fear, here, was of a disruption in the function of the divinely ordained world of signs whereby the outwardly visible provided a readable and reliable roadmap to the social order. No other single consumer item landed so squarely on the anxiety produced by the rising tide of consumerism.

Nevertheless, by the mid-eighteenth century, wig wearing had settled into sets of well-established conventions.[46] Its dangers were blunted as wearers used their wigs not to hide but, rather, to advertise their status. Lawyers and justices took to wearing one specific style (as indeed they still do), clergymen another, and even the common soldiery donned them on dress occasions. William Hogarth's satirical chart detailing the full range of the "Five Orders of Perriwigs" seen at George III's coronation treated each flamboyant style as if it were a genus of animal, giving it multiple views and careful measurement. One need only scan a sample of Hogarth's numerous prints to see the full range of wig styles teetering on the heads of dandies or slipping off a drunk's head and landing in the punch bowl. Rather than disrupting order, wigs became another marker of status within the great chain of being and were so naturalized within English culture that they were more objects of humor than fear.

In 1752, Washington purchased a "grey cut wig" for his eighteen-year-old younger brother Samuel.[47] The purchase shows that, as an older brother, Washington was concerned with having his younger siblings look their best as they entered society. The question, though, is how tightly can we tie the collection of wig curlers to Samuel Washington's wig? Probably not directly, if only because "cut wigs" did not require the use of curlers.

The written evidence of the purchase, though, is further evidence that the Washingtons were in touch with metropolitan trends, as were most gentry Virginians. It speaks to Washington's involvement with his family as well. But the curlers and their location on the site show another aspect of wigs. Whether or not Samuel's wig and the curlers were part of the same purchase or otherwise linked, the fact that the curlers concentrate in the yard, not the home, is telling. Normal practice would have called for a skilled craftsperson to be tapped at intervals to make sure a wig was clean and freshly curled. With care, a good wig could go for some time without major work, and of course the plainer the wig, the easier the care. In buying Samuel a simple cut gray wig, Washington ensured that cleaning would be less of concern than with a more elaborate white one. The most fashionable wigs of the day had the hair parted in the center, pressed down along the head (to accommodate a hat) and then ending in sets of small curls over the ears and tapering down the neck and back. Simpler wigs might end in one large ear curl and keep the tapers to a minimum.

Even if Samuel's wig did not need a high level of maintenance, the site's curlers still testify to on-site wig care, and their large number suggests something well beyond the simplest designs. Keeping all the various curls tied to the various sizes of curlers was good protection against moisture and gravity, a periwig's natural enemies. Although they were found all over the site, the largest number came from the yard, and the presence of many broken and discarded curlers all point to a specific workspace. Maintenance took skill, but it was also messy when powder and dyes were involved. Also, baking moist hair in a purpose-made oven was the common way to make curls—a task that was often a bit smelly if the hair burned. For these reasons, seeing this work taking place outside the home makes sense. The location of the curlers also suggests that the enslaved Washingtons were probably the craftspeople performing these tasks. This opens an important window into the functioning of the household.

It seems that someone living in the yard was skilled enough to have a set of wigmaker's tools. Indeed, it almost appears that there was something of a small artisanal shop working behind and around the Washingtons' home, and it is easy to imagine the craftsperson selling his or her skills. On-site maintenance may have been one of Mary's many economies, but this one is far more complicated than her skillful purchasing. This was a plantation economy that relied on the specialized skills of enslaved Africans to sustain gentry styles through objects produced in and shipped from England.

Taken in total, the artifacts from the site show an arc of contrasts for the Washington family. On one hand, we see samples of high style and intimacy with metropolitan trends. From fancy needlework to wigs and figurines, the Washingtons had many of the same things as had others of their class. But at the same time, they were adept at making their purchasing power go as far as it could by buying lower-cost versions of must-have objects. This, in effect, turned the objects into speech more than physical reality. It was more important to be able to *say* that one had this or that trinket or object than to actually have the best one possible. On top of that, very few Virginians would have had much of a chance to see better quality. Mary may have been good at stretching the family finances, but the audience for her gentry performances was not made up of the most sophisticated viewers. Rather, they were mostly local planters and merchants who were involved in their own ongoing colonial games of playing gentry. The Washingtons were aided immensely in their image production by the larger forces of an Atlantic world that both provided them with the goods they needed and ensured a somewhat lower standard for their uses.

The biggest consumer good on any home lot, however, is the home itself.[48] Measuring roughly thirty by fifty-one feet, the Washington's rectangular wooden-framed and clapboarded home stood at the conceptual center of the home lot. When Augustine purchased it from its builder and initial owner, William Strother, it was still in its original *L* shape. It sat on stone foundations cut from Stafford County's local Aquia sandstone. The same stone went into making the two large chimney bases that sat at either end of the house and was also the main constituent in a large and expertly made cellar that sat in the home's center, presumably under the central passage.

The home was painted brick-red, a common practice of the

day that gave less-than-durable wood a bit of weather protection while disguising it as brick to a casual and distant passerby. An Aquia sandstone porch platform and cellar entrance faced the river, all making the 1720s home looking down the steep bluff seem somewhat grander than it was. One could say that George's first lesson that appearances matter was taught to him by his home.

The home took two forms during the Washington occupancy. The one into which they moved was the *L*-form built by William Strother in the 1720s. Sometime after 1740 the new residents oversaw an extension that fleshed the floor plan out to a full rectangle. Athwart the home's center was a passageway that ran from the width of the home and tied the front space to the work yards out back. Once the home was its full size, a pair of family rooms flanked the hall and smaller rooms sat above those. Beneath the hall sat a stone-lined cellar that was the single largest bit of the home found in the excavations. Regional building patterns hold that a frame home like this was commonly one-and-one-half stories high. The small sections of thin lines of stone foundation footers attested to the building's fairly low height—thin walls are unable to support very tall constructions.

Scholars have come to call this sort of house design a central passage home, or a hall and parlor home, or sometimes simply a Virginia house. Its development dates back to adaptive changes to English building styles of the seventeenth century, when colonists matched English sensibilities and building traditions to New World realities and resources. By the time Washington was a child, the common home of families like his was defined by that large central passage hallway that not only divided the home into two separate sections but also created a busy multipurpose channel that could serve as storage area, workspace, and welcoming antechamber. A definitive single reason for this development has proven elusive. Fraser Neiman tied it to the beginnings of the widespread use of enslaved labor and the need to monitor and control movement in and around the home.[49] By the 1680s, though, there was a larger trend on both sides of the Atlantic whereby gentry home designs and room plans gradually became more restrictive spaces for the mix of masters and servants living and moving within them. English architect Roger North noted this trend by remarking, in 1698, that in his father's day, servants and masters often shared spaces while dining, for example, whereas by his own time "it hath been usual, to find a room elsewhere for them."[50] In Britain slavery could not have been the driving force, but certainly the practice played a role in changing ideas about labor in general, both where its practice was common and in the homes of others made rich from the practice yet distant from its daily realities.

Donald Linebaugh, on the other hand, tied it to regional climate and the desire to move chimneys away from the center of the home as they continued to build in other cooler regions such as New England.[51] This is also a compelling argument and one well rooted in the simple fact that encountering Virginia's heat was often a devastating experience for many wool-clad Englishmen. Whatever the reasons, by the 1730s these houses, with their well-defined, segregated domestic spaces and a large central halls, were well established all over the Chesapeake region, and gentry families such as the Washingtons had pioneered a way of living in and around these dwellings.

The key to how the homes functioned was access—granted to some, denied to others. Flanking family rooms were more guarded than the main hall. For example, visitors might have to wait on the porch tower or in the hall before gaining access to the more private spaces; others may never get beyond those many thresholds both indoors and out. Who came in and who did not reflected a social geography of class and connection that was itself a small version of the whole of white Virginia's society and simultaneously a unique set of personal relationships and individuals. At the same time, a select group of the enslaved had almost universal and ubiquitous access to all spaces in the home. These people were essential to gentry living in these spaces and so, ideally, were as common as furniture—vital and always at the ready, yet at the same time relegated to a social margin. Their presence disrupted many domestic ideals. The notion of privacy was challenged by their labor within this imagined private sphere, the cohesion of family was complicated by the near-constant presence of people whose membership in the extended clan was coerced and commercial, and the idea of ownership was contested by people who were as human as their owners and, at the same time, as much a possession as a ceramic figure on a mantelpiece. The home was the wooden skin that enclosed these complicated and ongoing entwined dramas of family life and human ownership.

But all this was above ground and so was lost to time. The home's main survival was the large stone-lined cellar that ran roughly in line with the hall. William Strother had overseen its building, and its excellent construction tells more about the home's quality than any other single detail. Carefully laid and well faced, the stones of the cellar show the care that went into making this interior feature. When built, this was a more than fitting gentry home, and it was still right in line with gentry aspirations when it became full of Washingtons. It was only in the 1760s and 1770s that it began to fade somewhat, as wealthier families built grander homes within sight of Ferry Farm. It was the home that most reflected the changes in the Washington family fortunes. Mary may have been able to manage her children's gentry training and their estates, but the family finances precluded its expansion or replacement. Once Washington became the full owner of Mount Vernon, he began a long set of renovations that radically transformed what had begun as a fairly simple frame home. While he was changing

Mount Vernon, Ferry Farm was becoming less and less the kind of home in which a gentry family would live. Washington's new home bore almost no resemblance to Ferry Farm, a statement of how much styles had changed in a few short decades and how far Washington had come from where he began.

Perhaps the most significant event in the home's life was a fire the family suffered in the early 1740s. The story of a major Washington home fire has been around for some time. The first reference was in a 1741 letter to Augustine from Richard Yates at their alma mater, the Appleby School. In the letter, Yates condoled with his friend for what he called his "late calamity wch. you suffered by fire."[52] Over the years, there has been very little consensus about the meaning of statement. Many, such as Moncure D. Conway, read the letter as referring to a fire at Mount Vernon or even at Pope's Creek that forced the family to move to Ferry Farm. Douglas Southall Freeman, though, read the letter as referring to a barn fire at Mount Vernon. But in 1945, Charles Wall suggested that actual "calamity" by fire was in fact not a fire at all but a reference to Lawrence Washington's military travails during the disastrous Siege of Cartagena six months before the letter's penning.[53]

David Humphreys's Washington biography included a note in which Washington himself recalled that "my father's house burned."[54] Although this is direct and incontrovertible, it remains difficult to see clearly exactly which of his father's homes this was or when was the fire. In fact, for much of his adulthood Washington called Ferry Farm his "mother's" house, and it would be noteworthy if he changed that habit in this one reference. On top of that, these documents have been read to support the story of the Pope's Creek home being destroyed by fire as well. Many biographers saw fire as the primary reason for the family's many relocations—first from Pope's Creek to Little Hunting Creek, then, at last, to Ferry Farm. Most associated the fire with Pope's Creek, arguing "that the family mansion was burned to the ground when he was a mere boy" or that the old home was pulled down or burned before the Revolution.[55]

Some writers added considerable detail to the story, such as Wayne Whipple, who in 1911 told readers that one of the family homes burned in the spring of 1739 from a fire that began as a "bon fire, made of a pile of rubbish in the garden," but when caught in the wind, "the blaze started in the shingles" of the roof."[56] A similar story began to circulate for Pope's Creek, this time set on Christmas Day forty years later. Although tied to Washington family members and credited as being passed down, there is no reliable reference to the tale before the end of the nineteenth century; in fact, the date of 1779 was probably a whole-cloth invention of Wakefield Association historian Charles Arthur Hoppin, based on the fact that the resident line of Washingtons changed homes in 1780. Hoppin added an 1820 reference to a burned house and concluded rather mysteriously that there had to have been a house fire in 1779.[57] That story quickly become orthodoxy by the time the site was becoming an object of national attention in the 1920s, aided by the fact that Rupert Hughes included it in his widely read biography.[58] The story is still a part of the site's interpretation.

Adding to this confusion is the fact that Parson Weems told a fire story of his own in his *Life of Washington*. In this case, the story was in the form of a dream that he claimed Mary had when George was but five years old. In the dream, George scampered "with nimbleness of a squirrel" up a providentially handy ladder and began to douse the fire, using a gourd ladle to carry water.[59] Although Weems's story was as much an invention as his many other tales, the fact remains that bits of Mary's dream have wended their way into many of the other supposedly historical fire stories. There are only so many ways a 1700s house fire could have begun, and almost all of them involve windblown sparks or an overflowing fireplace. Arson could have factored in as well, but in centuries of stories no one has tried to make that argument. Eighteenth-century Virginia had more than enough house and outbuilding fires to sustain any number of stories and garbled, conflated memories—there is no need to sort one out from the other—and similarities in their circumstances might not be that remarkable. That the site of the Washington birthplace was locally known as Burned House Point by the 1820s is enough to establish that *something* happened there, even if the dates, details, and archaeological evidence are all questionable.[60] Likewise, archaeological evidence at Ferry Farm shows there to have been a fire there also. What seems to have happened in the records is that, over time, a set of recollections have twisted and turned into a set of collected tales that have been massaged and applied to various places.

The best documentary evidence of the "calamity" having been at Ferry Farm is a 1795 letter from one Robert Douglas, a Scotsman and former Fredericksburg-area resident, that added another dimension to the discussion. Douglas wrote to Washington, recalling with a "very sore heart that on a Christmas Eve, his [Augustine's] great house was burned down and that he was Obliged with his good family to go and live in the kitchen."[61] Washington biographer Jack Warren, though, first brought the three fire references together in Ferry Farm's National Historic Landmark Nomination form.[62] Warren saw the fire as mattering because it became, after baptism, the first documented event in Washington's life. Despite all the speculation, the current consensus is that the fire in these documents was at Ferry Farm. Indeed, visitors to Mount Vernon's museum are treated to an animation showing the highlights of Washington's childhood, including a very quick, all-consuming house fire. Visitors to the Washington Birthplace, however, will learn of a Christmas Day 1779 fire that has a narrative attached to it that sounds very much like Mary Washington's dream, of which

Weems wrote, or like the tales told by biographers such as Benson Lossing or Wayne Whipple.

What has not been questioned in all this is the scale of these fires. Richard Yates's claim that this was a "calamity" has been enough for all to assume that the flames were utterly devastating. That fact has folded into the Hard 1740s narrative. The loss of the home to fire was only the first of a one–two punch that soon took Augustine from Washington—and with that loss, the denial of an English education and the full family estate's income. In this view, Washington and his kitchen-bound kinfolk began the decade with one disaster after another.

But the site's archaeology disrupts this narrative and complicates the picture considerably. Excavators found evidence of fire, but far from being an all-consuming calamity, it was a damaging but limited affair. It seems to have been limited to the back room—the protruding part of Strother's L. A large, earth-fast cellar located just before the room's main fireplace revealed evidence of fire and burned plaster—a sure sign of room, and possible ceiling, damage. But higher layers in the same cellar also contained remains of fresh plaster—signs of repair. Also, the stone-lined cellar showed no evidence of fire at all, as it would have had there been a real calamity. Whatever fire this house had seen must have been localized, limited, and not all that disruptive of daily life.

This damaging room fire became the catalyst for a home expansion, for it was right at this time that the Washingtons fleshed Strother's L out to a full rectangle. They expanded the overall living space of the home by at least two rooms and added a new fireplace at the rear. If the young George learned anything from this, it was that additions could transform a home—a knowledge he certainly showed at Mount Vernon.

The archaeology allows us to reconsider the simple terms of the Hard 1740s, as biographers have portrayed it, and its crucial role in that part of the self-made man narrative. Washington spent his childhood moving between gentry seats that were appropriate to his family's station, and Ferry Farm may have been the poorest of the three, but that is hard to know for sure. The archaeology of Mount Vernon in this period shows that Lawrence used his money to make a fine family seat. In this respect, biographers have been right: Mount Vernon was a fine and well-placed home, and Washington was understandably drawn there. It is far harder to say anything meaningful about what life was like at Pope's Creek. Despite the current interpretation of the Park Service site, the archaeology is far less conclusive; indeed, it is difficult to claim that we have even definitively located the family home yet, despite the large number of features excavated.[63] The site's artifact collection strongly resembles that of Ferry Farm and has noticeable gaps in it—particularly in the late 1740s and 1750s. It may be that Austin was living elsewhere at the time and that some of Washington's time with his uncle and cousins may have been at a place we have yet to identify. Ferry Farm remains the most substantive material text we have of Washington's childhood and the only one we can see in any detail.

So what does the place tell us about the most famous person it produced? Its position at the crossing of road and river has long been understood as being both an opportunity and an annoyance. The opportunities lay in the ships in the river and the wagons and riders moving westward. This daily reality opened Washington's eyes to possibilities elsewhere. The irritation was in the very busyness created by the constant comings and goings of others. Biographers have charted out how Washington's education and horizons suffered from his father's death and have related in varying shades Lawrence's attempt to send his brother to sea. The events are all well known—we know the players and the lines they speak. What we have never seen, though, is the stage and setting in which these dramas occurred.

The archaeology helps give Ferry Farm a character all its own; it lets us see some of the intimate realities people on the site knew every day yet never recorded. Ferry Farm was a place of artful deceptions, with things done on the cheap and yet done to great effect. It was often a place of pretense over substance, of artifice over actuality. Even though many colonial Britons were playing the same games of make-do, each household did it their own way and felt either pride or shame at what they achieved. Many biographers have made much of Washington's lack of formal learning and how he worked to overcome those deficits through dance classes, fencing lessons, and mastering fashion. What did it mean to such a man to have come of age in a place held together with constant aspiration? The combination of Mary's careful consumerism, plantation economies, and perfectly imperfect location made Ferry Farm the *only* place that could have directed Washington's energies as it did. Had he been anywhere else, the alchemy would have been just a tiny bit wrong, and he would have been something very different.

Archaeology's narrative of Washington's childhood sets the many Washington stories within wider discussions of British colonization and the Atlantic world. It becomes one part of a tale of commercial goods produced in one place, transported to another, and used in the delicate balancing act of gentry status. It is a tale of the social dynamics of free and enslaved and of how spaces and buildings conditioned daily interactions within a very small and intimate space. Whereas the biographers reached into their sources to extract what made Washington exceptional, archaeology instead looks at the things that were most typical about Washington's background and locates him in larger colonial and even human processes. Rather than looking at how he became separate and distinctive, it explores what he most shared in common. All of this reveals the specific nuances of the conceptual—some might say ideological—bedrock of assumptions, habits, and received practices on which Washington built his life. Just as an archaeological site is made up of the long-enduring subterranean material remains of past actions, so a man's choices and responses rest on his own subterranean makeup. A large part of the subterranean Washington was to be found at Ferry Farm.

4

FRUITS OF MORALITY AND FRUITS OF THE MARKET

Weems's Idyll at the Crossroads of War and Markets

> This fruit doth make my soul to thrive,
> It keeps my dying faith alive;
> Which makes my soul in haste to be;
> With Jesus Christ the apple tree.
>
> *Divine Hymns and Spiritual Songs,* 1784

On December 14, 1799, George Washington breathed his last in a second-floor room at his Mount Vernon estate. His countrymen mourned his loss, but in the nation's grief there was opportunity.

Sensing a market opening, Maryland-born preacher, author, itinerant bookseller, and fiddler Mason Locke Weems wrote to his printer partner, Mathew Carey, that the moment was perfect for a mass-appeal, nonpolitical biography of the Great Washington. "Washington, you know is gone," he declared, "but now, millions are gaping to read something about him, I am very nearly prim'd and cock'd for 'em."[1]

The most enduring result of that priming was Weems's 1806 *Life of Washington,* a loving, lore-ridden, evangelically inflected version of Washington's biography that was unquestionably Weems's literary masterpiece. To be sure, much of what Weems wrote has been questioned since it first appeared in print. But, for better or worse, Weems has left an enduring imprint on the literature about Washington.[2] His may not be the most authoritative or the best researched of the vast corpus of Washington biography, but it is no stretch to declare his Washington to be the most enduring and perhaps the best known. Moreover, his central project—to reveal a human, relatable Washington—has been unquestioned as the biographer's central task ever since Weems put pen to paper.

Weems is best known for the stories he is credited with inventing, rather than for the more mundane elements of the rest of his work. The most famous of these is the story of a seven-year-old George turning the edge of a new hatchet onto his father's most cherished English cherry tree and then confessing the misdeed to a father overjoyed at his son's honesty.[3] But that was only one of the stories Weems told of Ferry Farm. Most have been forgotten, overshadowed by the fame of that single tale.

Through his writing, Weems created a vision of Ferry Farm that wove its way into common understandings of the meaning of the land. Although his signature cherry tree was the most visible symbol of his body of stories, his seemingly forgotten stories were often just as important. We have seen in earlier chapters how Washington's biographers turned the murkiest part of their subject's life story into set of canonical moments and concerns, and the ways that Washington himself saw and used the land add another dimension to his childhood story. In this chapter we explore how these stories took root in the place most closely associated with that childhood. It was these stories that eclipsed all others and defined the meaning of the land itself.

Weems brought to his readers a uniquely Edenic vision of Virginia as represented by Ferry Farm. Significantly, he created that world in text just as the real Ferry Farm underwent a set of landscape transformations that remade it in a way Washington would never have recognized.[4] Some of those changes came at the hand of market forces, others from the many hands of military forces. Both influences, though, worked to make the years between the 1820 and the 1860s the period of Ferry Farm's most dramatic change since settlement first began in the early 1700s.

Just as the profound near-silence that hung over Washington's childhood created fertile ground for fabulists such as Weems, the similarly blank landscape of Ferry Farm became the canvas for later inventors of local tradition. What Weems helped enable was the creation of two different Ferry Farms. One of them was a written place that was a national possession; the other was a real, local place that moved to its own rhythms regardless of the national discussion. In time, those two landscapes converged as the stories came home to roost and make themselves realities. But before that, there was only an ordinary plot of land on the north bank of the Rappahannock, which was outwardly identical to its neighboring plots and notable mostly for one famous name from its past. And that famous person was best remembered, in this land, for being a child.

In crafting his study of how places take meaning, David Glassberg built on the work of social psychologists, noting that "special childhood places" can become "crucial anchors" for individual personal identity.[5] This idea holds that a significant portion of a person's sense of self-worth, belonging, and security can be very powerfully connected to the places in which one spent one's formative years. Alienation from—and changes to—those places are not thought to be traumas but do become part of the formation of individual personalities in one way or another. To historians struggling to integrate places into work that is often disconnected from space, this idea has an understandable utility. In its way, it can serve as a theoretically informed motto for the entire Ferry Farm enterprise. In fact, a version of that idea has cropped up time and again in the land's story—but usually followed by a singularly pregnant ellipsis: "Washington grew up here, so. . . ." I have already tried to connect Washington-the-person to the place and suggest ways that he may have understood his childhood home. So rather than using the place–personality connection to inform that pairing, I instead want to build on the idea in order to make sense of how

Ferry Farm—particularly Weems's version of it—took a specific and deceptive meaning for people raised far from its imagined lush fields of clover.

Ever since Washington's 1799 death, memorialists had fallen into the enduring habit of calling him "The Father of the Nation." As Jared Sparks noted (in the same decade as Ferry Farm was seeing great transformation), words about Washington were surrogates for the nation itself. The former rhetorical posture cast the nation as Washington's children; as Sparks opined, Washington's very life story was integrated into the national identity. For Ferry Farm, Weems's great success was in taking the deep investments implied by those two ideas and tying them to the landscape itself. In inventing his version of Washington's childhood and casting Ferry Farm as a foundational paradise stage for a coming-of-age tale, he made a simple mundane Virginia farm into something of a national possession.

The connection was, in part, rooted in the idea that foundational places play a special role in the formation of an individual's personality. Through Weems, Washington's childhood at Ferry Farm became a collective—or what James Young called a "collected"—memory of a single national childhood. Weems's Washington was a synecdoche for all children, perhaps even all Americans, living a life of rustic splendor in a Virginia paradise that produced fruit and moral lessons with equal abundance. However, that childhood and its setting entailed an act of overlooking wrapped in an outer layer of remembering—a process very much like the way that Marx saw the fetishization of commercial objects as masking the grim processes of their production. The popularity and mass retelling of Weems's stories, most especially the Cherry Tree, was part of the creation of American identity. But at the same time, it was part of American imagining at a time when the overall health of the American project was very much in doubt.

Weems helped Americans imagine a place and time of newness and promise, of effort-free bounty and character formation—in short, a perfect childhood, one lived, in this case, by someone easily recast as a secular saint.

In that act of crafted, shared memory, Ferry Farm served as both the setting for this story and its embodiment. For Americans confronting warfare, market collapses, sectionalism, and, finally, civil war, having stories and images of a place like Ferry Farm in mind was one of the many ways to bolster confidence in the national project. And even though most Americans never even knew its local name, they nevertheless knew that there was a place that produced Washington. They knew it because they had pictures of it on their walls and learned to read through its most famous story.

Most also did not know that the place with the charming old farmhouse, the wise father, and trees heavy with fruit was in the process of being devastated—first by market needs, and then by war. What they did know was an enduring association between Washington, a place, and a single iconic cherry tree, and that trio came to define not only Washington's childhood but also, crucially, the land where most of it took place. Because it was Weems who planted it in the American mind, we need to begin with understanding something of the man and his career.

The man who planted this vision in the American mind was born in 1759 to a large farming and merchant shipping family in Anne Arundel County, Maryland. Barely two generations of Weemses had lived in America, but Mason's father, David, worked hard to make up with numbers what they lacked in generations. Mason was the youngest (or, some say, one of the youngest) of nineteen children from two wives.[6] The actual contours of his childhood are understandably obscure, given his family's ordinariness, but his biographers have teased out and repeated a few details.

His early schooling was local, probably at the Kent Free School, which, charmingly, became Washington College. Two of his elder brothers, David Locke and William Locke, were busy in Annapolis's shipping trade, and most biographers believe that the young Weems made trips with them to their various ports of call along the coast and across the Atlantic. Like his most famous subject, Weems was a wanderer. But unlike Washington, Weems would come to know Britain firsthand. By the age of fourteen or so, the future Parson was bundled off to Scotland to study, although there is little proof to back this up; indeed, biographers have searched in vain for any Scots reference to the lad as a student, and none has emerged. Another longstanding story, also hard to verify, holds that he served a brief stint on a British warship during, ironically, the Revolution.

Less debatable, though, is the fact that his father passed away in 1779, leaving Weems only a "negro boy Nead" and a possibility of some acres, should some of his many older brothers die without heirs.[7] None did, and with that, Weems's main tie to his native state was undone. What became of Nead, we do not know.

Around 1780, Weems went (or returned) to Britain, this time to study divinity and become a minister in the same established church his countrymen were then fighting to escape. How, exactly, he found his way into the country has been the subject of some speculation. What is clear is that by 1784, he was finding it difficult to gain "admission to the sacred vineyard" of the Anglican ministry and found himself lacking influence or influential friends.[8] With his applications rejected and doors shut in his American face, Weems found himself at "a loss of time, money, and patience, sufficient to distract a stoic."[9] He reached out to his nation's new emissaries, John Adams and Benjamin Franklin, asking advice on the matter and even the possibility of seeking ordination in another sect, perhaps one in Holland, Sweden, or France. A solicitous Adams wrote back, offering to drop a good word and cautioning the not-yet-ordained divine against taking any oath in the Anglican Church until such a time as "the members of the church in America have digested some plan for their future government."[10] Franklin offered the same advice, suggesting Weems act as if "the British Isles were sunk in the sea" and seek ordination elsewhere—Ireland perhaps—where "the religion is the same, tho' there is a different set of Bishops and Archbishops."[11]

Weems was, in fact, one of many young men whose ministerial careers had been prejudiced by the war, and so there was good reason for Adams and Franklin to pay attention to Weems's plight. Adams later claimed that he had helped Weems procure "a more polite reception from the English clergy," an act he saw as helping not only Weems but also the new Episcopal Church as a whole.[12] Something fell into place, though, for in September 1784, Weems became an Anglican priest and soon returned to Maryland to take up the role of rector in his old home of Anne Arundel County, Maryland.[13] Soon, he had opened a school in the area, served several parishes, and may even have tweaked local sensibilities by welcoming the enslaved into his fellowship.[14]

But something was not quite right. A Maryland rectorship was a hard way to earn a living, even for the unmarried Weems. Matters surrounding the funding of the ministry were still unresolved in the wake of the Revolution's separation of the American Anglican Church (then called the Episcopal Church) from its state and tax-funded parent, and Maryland was never the richest place. By 1789, Rector Weems had packed up and headed south to see whether he could do better. He took up a new residence and a new living in Dumfries, Virginia, the address that landed him right in the shadow of Mount Vernon and the man there who would make Weems's name and reputation. By 1794, he had begun his fruitful association with printer Mathew Carey, the other man vital to making Weems.

Rather fittingly, his own biographers embellished Weems's actual life with colorful stories of questionable reliability. William

Mead, in 1857, recounted a tale of the young Weems in which the lad's persistent evening absences from his home caught the attention of a neighbor. Curious about Weems's odd behavior, the man "followed one of his regular excursions into the surrounding forest," only to learn that the boy had made a habit of visiting a "tumble down shanty." Therein, the future divine sat surrounded by "the poor children of the neighborhood" to whom he was "imparting the rudiments of common learning."[15] A different version of the same tale had the whole family so curious about Weems's activities that "a plan was laid whereby he was tracked." Their reward was to find the lad "surrounded by the bareheaded, barefooted, and half-clad children of the neighbourhood" who were benefiting from Weems's instruction. Another similar story later emerged, but this time concerning a somewhat older Weems and set during his divinity training in England. In this version, a concerned friend came to wonder about his late-night absences. His stealthy searching found the Weems in a "lowly cellar," there "exhorting to repentance a poor wretch."[16] These gems, in true Weemsian style, serve as imagined premonitions of the Parson's eventual future of traveling far from home to share edifying tales with the common people of the South.

Another story biographers related was that, as part of Weems's medical training in Edinburgh, he did a short stint as a surgeon on one of His Majesty's men-of-war. If the story were true, that would place the future "rector of Mount Vernon Parish" on a British warship right as his homeland, and the man who would bring him fame, began their long struggle for independence—an awkward possibility for biographers.

Weems may have returned to Maryland for a time before his divinity escapades. Lawrence Wroth wishfully saw the timing as meaning that Weems was "doubtless" motivated in his return by an "aversion to service against the struggling colonies."[17] Nevertheless, there is no record that the young "physician" offered his services in any capacity to the cause he would later champion. Emily Ellsworth Ford Skeel addressed the missing Revolutionary war years by filling out an appendix, in her invaluable three-volume collection of Weems's letters, with a list of the Weemses who did serve in the war. Harrold Kellock, seemingly made a bit uncomfortable at the Parson's noticeable invisibility during the war years, excused it by noting that Maryland "was not a theatre of war" and by stating, somewhat disingenuously, that the quite able young man was "hardly of fighting age then."[18] Kellock added, tellingly, "One likes to think" that perhaps Weems did his bit for the cause aboard one of the vessels of his family's association.[19] A pleasant thought, perhaps, but there seems to be no evidence that Weems had taken much of a revolutionary—or even political—stand until he did it in writing, long after the war's dangers were mere memories. Whatever his reasons for having priorities other than service, Weems's experiences with the Church of England would certainly have been enough to seal in him an enduring dislike of the one-time mother country and her ruling elites. He certainly matured into a full-fledged advocate for the land of his birth and a skilled maker of its heroes.

But it would take a while before patriotic themes flowed from his pen. All his early writing was of a singularly conventional moralistic—and singularly derivative—nature. Catherine Clinton has shown that issues of family relations and gendered matters were foremost in his mind. His first major work was a 1791 shortened reprint of an already venerable anti-masturbation tract, with the appropriately biblical title of *Onania.* One observer claimed to have seen Weems's musing against the "heinous sin of self-pollution and all its frightful consequences in both sexes" in "a good many hands," but usually more "as a matter of diversion than serious consideration."[20] Indeed, Weems seems to have "incurred a good deal of ridicule as well as serious blame by his odd publication." At least one recent scholar argues that the booklet failed largely because it chose prurience over substance and so was read more for a laugh than a lesson.[21] The Parson's future as a literary figure of fun may have begun early, with *Onania* playing a major role.

If there was a lesson to learn here about style, he did not heed it; his subsequent work kept the same tone. But his critics then, and more recently, may have missed a point that Weems himself did not: It mattered not whether people learned from his books or whether they laughed at them—so long as they bought them. His eye was always on quantity and not quality, and judged on those terms, he was a quick learner.

He followed *Onania* with a string of modest efforts, building on moral themes and somewhat humorous stories. As this side of his career developed, he continued to refine his own voice through regular preaching at churches in the area of Dumfries. He edited the collected sermons of more famous divines and a few moralizing tales by other authors and eventually landed on the almanac as a good vehicle. Those volumes were more acts of compiling and repackaging than of sustained composition. *The Virginia Almanac, The Bachelor's Almanac, The Lover's Almanac,* and others were short volumes perfect for tidbits of wit, advice, parable, and sermons. It was in these small bursts of prose that Weems refined his art.

Even though no longer a regular parish rector, he nevertheless continued to offer sermons where and when asked. As always, Weems had fans and foes. Some found the preacher to be "cheerful in his mien and that he might win men to religion."[22] His opponents, though, saw him as being too colloquial and emotional in approach and too "tedious in exhortation."[23] If Weems were destined for a career in the pulpit, those concerns would have taken one set of meanings. But Weems was on his way to becoming a writer for a humble popular audience. His readers wanted the colloquial and the emotional, while "tedious" preaching easily translated into prolific writing. Sermon by sermon, book sale by book sale, Weems was learning a craft.

By the time Washington lay dying, Weems was already well known in the area as a bit of a character, laden with fiddle, a thirst to preach, a load of books and subscriptions to sell, and a ledger full of orders to fill.

Biographers of both men have speculated about the relationship between Weems and Washington. There can be little doubt that the two knew each other, even if only as cordial neighbors. Given the number of visitors streaming in and out of Mount Vernon in the 1790s, the possibility that Weems visited the Washington home is less of a badge of honor than he might have wanted his readers to imagine. Likewise, that he may have filled a guest spot occasionally in Washington's local Pohick Parish Church pulpit, and in other area churches, is far from remarkable. There is no reason to imagine that the two men were confidants in any sense of the word. Nothing exists to hint that Weems had special access to Washington's thoughts or stories from his past. But, as Dixon Wecter wrote in his less-than-flattering profile of the man and his work, "naïve though he was, Weems knew the ways of ingratiation."[24] Francois Furstenburg wrote that "throughout his career, Weems cultivated the patronage of elite figures."[25] Weems also knew very well the promotional value of his noted neighbor's reputation when it came to selling books.

Either out of sincere devotion or cynical exploitation, he dedicated his 1799 *The Philanthropist* to Washington, in hopes that "you may live to see us all, your loving countrymen, catching from your fair example" a love of God and country. Weems then signed his dedication "your very sincere friend and Masonic brother."[26] It was a deft little bit of positioning and well played, in a small book that was a paean to the values of the Revolution.[27] Later that year, after

Washington's death, he wrote to Mathew Carey of his intention to begin writing what would eventually become his masterwork.

When scholars have discussed Weems's *Life of Washington,* it has usually been in aid of a few specific causes. One has been its value as a historical biography, but that discussion ended long ago, and not in the Parson's favor. More recently, Cathy Davidson made much of Weems's remarkable abilities as a marketer. Weems was "the most successful" and "the most popular" of the early American book peddlers, a diligence that earned him a remarkable 25 percent commission on his sales, whereas others were settling for 5 percent.[28] Other scholars have looked more into the logic and language of the man's work. Scott Casper saw in the book an important moment in the development of American biography as a genre—the turn to the probing personal biography as a look into the inner workings of its subject's soul, character, and motivations, as opposed to a recitation of deeds.[29] Francois Furstenburg and Peter Onuf both saw Weems's work as a voice for unity amid an early national politics that pitted elites against common folk, region against region, and party against party. Weems positioned himself as a moderating force seeking to silence schisms and emphasize a shared national meaning and mission. Whether this was sincere politics or a clever way to sell books to all sides is an open question. As with *The Philosopher's* call for unity, Weems's Washington was meant to be a unifying figure set against the horrid possibilities of division, or worse, civil war. Furstenburg summed up Weems's work on this score by claiming that "his texts helped to bind a nation together, and they succeeded for a time."[30]

Weems the preacher, Weems the partisan, Weems the bookseller, and Weems the historian we have seen. What has eluded examination, though, is Weems the observer and creator of landscapes and environments. This concern has an obvious resonance for Ferry Farm, the setting for his most famous stories and the landscape he brought, through writing, to Americans who would never see the place firsthand. Landscape, here, is the tie to memories collective and personal, as indeed Weems himself told us in his little book. Washington grew from the land, both physically and metaphorically. In Weems's hands, the land produced Washington memories that he told his readers were both true and false while at the same time serving as a perfected America. The land produced, the land reflected, the land knew, and over and over again, the land remembered.

But at first, the land was not really a part of the book. The earliest versions of Weems's *Life of Washington* were essentially expanded pamphlets, hurriedly assembled and rolled out in the largest possible numbers for quick sale. As sales and orders of what he called "our little book" increased, Weems knew he was onto a good thing.[31] He wrote to his publisher, Mathew Carey (an otherwise business-savvy man who was initially not entirely persuaded by Weems's sense that he was onto something big), that he wanted to adorn the frontispiece with a nice picture of his subject, perhaps even "turning to Mrs. Washington" for a dedication.[32] Soon, though, Carey was printing copies in Philadelphia, and Weems was selling them far and wide. In August 1800, he wrote to Carey that "you may thank Washington and The Bachelor for most of the remittances made you," and when resupply was slow, Weems was almost in a panic.[33] "Washington" (as he called the book in his letters) rapidly became "the best ammunition I ever had in my cartouch box yet," and with each new printing, he folded in new tales and details—all penned by him, either by candlelight in some roadside tavern or during his brief visits back home to Dumfries.[34] In 1806, he added the Cherry Tree story, and by 1809 the book was far thicker than when it had begun. He had even achieved some clarity about the part of his work that would be most memorable. He wrote to Carey, in January of that year, that he was "setting Washington before the youth of our country."[35] Even though he had been editing and adding over the years, he still felt he had barely scratched his topic's surface and not fully tapped the book's potential. He told Carey that we would "sometimes mourn" that he "ever let it go out" of his hand and that "several more chapters, chapters entire, ought still to be added," and that there were "many passages that are capable of being wrought up to a far more interesting height."[36] Weems may well have been a master salesman and champion ingratiator, but it also seems that, at least by 1809, he had become a real writer—perfectionist, detailed, concerned about his craft, and eager to get just a bit more on the page. More than any other project, it was his *Life of Washington* that brought him to that station.

In the year 1809, the project was finished, even if Weems still had more he wanted to add. Over the years of writing, he had traveled all along the southeastern seaboard, and he knew its people well. He passed through Fredericksburg many times and probably knew the town as well. He used local printers to keep his stock up and no doubt had visited Ferry Farm on one occasion or another. The main road down the Northern Neck still began hard by the site of the old Washington home, and the same ferry run that had annoyed Washington more than half a century before was still taking travelers such as Weems back and forth across the Rappahannock.

He made two specific references to the site in a way that suggested familiarity with the place and its history. In one, he noted that visitors came to the site regularly and mistook it for the home of Washington's birth. This is an easy and understandable error that dates back to at least 1777, when Philadelphia bookseller Ebenezer Hazard mistakenly labeled the farm as "the Hill upon which Genl. Washington was born."[37] Weems turned the conflation of places to his own advantage by calling it out as an untruth. Patriotic visitors may look at the home and say "here is the house where the Great Washington was born," but Weems quickly retorted, "but it is all a mistake," reminding his readers that Washington was, in fact, born in Westmoreland County.[38] With this correction, Weems claimed the mantle of truthful raconteur of past events, an author who was trustable while creating his own tales. Crucially, though, he relied on Ferry Farm's actual physicality to establish his credibility.

Weems also made use of the old home's appearance. The site's archaeology revealed that the home—albeit dramatically altered over the century of its life—was standing until sometime in the 1820s. Weems therefore would have known a far more ramshackle and shopworn version of the old home than Washington would have known. His descriptions reflected that. Weems referred to the home as having a "front of faded red" and being "weatherbeaten," both descriptors that emphasized the kind of rural, rustic Washington background that Weems wanted to convey. But at the same time, there was an actual home to be observed, and from what we can see, it would have been in just such a state.[39] The homespun quality of Weems's Washington tales have usually been understood as resulting from what Francois Furstenburg called a "complex back and forth" between the author and his readers.[40] He wrote in their voices and used their sensibilities to present them with his distillation of a far larger American—and even Atlantic—world of ideas, political currents, and religious sentiment. It was this role as a purveyor to, and arbiter for, the masses that made Weems matter.

But at the same time, his descriptions were in dialogue with observable landscapes and places. A rustic Washington childhood may have made good marketing and political sense for readers who would have been able to see their own lives mirrored in that of the Great Washington. But it could not have stuck had there been a grand and enduring mansion home sitting at Ferry Farm, attracting visitors and providing testimony to a very different family life. The circa 1800 condition of the neglected and dilapidated old Washington home enabled Weems's storytelling and may even have served as the first source and main proof of the rusticity that became a central part of the self-made man narrative and other themes in the corpus of Washington biography. In this way, important Washington meaning was itself, in part, a product of a material reality that was there to be seen on a rise of land overlooking the Rappahannock.

Weems certainly invented a fabulous landscape, but he built on a familiarity with the real one and ones just like it. While rooting his tales in visible material realities, Weems also self-consciously made Ferry Farm into a special slice of Eden. Here was a place where a young George could "look in silence on the wide wilderness of fruit" and where the "chase of the butterfly" could exhaust the young innocent, who could then lay "himself down on his grassy couch" and sleep, all the while serenaded by "little crickets."[41] Here a godlike, forgiving father could sweep out his arm in any direction and show his son the bounty that sprang from the fertile earth, seemingly without any effort at all. Fruit abounded, sweet flowers opened for his "pug nose," and the "bubbling spring" was cool and awaiting his thirst. Even the animals knew their role and played it gladly: "Silver fish" fairly jumped into the net, "good cows" were there to "give him milk," gentle "beautiful horses" stood ready "for him to ride," bees buzzed to and fro only to "make sweet honey for his sweeter mouth," and the "little lambs" were eager to give up their wool to make "beautiful clothes for him."[42] Just as Adam had all he could want in his garden, so too Washington had all he could want in this new American Eden.

The centerpiece of this envisioned landscape was the Cabbage Seed tale. When George discovered these clever plants, he came running to his father to share the news of "such a sight," which "never did grow there by chance."[43] Indeed, it did not, and Augustine quickly unmasked his game, and through him Weems explains that the lad, indeed, had a true father in heaven and that, thanks to him, nothing happened by chance—indeed, he was the sole author of all of the earth's bounty that was there for George to enjoy. The tale has a simple lesson in faith, but it also is a statement about the land itself. It was likewise no accident that this land grew this lad. The land that grew Washington's name becomes, through this tale, a sort of earthly producer of the man and a repository for his memory.

Weems's Ferry Farm was a Virginia Eden, and like its biblical counterpart, it also had its trees. They came in two forms in Weems's writing: imagined, actual trees, and trees that were metaphors for Washington himself.

Young George was once "but an acorn, which a pig could have demolished," but eventually grew to be "the oak whose giant arms throw a darkening shade over distant acres."[44] Weems defended his project by claiming that it was good for readers to know about the "soil and situation" that produced "such noble trees" as Washington and his siblings. Parents would be well advised to listen as Weems related "how moved the steps of the youthful Washington," whose worth would become greater than "all the oaks of old Bashan" and that of "the red spicy cedars of Lebanon."

Not only was George like a tree, but also trees were powerful symbols of bounty and risk at Ferry Farm. In one anecdote, Washington walked into an orchard with an unnamed cousin who recounted (allegedly to Weems) that the "whole earth, as far as we could see, was strewed with fruit" and above that, "the trees were bending under the weight of apples."[45] The lesson of the tale was one of generosity, as Augustine reminded George of a past act of selfishness in the face of such plenty. He pointed out to his contrite son that "wherever you turn your eyes, you see the trees loaded with fine fruit; many of them indeed breaking down" from that weight.

Those apples taught lessons of sharing God's bounty, and Ferry Farm's most famous tree, of course, was enlisted in the cause of honesty. Weems's "English cherry-tree" incident highlighted not only George's truth telling but also his father's joy at seeing such virtue. It is worth noting that Weems's original text left the actual fate of the tree somewhat a matter for speculation. Although Augustine stated that George had "killed my tree" in the encounter, Weems the narrator wrote that George had "barked" the tree "so terribly, that I don't believe the tree ever got the better of it." This was a fabulous, and ultimately useful, literary sleight of hand. On one hand, Washington commits the biblical sin of killing a fruit tree and performs the healing act of confession to receive fatherly absolution and rapturous love in what is a perfect Christian parable. But on the other hand, there is always the chance that little George was guilty of nothing more than some youthful vandalism. Generations of Weems devotees at Ferry Farm would latch onto this little detail and allow the tree to survive long after the tale—and even allow it to produce offspring. This little wink from the author set in motion Cherry Tree possibilities that he never could have imagined. It also was a defining moment in Ferry Farm's history.

Weems's Ferry Farm, then, was made up of a few core constituents. One was an aging home—itself a shadow of what it had once been—whose dilapidation, projected back to the days of Washington's youth, made a viable foundation for a Washington self-made man story line. Another was an environment filled with all the bounty of a perfect English American farm. The lush and verdant nature of the land silenced the labor—particularly the enslaved labor—that went into all such production and instead made richness a gift of the land and of God. The land rewarded virtue with bounty, and the bounty itself taught virtue. The third element of Weems's Ferry Farm consisted of the trees, both ones that were symbols for Washington and the ones that gave shade and fruit while also serving as vehicles for other moral lessons.

This was the Ferry Farm that most Americans would come to

know, even if they never knew the name of the place or even gave it a second thought. Weems's *Life of Washington* went through multiple printings, which he and Mathew Carey oversaw. But bits of his story took on lives of their own. Sections were selected and reprinted—both in his own words and paraphrased—in almanacs, newspapers, and all manner of publications, wherever editors wanted to fill their pages with proven material. This process brought one story, above all others, to forefront and made it Weems's greatest contribution to American culture: that of the Cherry Tree and the Boy Who Could Not Tell a Lie. Its simple message and colorful imagery made it useful, its short, discreet, anecdotal nature made it easily reprintable, and its use of Washington as its main character gave it pedigree.

Artists also picked up on the tale, creating wall hangings, handbills, and book illustrations that showed the boy, the tree, and the father—a trio that any Trinitarian Christian would recognize, and one that cast the tree itself in a curious light. The illustrations all included some imagining of the Washington home and Ferry Farm itself. They carried on Weems's themes of fruit-heavy trees and the limitless bounty of a gracious land. But it was through writing that Ferry Farm reached it largest audiences.

Weems understood that he was creating a fabulous set of anecdotes designed to teach children morals and patriotism in one package. By the 1820s, though, producers of children's readers had begun to use the story in their history books and practice readers, an addition that became more common closer to the 1832 centennial of Washington's birth. These compilers and publishers added teaching children to read to Weems's own goals. The most significant of these schoolbook producers was an Ohio minister and teacher named William Holmes McGuffey. McGuffey was born in Washington County, Pennsylvania and educated at Washington College in Ohio, so the Great Washington could never have been too far from his heart. Like Weems, McGuffey was committed to the broad evangelical project in America and was equally committed to selling books. His *Eclectic Reader* went through numerous printings, with each new edition adding a bit here and changing a bit there, until they had sold close to 120 million copies in just under a century.[46] McGuffey's first version of the Cherry Tree story appeared in his fourth edition and thereafter became a staple of the book but with a few crucial changes, the main one being some formalizing of language; for example, Weems's original "Pa, do I ever tell lies?" became "Father, do I ever tell lies?" The story appeared most frequently in the readers designed for younger pupils, so in that way McGuffey ensured that the largest possible number of nineteenth-century Americans would first experience literacy through some version of Weems's Cherry Tree story.

Other writers picked up on the tale, repeating it in varying forms. In some versions, Washington chopped the tree down, and others were truer to Weems's more ambiguous chopping. The story was also enlisted for various causes—although, in time, it would become a mere trope for cartoonists and a way to sell cars each February. The most interesting use was William Thayer's reworking of the tale so that it had an abolitionist moral. In his version, young George's confession came only after his father assumed it was an enslaved African who committed the vandalism. Once George learned of his father's intention to punish one of his people unfairly, he bravely came forth and confessed saying, "Don't whip poor Jerry: if somebody must be whipped, let it be me; for it was I, and not Jerry, that cut the cherry-tree."[47]

Weems's stories and style also found a champion in a New York–born writer named Benson Lossing. Through a series of much reprinted and heavily illustrated "sketch books," Lossing took on Weems's mantle as the great American historical fabulist and popularizer.[48] His interests were similar to Weems's, and like the Parson, he wrote appeals for unity through a shared history as the nation teetered on the edge of calamitous sectional conflict. Lossing wrote works that were part history, part folklore, and part travelogue but always emphasized the realness and visitability of the places he described. In that way, Lossing is one of the unsung heroes in the birth of American historical tourism.

In his 1852 *Pictoral Field-Book of the American Revolution*, Lossing penned a standard, brief Washington biography that made some use of Weems's Washington and praised the author, stating that despite his flaws, he was "a man of great benevolence" and a "very successful" bookseller—a quality to which Lossing certainly could relate.[49] He also later added tales he worked out with George Washington Parke Custis, the self-promoting adopted grandson of the Great Washington. From Parke Custis, Lossing cribbed a second version of the Cherry Tree, except in this one it was a wild colt at the center of the tale and it was Mary who confronted a seventeen-year-old George about his having ridden this favorite horse to death. The moral was the same, as were the Washington attributes of strength and honesty. This time, though, the tale was recast and valuably connected to a vouching family member, whereas Weems's Cherry Tree rested on the tale of an unnamed "excellent lady," who Weems hinted may or may not have been kin to the family.[50]

When he visited Ferry Farm in 1848, Lossing claimed there was "nothing of interest being left upon the soil," and so the great tourist passed on his chance to walk over the land. Indeed, he had it on good authority from locals that the Washington's "mansion house" had "long since gone to decay and disappeared," leaving little that warranted a trip in the rain that then blanketed the town.[51] He contented himself with a "distant view" of the farm's "rolling acres" as he left town for points south.[52]

Lossing's great contribution to the imagined Ferry Farm came in the form of a small sketch of what he called the "Residence of the Washington Family"—a specific and lithographed reference to Weems's "weatherbeaten" old home, still visible in his day but long gone by the 1850s, when Lossing visited. Lossing described the home as having had four rooms and an "enormous chimney at each end."[53] Since, unlike Weems, he never saw the place, Lossing claimed to have received his vision from Virginia painter John Gadsby Chapman, who painted the ruined home on the eve of the Washington birth centennial anniversary nearly two decades before Lossing's visit. Soon after the publication of the *Pictoral Field-Book,* the New York lithography firm of Currier and Ives created its own colored print of the home but mistakenly labeled it Washington's Birthplace, an error that echoed the confusion Weems mentioned while helping keep the conflation of the two places alive. Flawed though their renderings may have been, the combination of Weems, McGuffey, Lossing, and Currier and Ives ensured that Ferry Farm would be one of the best-known and most gazed-upon American places that most Americans could not have named.

Lossing's drawing was based on a chain of imagination and hearsay. But it was a clever rendering and an effective one as well. As late the 1930s, experts were still citing the sketch as authoritative, and its echoes are still part of museum interpretation today; an animated version of Lossing's "Residence" makes a cameo appearance, for example, in Mount Vernon's presentation of Washington's childhood.

Works of art and literature such as these addressed people's anxieties by producing for them not the world as it was but the world as they wished it to be. Nineteenth-century Americans were singularly adept at mediating their fantasies and fears through art. The same vehicles were also central in creating a new American identity—perhaps an act of conjuring as ambitious as the creation of the republic itself. Ferry Farm's written version played a role in this process in a few significant ways.

Changes wrought by an increasing pace of industrialization, the movement of peoples, and the need to claim a past as an antecedent for the new nation's present increased the appeal of historical paintings and made ruins a fit topic for paintings. When John Gadsby Chapman painted Ferry Farm as a stone ruin in 1831, his work drew on European trends while suggesting that America had an art-worthy past all its own. His rendering of the sun-dappled remains of the Washington home wistfully hinted at a sense of the passing of the Revolutionary generation, a concern then coming into focus for many of his countrymen. By combining Washington and ruins, Chapman brought American content to European themes. Ralph Waldo Emerson's 1837 claim that "we have listened too long to the courtly muses of Europe" was a call that many could have uttered—and did.[54] Indeed, Chapman himself later called on Americans to reject "the cast-off frippery of European garrets and workshops" and draw inspiration from the "vast resources of mind and matter" that America possessed in its own right.[55] Hudson River School painters, such as Thomas Cole and Asher Durand, used a similar logic and created large, lush green paintings of sweeping vistas that were as much a celebration of the American landscape as they were masks for changes made by the Erie Canal, growing cities, and factory towns.[56]

In that way, part of creating a shared American landscape vision was through hiding the changes that challenged the ideal. While Weems and others helped spread Weems's Ferry Farm vision, the real Ferry Farm was undergoing a set of landscape changes that contrasted sharply with the imagined place Americans were coming to know.

Washington sold off the land in 1774 to Hugh Mercer, who eventually left it to his heirs, who in time sold it off to the Coalter family who consolidated it into their larger holdings along the river. When Washington surveyed the land, he made it clear that the back acres onto Stafford Heights were still heavily wooded. Those trees included the same growths that had been there back to before English settlement began, just over a century before Washington's survey. By the 1830s, the land was in the hands of a pair of relocated northern businessmen named Joseph Mann and Thomas Teasdale. Both had come to Virginia as part of a larger movement of northern speculators and ambitious men looking to buy cheap land and find a way to make it pay. What we know of them comes from the written detritus of the collapse of their Ferry Farm plans.

Mann and Teasdale's efforts concentrated mostly on the possible speculative value of the land as the railroad planned on pushing into the county from Washington, DC and crossing the Rappahannock into Fredericksburg. They also farmed the land, but their main enterprise was broomcorn for resale and manufacture. Mann clearly saw this as a growing concern and sought out skilled "broom tiers," in Massachusetts and New Hampshire, to relocate and work the shop in exchange for a wage and *"good and wholesome board."*[57] The problem was that the business proved harder than imagined. On top of that, the location of a possible railroad crossing became the subject of a protracted fight between advocates of an upper crossing and those—such as Mann and Teasdale—who wanted a lower crossing, thus shutting down hopes of a quick, profitable sale.

At some point during this slow fading of the broom enterprise and the dying embers of land speculation, the owners began to turn to the other valuable resources the land held in order to make money: the back acres of the land, those that stretched up the rise of land onto Stafford Heights and beyond the old-growth timber stands. The various lawsuits and countersuits between Mann and Teasdale make it clear that Mann had been cutting wood from the land and selling it. Teasdale objected in court that the shared resource was being monetized by one partner and not for the benefit of both. Indeed, Teasdale claimed that this was no small, isolated event but rather a pattern through which Mann had "converted and misapplied" and "occasioned the conversion and misapplication" of large sums derived from the land.[58]

In the 1830s and 1840s, Fredericksburg was in an expansion phase.[59] New, mostly frame-built homes were springing up at the edges of town and on nearby fields. The new railroad was in the area, cutting a path down to Richmond and laying tracks and ties while consuming cord after cord of cut wood for engines that had not yet switched to coal.[60] Wooden ships and barges sat at the town's upper and lower wharfs and at Falmouth on the opposite bank, all needing wood for repairs and ready to ship out quantities of the stuff if anyone called for it. In short, wood was one of the most readily used commodities of the day, and even though the Ferry Farm tree stands had been in place before European settlement, to men such as Mann and Teasdale (and many others) they were merely resources for sale. Tree by tree, the place famous for its mythical trees lost its real ones.

The mythical trees proved far more enduring than their quotidian cousins. The great meeting of Ferry Farm's mythical memory and the reality of its landscape happened when Northern military strategists realized that Fredericksburg was an essential stepping stone on their march to Richmond and an end to the rebellion that began in the spring of 1861. With its meeting of rail, road, and river, the city was perfectly suited to be a major staging ground for actions farther south. On top of that, Fredericksburg was, by Virginia standards, a major city. Its capture would be something of a symbolic victory in a war whose planners imagined early on that symbolic victories would be enough. So, in the spring of 1862—before the war had begun to show its grimmest face—Fredericksburg fell to a small Union force. For that whole summer, men from distant places such as New York, Minnesota, and Wisconsin conducted armed patrols in town, to the scowls and occasional insults of the town's residents, most of whom chose to stay in their occupied hometown.

Ferry Farm played a central role in this affair as its acres became the occupiers' tent-filled camp. Invading soldiers crossed over the river several times a day via a massive pontoon bridge made atop a line of canal boats; day and night they came and went in a schedule dictated by guard details and officers' orders. Occasionally a local resident would come across to sneak a peek or sell some goods and then would go back over. A steady of stream of enslaved Africans used the bridge—and every available crossing—to reach the federal lines and there discover freedom; that was largely a one-way crossing, with few looking back. Their quiet but tidal migration to places such as Ferry Farm, and wherever the army settled, occasioned the central crisis of the war and hastened the collapse of slavery itself.

It was these people who also provided the soldiers at Ferry Farm with local stories that brought Washington into focus. But, as their letters make clear, it was Weems's Washington that the occupiers were most inclined to see. To a whole range of visitors—from President Lincoln himself, who visited the "Cherry Tree Farm" during his inspection of his army's newly taken city, to a small host of still-not-battle-scarred young men—Weems's creation was the most significant thing about this landscape.[61]

The newly enlisted farm boys noticed the quality of the land and remarked on how fine the area still was in 1862. More than a few commented on the fine field of clover that covered the acres—a reference to Weems's "clover-covered pastures" that he associated with Washington for his readers.[62] The old Washington home was long gone, but by the 1850s a local farmer named Winter Bray had built a new farmstead in the same place—his work even incorporated some of the old stones. Building conflation was something of a Ferry Farm tradition, and recycling building materials only blurred lines. So it is understandable that the soldiers readily imagined that the Bray buildings were in fact those of the Washington "old homestead" itself, a mistaken identity that did not keep them from pulling apart the buildings "for fuel and to assist in making comfortable the headquarters of the nearest regiments."[63]

Most of the writers, though, simply repeated their versions of Weems's tales of Washington's time on the Rappahannock. To them, Ferry Farm was the "'ol' plantation' where Gen. Washington spent the early days of his life," although some wrote about their time at "Ferry Farm where Washington was born," keeping alive the birthplace confusion.[64] In either case, the soldiers described the place with the grandest of Weemsian sentiments. One soldier wrote to a Wisconsin newspaper that this was the place where "The Father of the American Republic" first took into "his young mind, those principals of love, purity, and fidelity" which so shaped his life's course. One soldier mused about the sad state of the current conflict and wondered in print, "When will the Washington of our crisis appear?"[65]

A few remembered Weems's story of young George planting his name in seeds and then, as one soldier put it, found his name growing in the cabbage bed."[66] But most simply described the farm as "where little George hacked the cherry tree" or where "little Geo" "went with his little hatchet," an event through which "we all have been, morally, much benefited, of course."[67]

An "old cherry tree" growing on the farm had been "nearly all cut into pieces" by soldiers who used its wood to "make all sorts of crosses, pipes, rings, etc., that can be sent away by mail." Some, at the time, claimed this to have indeed been "the original tree of the famous hatchet story," a claim that reflects a clever and close reading of Weems's original version of the story, leaving open the possibility that the tree survived young George's abuse.[68] Other soldiers gathered up cherry pits from Ferry Farm and mailed them home so that Northern farms could be graced with trees descended from the most famous cherry of them all. The bravest of the soldiers—or perhaps the most Weems/Washington-devoted—went so far as to pass time at the river's bank, "attempting to throw a stone across the Rappahannock," even with cannon shot "constantly flying each way" over their heads. Most failed, except for "a huge fellow from Michigan."[69]

Freed from local white guidance (relations with residents were understandably strained, at best) the soldiers were able to see Ferry Farm largely as they chose. Newly freed Africans offered some stories of Washington and some local news, but more often it was Weems who was their principal guide in making the place meaningful.

By connecting their time at Ferry Farm to Washington lore, soldiers centered their encampment at the heart of rustic American patriotism. The place and its connection to the nation's still premier military leader and first president, and tales of cherry trees, became symbolic of the Republic these men were fighting to preserve. Moreover, many resorted to the longstanding language of Washington deification to touch on what mattered about the place, expressing anger and sorrow that this "consecrated" or "hallowed" ground should be so "desecrated" by the "hell deserving bandits" of the South.[70]

Blaming Southerners for the conditions they saw was nothing new to Northern visitors. Frederick Law Olmstead observed, in his 1850s tour, that Virginia's "shabby and half finished cottages" sitting near acres of "poor corn half smothered in weeds" were an embarrassment, compared with the industrious farmers he knew in his native New York.[71] Though a Scotsman, James Sterling spoke for many when he noted that Minnesota had been inhabited by Anglo Saxons not more than a few decades, and yet it had more civilized amenities than did South Carolina for all its nearly two centuries of settlement. Southern cities were "ill paved and utterly in want of sewerage," and in all his 1850s travels he had "met no well-made road," a complaint echoing those of Charles Dickens, who found Stafford County to be a "dreary and uninteresting" expanse.[72] Soldiers often viewed the South through similarly racially tinged and scornful eyes. John Haley, the marvelous Civil War diarist, summed up the view of many Northerners, seeing first that nature had been lavish in her gifts to the South but then that the infernal mix of slavery and the consequent degradation of whites left the land literally in the dust.

Ferry Farm thus was something of an island, a Southern landscape that Northerners could appreciate but really only because it had been Washington's home. Even then, their understanding of the place came from enslaved Africans they easily derided and a Southern, showboating parson who made up his stories. Ferry Farm's special status did not keep the land, or the whole surrounding region, from suffering.

The archaeological record shows how the effects of war came to rest on Ferry Farm's buildings.[73] The first occupation, in the summer of 1862, was peaceful enough, despite some dirty looks. When the soldiers stole a chicken or kicked over a fence, their officers told them to make good the damage. But as the war progressed and casualties mounted, such niceties fell by the wayside. As the Union Army came back again and again to Fredericksburg, Stafford and Spotsylvania Counties, and the river crossing right at Ferry Farm, the land took it on the chin. One by one, the buildings the soldiers imagined had once housed Washington himself came down, and their cellars became open pits for damaged canteens, old clothes, and abandoned munitions. The soldiers dug long trenches right through the core of the Washington home lot and threw up impromptu breastworks containing fragments of Washington-family table service and wig curlers.

Meanwhile, the trees that had become the land's most enduring symbol fell, as well. Mann had cleared much of the land, but
photographs and drawings from the early days of the war show the
Bray buildings standing and still shaded by the hardwoods Southerners typically cultivated near their homes. Alfred Waud sketched
the farmstead and its distinctive barn and cupola, in a sweeping
view of Fredericksburg and the dug-in gun emplacements on the
eve of the December 1862 battle that devastated the town. One
large tree (presumably a walnut) stood alone in the middle of the
fields. Over the next two years, photographers showed that Waud's
tree did not last the year. After that, soldiers reduced all of the Bray
home lot trees to stumps, while buildings went into winter shelters
and cook fires, one board at a time. In contrast to the heavily treed
floodplain and hillside one now sees on these same acres, Civil
War Ferry Farm looked more like a place in Kansas or the Crimea.

Northerners and other observers easily criticized Southern
land use patterns and readily connected what they saw to the slave
system and the racial commerce it engendered. This critique helped
justify a new level of destruction, which in turn became further
evidence of the inadequacy of Southerners as able stewards in the
years after the war. However, Ferry Farm's actual emptiness was due
more to the same sorts of market forces that were then denuding
many Northern hillsides than to the economic and racial realities
that understandably caught visitors' eyes. But the war over the
future of that system finished the job that had begun back in the
early 1700s when the first Englishmen settling the area put axe to
tree—an act so vital to the process of settlement, the marking of
property boundaries, and the making of a nation that Weems wove
it into the central tale of Washington's early years. His readers, in
turn, made the act of chopping central to the very meaning of Ferry
Farm, even as soldiers in one year chopped down cherry trees from
which, the year before, other soldiers had harvested patriotic pits.

By the time the war was over and new people had come into the area to settle it almost as if for the first time, there was nothing above ground to recall anything or anyone standing on the land a short five years earlier. The main artifact was the cleared, empty, pockmarked, and treeless land itself—a crowning (not to say inevitable) achievement of a long process of remaking the land to suit human commercial purposes. But that transformation had been so thorough that it rendered itself and its outcomes all but invisible. Land was land, and even though James Deetz noted that the landscape had an "all-pervasive quality," making it the biggest artifact of all, he needed to make that claim only because that fact was not self-evident.[74] Ferry Farm was indeed a cultural statement: Its plain and hillside were empty because they had been set on that course long ago, and its central story of tree killing turned out to be not only a memory but also a charge and license.

But the Cherry Tree endured even in a bare and ordinary landscape. By the beginning of the twentieth century it had become an informal symbol for the land. The farmer then owning the land invoked it in his advertisements. Visitors came by—in ever greater numbers as the automobile became more common—to see the sites at the Cherry Tree Farm. These included a large tree near a set of newly built farm buildings that many were happy to call the Cherry Tree. Snapshots caught proud guests standing by the venerable relic, some smiling at the camera, others gazing into the distance. As the tree aged, concerned citizens set up frames to keep it standing; later, as it was near to falling over, its fans set a bronze plaque at its base. By the 1950s there were more cherry trees planted by patriotic Cub Scouts and other well-meaning enthusiasts, and soon after that, backers were soliciting funds for a "character-building boy's home" on the site where Washington famously said, "I cannot a tell a lie, Pa."[75] The home they built and its promotional materials were all adorned with cherries, hatchets, and images of little George at what had long been his childhood's defining moment. Historical preservationists vacillated between celebrating the old tree and distancing themselves from it, but in both cases the tree's effect was a simple reality even if the event was not. Even when Walmart came to the landscape in the 1990s, its plans called for cherry trees to be a part of its plaza's design.

Such was the effect that Weems had on the landscape. His invention took root with more effect than any actual Washington story ever could have. There is a common assumption that historicity attaches to place and things because they are old—or at least, as David Lowenthaul taught us, because they appear old. Yet historicity has a hard time attaching to empty land, no matter how historical it is; it seems to want objects to attach to. Even when landscapes are considered to be special or sacred, they still require some sort of extra action to fulfill their promise. The erection of monuments on Civil War battlefields is one locally resonant example of this process at work. By 1985, commerce and war had left the home of Weems's Cherry Tree a blank slate with residual meaning but no place for it to land. As we will see in the next chapter, people invented the objects their history required.

But amidst these invented objects, Weems's always loomed largest. He had created his narrative to teach the basics of ethical behavior and to help unify the nation around the depoliticized veneration of a prominent national hero. One side effect of that project was the setting in motion of a set of stories that brought a single landscape to a national audience. The shared view of that land became a sort of narrative spine for the place—the cohering set of stories that locked Washington to place while creating a precedent for historical invention on the land. Similar processes took place—indeed are taking place—at historical sites everywhere. What makes Ferry Farm special is the Washington connection, though not the one usually mentioned. Thanks to Weems, Washington's name not only grew from the land but also cast a permanent shadow on it. His writing focused a certain kind of long-term attention on the land, a continuous, albeit inconsistent gaze that enabled a rich documentary record through which we can see the tacks and turns of the creation of landscape meaning. Washington's greatest gift to Ferry Farm was his celebrity and the discussion it engendered. It is clear that Washington himself cared not a fig for the fate of his childhood home once he had moved his mother off and sold the place. But Weems dusted off the old place and wrote Washington across it.

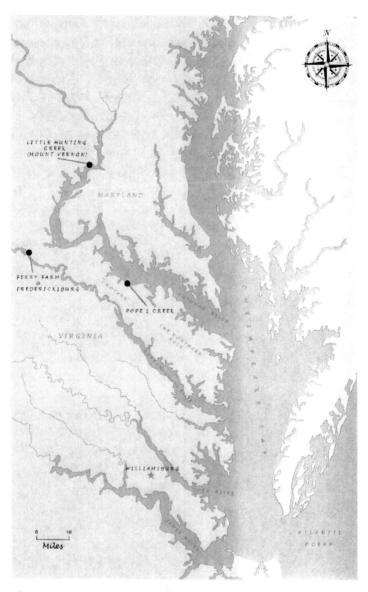

The Virginia of Washington's childhood showing some of the main locations mentioned in this book.

Ferry Farm and the small white Surveying Office today in the left distance. Little survives of the farm buildings that occupied the land in the centuries after the Washington occupancy. The archeology site sits just behind the white walls of the Surveyor's Office. Photo: Philip Levy.

Above: There is no authenticated painting of Mary Washington, but many artists have offered fanciful versions. This one by an unknown painter is the most reproduced. It is notable for its projection of George Washington's features onto the imagined face of his mother. Photo: Anon.

Facing page, top: As part of the 1932 bicentennial of Washington's birthday, the federal commission overseeing the festivities mapped out Washington's 1771 survey of Ferry Farm. It captures a few of the contemporary landmarks and cleverly inserted excerpts from the original document reprinted in Washington's handwriting. Nevertheless, parts of the survey are missing and recent reanalysis suggests that it is riven with small but significant errors. Photo: *The George Washington Atlas*.

Facing page, bottom: The cover page of the Historic American Building Survey report makes clear the confusion around the Surveying Office's age and identification. On one hand, the report repeats the name "George Washington Surveying Office" but, on the other hand, quickly walks back that name by claiming it to be merely a "local appellation." This is a wonderful illustration of how proponents of the building were able to harmonize a historical claim with suspicion of that same claim. Photo: Library of Congress.

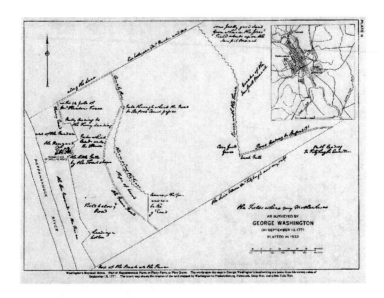

AS SURVEYED BY
GEORGE WASHINGTON
ON SEPTEMBER 13, 1771
PLATTED IN 1932

Washington's Boyhood Home. Part of Rappahannock Farm, or Ferry Farm, or Pine Grove. The words upon the map in George Washington's handwriting are taken from his survey notes of September 13, 1771. The insert map shows the relation of the land mapped by Washington to Fredericksburg, Falmouth, Deep Run, and Little Falls Run.

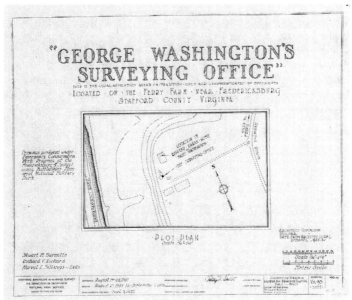

"GEORGE WASHINGTON'S SURVEYING OFFICE"
THIS IS THE LOCAL APPELLATION BASED ON TRADITION ONLY AND UNAUTHENTICATED BY DOCUMENTS
· LOCATED · ON · THE · FERRY · FARM · NEAR · FREDERICKSBURG ·
· STAFFORD · COUNTY · VIRGINIA ·

PLOT PLAN
Scale 1"=50'

Stuart M. Barnette
Richard V. Lockard
Marvel E. Selfridge — Dels.

Scale 1/8"=1'-0"
Metric Scale

This image of Fredericksburg from late in the Civil War shows the old Washington Farm in the center left. It is a fine illustration of just how bare the land had become by then. The fields in the foreground before the ravine are the same ones Washington surveyed in 1771. Close inspection of the high resolution rendering available in the Library of Congress's Civil War Photograph online collection shows the damage done to the farm. Photo: Library of Congress.

This circa 1920 image shows the old Corson home on the left as attached to the Surveying Office sheltered by its own second roof. The still young ailanthus tree sits to its right and beyond that, the home J. B. Colbert built where the Corson home originally sat—both atop the ruins of a Washington family kitchen. This wonderful image shows the intentional neglect of the Surveying Office. Photo: The George Washington Foundation.

A 1950s shot showing the Surveying Office and the Corson home, soon to be demolished. Note the rapid growth of the ailanthus tree and the damage its roots are visibly doing to the chimney base and foundation. Photo: The George Washington Foundation.

5

"THE LOCAL APPELLATION BASED ON TRADITION ONLY"

Making History from Promotion at George Washington's Surveying Office

Let others echo Rupert Hughes
And mix up motes and beams—
The anecdotes that I peruse
Were told by Parson Weems
Above iconoclastic views
That little hatchet gleams!
"I cannot tell a lie," I choose
The Washington of Weems

Lydia Chatton, 1909[1]

In 1909, a Fredericksburg dry-goods seller named James Beverly Colbert embarked on one of the oddest and most improbable preservation efforts. The first hint of his ambitions was in a September 9 local newspaper announcement heralding that Colbert had bought what it suddenly called "The George Washington Farm."[2]

It was not news that the small parcel of land just opposite the city's wharf across the narrow Rappahannock River was the place where George Washington lived as a child. A small but steady stream of visitors and some local storytellers kept that distant memory alive. But ever since Washington had sold the land and ended all family ties to the place, his famed name had faded more and more from the landscape. Gone, too, were any traces of the farmstead the Washingtons had once called home. A succession of later buildings replaced them, and it was the latest of these that Colbert bought and rechristened the George Washington Farm. Although few people knew the details of the Washington family's early history, almost everyone knew the most famous tale from those years—the story of the little boy who chopped at his father's cherry tree and then could not tell a lie. There may have been no relic from those early days on the farm, but there was the well-known story, unquestionably its most famous, useful, and problematic feature.

Thus, Colbert faced a unique problem. He understood that his new property carried a great American name, perhaps the greatest one possible. His plan was to capitalize on that celebrity, first as marketing for his crops and hogs; his promotion boasted that customers could buy "the best alfalfa hay" from the "old home where Mary Washington lived" and where "the famous Cherry Tree grew."[3] But he also planned to turn his new farm into an attraction and even an object of veneration—a shrine to the Great Washington who once killed the cherry tree on this same land. He wanted to turn celebrity and storytelling into a commodity and sell the farm to a buyer, or buyers, at the best possible price. It was a plan as rooted in a patriotic spirit as it was in a New South commercial spirit—as if there were a contradiction.

But how does one take a landscape devoid of anything anyone local would have called "historical" and turn it into a national historical site? How does one make a shrine to a story, especially one that was rapidly losing its credibility amid the same people driving other preservation efforts? In other words, where does history lie in a landscape? Is it an attribute or an aspiration?

From memorials to battlefields to the homes of famous people, invested groups have tussled over meanings of historical places. But in each of these many cases, the essence of historicity was evident and accepted—exalted, even, by disagreement. After all, why fight if nothing important was at stake? But the George Washington Farm, or the Cherry Tree Farm as it was often called, presents a unique and challenging problem. Although its Washington past was very real, it has been best remembered as the site of the Cherry Tree story, a dubious honor at best. Its post–Washington family history has usually therefore been more about Weems than Washington. Faced with a Washington historical place devoid of any obvious Washington remnants, project backers and well-intentioned enthusiasts found a way to create the visible amid the folkloric and the invisible—to invest Washington meaning, historicity, and preservability in one simple 1870s farm building into George Washington's Surveying Office, imagined as the only physical survival from the much-storied childhood days.

Just as the biographers, Washington himself, and later Parson Weems and archaeology all created their entwined narratives of place and childhood for Ferry Farm, historical preservation also created its own sets of stories. What began in the first decades of the twentieth century reached its fruition at the century's end, when Walmart sold its stake in the land to what soon became the George Washington Foundation and the land became a preserved historical site. The biographers made Ferry Farm a trope of the wild, the poor, and the problematically maternal. Weems had a role in that, but his main contribution was in giving the land its enduring arboreal symbol and setting it as a moment in the ongoing discussion of the ideal American family. Preservationists, though, had to bring something called history. In doing so, they tapped into a process of invention that Weems set in motion but applied it to something other than the usual tree. Thus, the Surveying Office was born through a new fable that linked the land to something far more objectively historical than the Cherry Tree, which many, at the time, believed still stood a few feet away from the building. The preservation narrative of place latched onto the resonant surveyor portion of Washington's story and manifested it in the landscape that surveying pulled him away from through a single nineteenth-century structure. The cherry tree was a powerful icon, but even its supporters knew they were walking a line between fantasy and history. Lydia Chatton's little bit of doggerel captures the awareness that in holding onto Weems, one was doing something self-marginalizing or in some way transgressive. Travel writer George Allan England later claimed that, through time and retelling, the old tree had "crystallized into solid reality" even though his defiance of the anti-Weems establishment was itself also a tacit recognition that the story was, in some important way, not reality.[4]

Not so the Surveying Office. Here was something undoubtedly real, at least in its material sense. Although there were real cherry trees on the land (and would be until archaeology killed off the last of them), all were leftovers from generations of well-intentioned commemorators offering a little February tribute to Washington. By the early 1900s, the story at the root of each cherry tree had long been questionable. Washington's surveying, though, was historical beyond question, though, and was perhaps the single most important outcome of his life at Ferry Farm. Washington's own personal wealth stemmed first from surveying, but his work itself was also part of a larger continental expansion—an issue still very much on the minds of Americans when the Surveying Office story emerged. The biographers marked surveying as a major break in the Washington childhood narrative. It was the point in the story where the narrative generally shifted from the more mythological and conjectural childhood to the most avowedly historical phase of young adulthood. The backers of the Surveying Office story did a version of this themselves, using the building as a way to move beyond Weems's problematic stories and transition into the historical, even though doing so centered on an invention as obviously invented as the cherry tree that stood near the building.

The Surveying Office's odd story also brings together concerns from two different streams of scholarship. One is the historiography of historical preservation, a literature with a very sensitive ear for the tones of disagreements between parties seeking to enshrine this or that valuation of the past.[5] The other is the somewhat smaller literature on what James Cook called the "artful deception," a form of deception that invites its audience to both believe and disbelieve and manages to profit both ways.

In describing the logic and motivations of the Virginians behind this era's many preservation projects, James Lindgren noted that those members of the social elite "scoured history" to find what he pinpointed as "pleasing myths and telling legends which could enhance elite hegemony."[6] This could not have been truer in Fredericksburg, Virginia, a place discussed in detail in Lindgren's work.[7] Seth Bruggeman has revisited some of these same social elites to call attention to how they fought (mostly among themselves) over the meanings of Washington as they tugged and pulled in favor of their own competing visions of the place of his birth.[8] Those preservationists were not the ones who rallied to the cause of Colbert's Surveying Office, however; in fact, a few were active opponents.

The crucial issue was defining the "pleasing myths" to which Lindgren referred. Whereas most readers would put the emphasis on the word *myths* in that phrase, the Surveying Office story places the stress on the word *pleasing*. Promoters were faced with a landscape of impeccable historical pedigree but lacking any tactile link to its marketable past. They had a landscape long famous for being the site of the best-known incident in Washington's celebrated childhood. But that incident was a well-known lie and increasingly becoming a problematic association, as those most invested in preserving Washington's memory abandoned the tale; the "myth" became less "pleasing" to those pursuing serious ventures. The response was to imbue a later building with a whole new set of Washington meanings—in essence, to fight invention with invention.

The Surveying Office provides a chance to mark the differences between an "artful deception" involving history and an "invented tradition," both of which are themes in public historical sites. Weems's Cherry Tree is one of the latter breed, created and sold to serve a specific moral purpose in the Early Republic. Weems located the tale's origin in the memory of a local old woman, and once the story was deployed, it could attach to the land as it might. By Colbert's day, one large tree on the land was "said to be" the original, or maybe a scion of the original. That identification let it become a touchstone for all the patriotic family values Weems wanted Washington's childhood to impart. It had become like Hugh Trevor-Roper's discussion of a Scotsman's clan tartan, or Yael Zerubavel's vision of Yosef Trumpledor's last words at the battle of Tel Chai—untrue things believed to be true, in aid of some naturalized unifying project.[9]

The Surveying Office carried some of these traits, but was also too sudden, contrived, and narrowly accepted and promoted to qualify as tradition. Its sudden rise in one expedient moment makes it akin to the celebrated half-fish half-not-fish Fiji Mermaid or the tricks of P. T. Barnum—an almost winking deception, calculatingly deployed for short-term gain, rather than a slowly accruing, polyvocal, multiauthor memory. Such "hoaxes" could be as enjoyable for those seeking to unmask the deception as for those that believed them. That is what was "delightful," to use Andrea Stulman Dennett's description.[10] The building's sudden emergence as a historical site, or perhaps even more—perhaps a precious link to George Washington and a reliable repository for the moral lessons assumed in his childhood, and all facilitated by what might have been its own otherwise unsung P. T. Barnum—represents a unique convergence of meanings for, and uses of, the Washington stories.

By the time Colbert bought the land, it had seen two successive post-Washington farmsteads, and it had been at the center of a wartime occupation and twice been a battlefield. Over time, its various owners had hoped to turn its acres into a new town opposite Fredericksburg, others wanted it to be the route for a new railroad, and still others sought only good crops—feed crops and broomcorn, mostly. In nearly one hundred years, though, what was missing was Washington. Locals do not appear to have cared all that much; in fact, it was outsiders, mostly, who associated what they sometimes tellingly called the Cherry Tree Farm with Washington.

All of that changed when Colbert took possession of the George Washington Farm. For the first time since Washington actually owned the land, that famous name took pride of place.

Colbert's motivations are hard, but not impossible, to divine. He wanted to associate his businesses with the cachet of the Washington name. Colbert was a rough, homespun character from the nearby rural hinterland of Massaponax. He was born just after the end of the war that devastated his native Spotsylvania County. Like many, he came to Fredericksburg to make a postwar commercial fortune. He settled on dry goods, but soon he owned a saloon, a small hotel, and ice works and had interests in other going concerns. His purchase of the Washington Farm put him back in professional farming and also allowed him to live closer to his ice factory at Cold Spring. He was locally well known, even if he was not amid the town's upper social echelons. He never held public office, but he was known for public brawling and rather heavy-handed business practices. In the early 1900s, as local elite families were warming to historical projects, J. B. Colbert was certainly not in that company. Nevertheless, he knew the value of the farm and quickly moved to tie his name and his businesses to Washington.

The city had just gone through a wrenching struggle over the gravesite of Mary Washington. An 1830s attempt to mark Mary's grave ground to a halt and left a half-built stone monument on the site. By the 1880s the place was a forgotten eyesore, and as the town rebuilt after the Civil War, selling it for housing made good sense. The conflict that emerged pitted land developers who wanted to sell Mary's grave at auction against a host of local and national commemorators roused to action by the sales advertisement. Commemorators dragged the developers into court and eventually blocked the sale. Next, a group of matrons raised the money to erect a newly dedicated monument to Mary on the western side of town. The fight also showed that invocations of the Washington name could be quite powerful. The struggle over Mary's grave caught national attention and drew in money from all over the nation as patriotic-minded citizens contributed funds to ensure that Mary's last resting place would be fittingly marked.[11]

Colbert had a front-row seat for all of this—both figuratively and literally, as his in-town home sat almost in the shadow of the monument. So it is a fair assumption that the sudden reawakening of the Washington name at Ferry Farm in 1909 was not just chance. The monument controversy showed Colbert that there were outside moneyed interests ready to open their purses for causes that bore the Washington name. There is no reason to suspect that a full-scale landscape preservation effort was in Colbert's initial plans, but he certainly sought to use his new farm's Washington name for his own personal profit. The first manifestations of that show up in something as simple as his farm stationery. The new farm title blared from the top of the page, "The George Washington Farm—J. B. Colbert, Proprietor," and with that was a rough copy of Gilbert Stuart's famed Washington portrait.[12] The letterhead filled a full quarter of each page and boasted "Old home where Mary Washington Lived and the Famous Cherry Tree grew," and "Old home where Geo. Washington lived and threw the Silver Dollar across the Rappahannock."[13]

Colbert's immediate goals were certainly to associate his own business with the land's prestigious former resident. But the main vehicle to that goal was Weems's set of stories, as opposed to simple invocation of a more historical Washington. The Washington past was bankable only when seen through Weemsian lenses. His actions worked to reinscribe Weems's history in the landscape—to take the old stories and recast them in new guises and in aid of new projects. Like an early version of a President's Day car sale advertisement, Colbert used Weems's best-selling stories to sell his own produce and position himself as a man of substance—both as a farmer and as a patriotic American.

But Weems was a two-sided coin. In the early twentieth century, "serious" people took a dim view of the Parson and his false stories. Some of this was due to the professionalization of historical writing itself. In his 1897 address to the American Historical Association, John W. Burgess noted that "the arranging of the facts of history in the forms and conclusions of science will only lift history to a higher plane."[14] This embrace of science put the objective crosshairs on artists such as Mason Locke Weems and later imitators such as Benson Lossing, both of whom defined the style of American history writing in the 1800s.[15] A history genre writing that mixed moral lessons, personal anecdotes, patriotic treacle, and historical tidbits became derided and dismissed as fabulism.

Colbert could hardly have been aware of these trends taking shape in distant ivy-covered halls. But his small invocation of Weems, and his strengthening of the Parson's hold over Ferry Farm's land and story, set the land itself solidly on the side of the fabulists. Whereas Mount Vernon was enjoying a half a century of being the lovingly preserved home the General pined for as his Cincinnatus-like honor called him to service, Ferry Farm could best lay claim to Washington through fairytales. If Weems and his ilk had to be cleared away, then what of a place that made its primary claim to Washington through the language of Weems's best-known lie? Such places could hardly be considered historical right at the moment that the nation was discovering that it had a past worthy of preservation and a time when preservationists themselves were deeply invested in saving exactly the kind of "history" that the likes of Burgess smiled on.

Ferry Farm as a historical place therefore faced a singularly challenging problem—indeed, an utterly unique one in the annals of American preservation. It had a longstanding and well-documented link to something most Americans would have agreed was important: Washington's childhood. But at the same time, that childhood was the subject of some of the most famous lies of American storytelling, making almost every mention of it fraught with the tension between the competing discourses of folklore and history. This tension was a major part of why Washington biographers relied more and more on knocking Weems in their work. Ridiculing Weems became a way to establish oneself as valid, truthful, reliable, and not mythic—everything a modern historian should be.

But by the time Europe was tearing itself apart in world war, bits of Weems's Washington were sprouting anew under Colbert's cultivation. The evidence is largely photographic. A small handful of yellowing snapshots show visitors standing proudly near some crucial areas on the Colbert's Washington Farm. One area was a large, ragged tree that stood near where the land dropped down to the floodplain. One visitor in a suit and driving cap stands as if at attention, gazing past the tree onto the out-of-frame Rappahannock. Handwritten captions date the collection of images to 1917 and reveal that the tree was "the Cherry Tree." Another shows a woman smiling for the camera, her hand lovingly resting on the trunk. For the next few decades, visitors like these stood next to the tree and noted seriously or humorously that this was, or was a descendant of, the famed tree of Weems's writing.

There are a few things we can say for certain about that particular tree. One is that it did not date to before the Civil War. Wartime photographs of the site leave no doubt that there were no trees standing on that part of the land after 1863. These are the same photographs that show the empty landscape, which made such a contrast to the verdant Eden imagined and promoted by Weems. Another certainty is that recent archaeology of the site shows that this tree actually sat right in what had been an open-yard area during the Washington occupancy of the 1740s through the 1770s.[16] There is no reason to ascribe any venerability to this particular tree—it was as new as the 1870s farmstead built by the Corson family after the war.

Nevertheless, around World War I it became a stand-in for the legendary original. As Weems's standing with scholars fell, there were nevertheless those unwilling to let go of the old stories. Weems's vision was not only well entrenched and still influential (if only as a counterpoint), his stories took on new meanings even as they fell in esteem.

Other photos have visitors posed next to a simple wood-framed farm office, which sat at the end of the farm's driveway. This was probably the oldest-looking building on the site, although the only extant landscape photo to show the whole farm reveals it as just another part of the Corson postwar complex. Nevertheless, whereas the home and low milking barns were all constructed in contemporary styles, the farm office was different. It was built in a long-enduring local vernacular style. High peaked roof with cedar shakes, small brick chimney, and rough clapboards were part of countless similar small offices all over the region. One pops up in one of the Civil War's best-known Fredericksburg photographs. The image shows a group of singularly young-looking Confederate soldiers staring at the camera from the town side of the wrecked rail bridge. Sitting on Marye's Heights behind them is a dead ringer for the Corson office—one example of many.

But soon after Colbert bought Ferry Farm, visitors and their cameras paid special attention to the farm office at the end of lane.

A story had begun to coalesce around the building, even though the tale's origins and originator were equally unclear.

What is clear, though, is that the story took on a life of its own. One of its first high-profile treatments came from socialist utopian science fiction writer and journalist George Allan England, who placed the building at the center of a 1925 piece he penned about Ferry Farm for the *Daughters of the American Revolution Magazine*.[17] England was then making his living collecting travel stories along his many adventures. During a pass through Fredericksburg, he was charmed by a series of preservation efforts he saw locally. Mary Washington's grave had awakened a preservation impulse that soon spread to local structures, including the homes of Mary Washington, Charles Washington, and Fielding and Betty Washington Lewis. Preservation served many purposes in this town so recently shattered by the Civil War. It gave the place an American past that was far less painful to discuss and remember amid bullet-marked buildings and thousands of graves.[18] It also spoke to larger anxieties engendered by decades of market-driven changes, as the city became a New South place of commerce and manufacturing.

But for a passerby such as England, preservation was all Old South charm and simple patriotic public spirit. England dressed up in mock-colonial garb to help raise funds to save the Lewises' home, "Kenmore," for posterity.[19] But it was ultimately Ferry Farm across the river that he claimed as his own favorite project, via essays he wrote for magazines and major newspapers. His 1925 essay revealed the reason people had been standing in stately fashion in front of the old Corson farm office. England's essay became a main player in remaking this ordinary building as the George Washington's Surveying Office—the last "humble but priceless" material tie to Washington's childhood.[20]

England had learned this creative tale in the area—most likely from Colbert himself. The question of who invented this useful and well-thought-through association remains open, though. Associating the building with surveying was nothing short of brilliant. Of all the land's stories, the birth of Washington's surveying career was the most "historical" and certainly the most nationally significant. Surveying made Washington rich before he was twenty years old; it got him his colonial office and began his lifelong pattern of land acquisition. But it also was a crucial part of expanding colonial settlements. Surveyors, with their measuring chains, quadrants, and recording books, were often the first heralds of English expansion—small wonder that Indians learned to take shots at backcountry surveying parties when they spotted them too close to their homes.

The significance of surveying to Washington's life and the larger colonial story was only then fully emerging within the long parade of Washington biography. Weems himself barely mentioned Washington's enormously prosperous career in the woods, passing it over as a brief phase in which he lived "the laborious life of a woodsman."[21] John Marshall mentioned only that Washington had acquired great "information respecting vacant lands" and later put it to use "to the increase of his private fortune."[22] Likewise, Washington Irving saw surveying mostly as having toughened him for a future military career.[23] Most nineteenth-century writers saw the surveying as a significant break between childhood and maturity, but most also tended to see is a toughening up, or preparation, for later military adventures. There was no meaningful change in this tone until Henry Cabot Lodge associated the "rough life, but a manly and robust one" surveying offered with something more resonant than mere prelude. For Lodge, surveying—an act already pregnant with images of domination and conquest—and its tough practitioners ensured that Washington would not be "weak or effeminate."[24] Lodge also called this job a "profession," a word that instantly made Washington himself a professional. That idea was picked up by George Allan England's and J. B. Colbert's contemporaries, Rupert Hughes and William Woodward, who respectively lauded Washington's drafting as "so exquisitely exact that his surveys are found faultless to this day" and noted that he always composed in a "neat, clear manner."[25]

Invoking surveying as the building's new story situated it within a set of meaningful, but also very contemporary, Washington concerns. Following Lodge, it spoke to manliness, and there could be no better role model than Washington, the boy who grew to be a great man at this place. England himself even suggested that Boy Scouts of America might want to adopt the land as their own, arguing that they would be "inspired by the boyhood home of America's greatest boy—and man—George Washington!"[26]

According to the 1920s Washington biographers, the Surveying Office spoke to that most relatable and respectable of Washington traits: his professionalism. Oddly anachronistic traits such as that were vital bridges that made the otherwise marble man seem real and meaningful.

The Surveyor Office story emerged right as the nation was having its own debates about expansion and borders. Frederick Jackson Turner's celebrated 1893 lament over the end of the democracy-making "frontier" gave voice to an anxiety that the claiming of new lands was central to the American project.[27] Without new land, could the nation survive? Colonial enterprises in Cuba, Haiti, and the Philippines were one possible answer to the problem. As a travel writer, England expressed some muted approval of these actions by romanticizing the subjects of imperialism and celebrating the ships, planes, and soldiers backing it up. He took a greater interest, though, in a small but significant movement advocating the annexation of Newfoundland and Labrador. The advantages of northern expansion were mainly that the people of these provinces were themselves from the same good Anglo Saxon stock as were the would-be colonizers. All the political, social, and possibly evolutionary problems posed by prolonged contact with racial inferiors in alien climates were nonexistent in northern expansion.[28] In the early 1920s, England even toured the Canadian provinces and wrote extensively about local characters, dialects, and economies.[29] His work made much of charting the uncharted and seeing the previously unseen. His very self-conscious stance as the quintessential explorer and writer mirrored the kind of admiration Woodward and Hughes expressed for Washington's own neat and meticulous survey records.

England saw himself as an embodiment of those values, played out in his own literary surveys of foreign parts ready for the taking. Even if he was unaware of it, the resonances of an actual physical link to Washington's personally and politically consequential career as a surveyor spoke to real desires and concerns that both he and his audience shared. That is a lot to place at the antique doorstep of a small Virginia farm building, but each preservation or commemoration effort is always about much more than the stated project at hand. And in this case, there was another sting in England's essay. Not only was there a surviving relic to Washington, but also the building and the land needed to be preserved.

England urged the Daughters to make Ferry Farm their own cause and to save it from ruin as they had so many other relics of a vanishing past. Indeed, if they did not, time would take its devastating toll. Already the "little house" with its "ancient and handmade shingles and clapboards" was showing "marked signs of deterioration," which "if not soon arrested" would certainly lead to the loss of this "irreplaceable landmark of pre-Revolutionary days and Washington memories." He concluded that whereas "Lincoln's birthplace is protected by imposing marble," this "soul-stirring Washington antiquity" sits vulnerable to "destruction by the weather or fire."[30]

Three things happened in that essay. One was that the Surveying Office story had found its bard. A tale that could not have been two decades old (it being unlikely that the previous owners, the Corsons, would have dated a building to Washington's day that they themselves had erected) was suddenly reaching national audiences right when they were seeking out ways to connect with their colonial forebears. The second was a prolonged real estate advertisement. Not only did that farm have a living link to Washington, it was also open for business. The third was the spirit of Parson Weems, remade and doing itself one better.

When Weems described Ferry Farm in his *Life of Washington,* he pulled off a fine trick. Rather than recounting his stories as his own, he claimed to have learned them from local old folks—one "aged lady," whom he called "a distant relative" of the Washingtons, in particular.[31] More than the fabrication of the Cherry Tree tale itself, that attribution has caused the most problems over the years. It was his use of the style of the sourcing scholar that has been most vexing to others who make the same claim to being truth tellers based on their own sourcing.

He did a similar thing in relation to Ferry Farm's Washington home itself. He described what would have been a nearly eighty-year-old building as having a "low and modest front of faded red," a perfectly believable claim given the evidence.[32] But he situated his description within a tricky twist. He noted that visitors were wont to come to the site "with emotions unutterable" and "exclaim, 'here is the house where the Great Washington was born!'"[33] Weems went on immediately to note the error of those tourists—a very real and understandable error attested to by other contemporary sources as well. The Parson next wrote, "But it is all a mistake, for he was born, as I said, at Pope's creek (sic)."[34] Weems was, of course, correct, but his little game of error correction was a crafty way to set himself up as reliable, a voice readers can trust to correct misconceptions.

It was a sort of cover for the rest of his version of Washington's childhood, all done with a wink at his audience.

The Surveying Office story pulled off the same sort of trick, minus the wink. Weems knew what he was doing, whereas England was a true believer. He had learned the tale and saw no reason to doubt it. The undeniable record of Washington's surveying served as a reservoir of truth that washed over the fiction of the old farm office's new designation. That was pure Weemsian storytelling: the blending of the real and made-up in ways in which the solidity of one shored up the weakness of the other.

Pretty soon others were chiming in. One was colonial historian Joseph Dillaway Sawyer, who visited Ferry Farm in the early 1920s to do research for his two-volume opus, *Washington*.[35]

Sawyer folded the story into another level of truth telling. The colonial revival–informed 1920s saw a major uptick in Washington interest, thanks to the approach of his two hundredth birthday in 1932.[36] Once again, millions were gaping to learn of the great man, and there was no shortage of writers ready to give them what they wanted, as Weems had done nearly two centuries earlier. The two titans of this decade's Washington biography were Rupert Hughes and William Woodward.

Both writers were turning their already skilled hands to historical biography. Both based their work principally on a reread of older biographies and fresh reads of the Washington papers to produce new works in a newer style—sharp, pointed writing in an almost journalistic voice. Woodward called history "news from the past," and both presented Washington in ways that made sense to their Roaring Twenties audiences.[37] They made Washington familiar, a businessman concerned with the same things that preoccupied contemporary Americans, ordinary even by the standards of the day. The project of making Washington real and relatable was just the one that Weems had long ago embarked on. Both turned on the old hero worship style of biography, preferring to see all warts wherever possible. In their hands, Washington became rough, rude, even grasping and spiteful—nothing like the marble man of old, and certainly not the pious moral exemplar Weems had created.

Ever since Henry Cabot Lodge had issued his fatwa against the Parson, writing that "until Weems is weighed and disposed of, we cannot even begin an attempt to get at the real Washington,"[38] Weems—the man who had sought to bring Washington to the masses—had become the main obstacle to that selfsame project.

Enter Woodward and Hughes, "debunkers" both, as Edward Lengel has recently termed them.[39] Both of those authors achieved their aims by relying on newly published primary sources and positioning themselves as truth tellers, claiming to take their subject outside the usual entrapments of puff, patriotism, and piety. Weems-as-villain had a special role to play in that truth-telling project. Hughes accused the Parson of stealing a few of his "fairy stories" and otherwise filling in gaps in the Washington childhood story with a "slush of plagiarism and piety."[40] Woodward dismissed Weems with the brush of his hand, calling the "Cannot-Tell-a-Lie incident" a "brazen piece of fiction" and leaving it at that.[41] It was becoming a necessary commonplace of the genre to take a swipe at Weems when discussing Washington's childhood, and Hughes and Woodward both benefited by setting up their own contrasts before reviewers might compare.

Sawyer was not the bestseller that Woodward and Hughes were, but he was a substantive scholar swimming in the same waters. He used clout, detail, a frequent invocation of place, and especially photographs as his way to validate himself as truthful. He peppered his biography's pages with images of the British homes and haunts of Washington's ancestors, photographs and drawings from the birthplace site in Westmoreland County, and images from Ferry

Farm, which he noted also went by the names the Washington Farm and the Cherry Tree Farm.[42]

The text did not win friends. One hostile reviewer wrote that "those preferring myths" would find in Sawyer a corrective to the likes of Woodward and Hughes.[43] But even so, the same critic claimed that Sawyer's book "finds its chief merit we think in its more than 250 illustrations."[44] One of those illustrations, dating from a 1923 visit, showed what Sawyer called "the alleged descendant of the cherry tree" of Parson Weems fame. In the text, he addressed the Parson head-on, calling him "a character" and noting that he "certainly struck the popular fancy when he launched the cherry-tree tale," which Sawyer nevertheless considered of "dubious dependability."[45] Though a dismissal, it was a far more generous dismissal than others. It was also a curious Weemsian sleight of hand, which invoked the claim (in this case that the cherry tree still stood) while also seeming to stay aloof from the premise. Sawyer teased the issue a bit more by suggesting that a sturdy new shoot grew from the base of the tree—a clever suggestion that the story, if not the tree itself, was still alive and well.

But what made his creative handling of the tree so remarkable was that, while grinning at tales like the Cherry Tree, he offered the Surveying Office as a real tie to Washington—a genuine link to the past. Sawyer related that despite the fact that "the old farm buildings have disappeared," the Surveying Office was "the only building remaining" to create an "indissoluble" link to the farm's past. What's more, Sawyer singled Colbert out for special praise for his care in maintaining such a treasure—a treasure made all the more valuable for its very factuality in the face of folklore such as the Cherry Tree.[46]

Such solid, real, and meaningful ways to connect to Washington obviated kiddie stories, even while the land still produced them. Sawyer offered both the legend and the putative reality of the building as a linked contrast to fictional cherry trees—trees he nevertheless included in his text and photographs. It was an irony the Parson himself would have enjoyed. Weems had used his own correcting of the then-common mistake about the location of Washington's birthplace to assure his readers he would not steer them the wrong way. Sawyer used the Surveying Office in a similar way, offering a false claim dressed up as real that would become a replacement for other well-known falsehoods.

Thanks to England, Sawyer, and a few others who gradually picked up on the tale, a local story that took shape sometime after Colbert's purchase began to reach national ears and become both a parallel to and a replacement for the Cherry Tree. Colbert did what he could to ensure that his treasure bore the mantel of historicity, sometimes in conflicted ways. On one hand, he moved part of the old Corson House across the land and attached it directly to the Surveying Office. The result was an odd hodgepodge of utilitarian conjoined buildings that was far from being a celebration of Washington. Evidence is thin, but it seems that Colbert used the Corson House as an on-site historical hostel, allowing visitors to spend a night in commune with Washington. He certainly was welcoming visitors and offering tours, and more than a few no doubt stayed at his in-town hotel.

The Corson house was itself an interesting construction. The photographic record shows the Corson house as being really two attached buildings. The older part was a small, slope-roofed, rustic homestead with a large chimney on one end. The Corson family bought the land after the Civil War when they came down from Pennsylvania, to a place that was as poor as it could be. Their buildings reflect that poverty in that they had to rely on the most deeply rooted of local building practices and simple local materials. The older part of the home, like the Surveying Office itself, was simple and would have been suited to the land one hundred years earlier. An 1885 travelogue about Fredericksburg and its Washington connections, in *Frank Leslie's Popular Monthly* magazine, featured a stylized drawing of this small house, with the town in the background.[47] The article claimed that Washington "pictures adorn the interior of the cottage," a plausible description of the décor because the family was said to have boasted about their Revolutionary ancestors. The family also purchased some of the land that had been part of Augustine's Accokeek mining activities. It seems that the new arrivals had Washington very much on their minds. *Frank Leslie's* readers also learned that the Corsons had gone to the trouble of excavating the original Washington family–era kitchen cellar so as to set their new home directly on the same foundation.[48] If that last claim was true, then the original, older part of the Corson home was itself, indeed, a domestic private tribute to Washington and his childhood.

The second part of the home was a completely different animal. It was a two-and-one-half story balloon frame, of a type that was then filling Fredericksburg's city blocks. Its construction probably postdated the 1885 *Frank Leslie's* article, and its overall appearance was far too new for it to have seemed historical to anyone at the time.

Yet it was that half of the home that Colbert moved over to the Surveying Office site and set up on a new concrete foundation while scrapping the older part of the house. With the homesite that *Frank Leslie's* had described being cleared, Colbert then had built a new home that incorporated the old Washington-era cellar. It is impossible to say just what stories the Corsons may have passed on to Colbert when he bought the farm they had rebuilt. The fact that the *Frank Leslie's* story made no mention of the Surveying Office, in a piece that was eager to make every historical connection it could, is a loud hint that its imagined historicity simply did not yet exist. It is unlikely that the Surveying Office would have been passed off as a Washington survival at that stage. But it is also clear that stories about the Corson home and its Washington cellar were common currency. The confusing mix of old stones, buildings built on the sites of older ones, and buildings that may have been old all proved a productive seedbed. It may well have been in Colbert's mind as his work crews hauled a two-story wooden box from one part of the home lot to the other and attached it to the building he thought was the farm's most important.

But even though Colbert treated his small treasure as more or less another farm building, he also took steps to reveal it as special. He placed a large tin roof over the entire office, an entirely separate construction that shielded the old building and its aging wooden shake roof from the elements that had so worried England. Photographs suggest that this protective roof may have been made up of parts of the older Corson house roof. The result of that curious building work was a homespun oddity as crude and cobbled together as was Barnum's Fiji Mermaid. Colbert's second roof sat on posts over the aging Surveying Office, so that the whole piggybacked monstrosity called attention to itself, as much for its freakishness as its supposed historical care and concern. It nevertheless became a sight to see, and numerous visitors' photos show the Surveying Office snugly tucked in under its own freestanding shelter and braced on one side by the moved Corson House, while on the far end a little hole cut through the tin allowed the old brick chimney to poke though. The extra, protective roof was at once an extravagance and a useful and highly visible sign that there was something worth special care, however homemade that care was.

Colbert used a cultivated neglect to his advantage. Whereas the attached and neighboring buildings all bore fresh coats of white paint, he held his brush quite deliberately from the Surveying Office, allowing it to gray, fade, and decay all in plain sight. He allowed the mortar of the brick chimney to wash out, leaving it unrepaired, and allowed much of the stone foundation (ironically, made from stones originally used in the Washington family home) to show through rotting clapboards. All of this was aided by the region's prevailing poverty at the time of the building's construction. The dated building style and materials allowed the office to seem much older than it was. That meant that something as simple as a regime of neglect could leave a dramatic mark. The effect was twofold. The curling, aged wood invoked the past and added an air of hoariness, and the dilapidation itself was a crucial and useful selling point for those concerned about saving old treasures. Just as P. T. Barnum needed to maintain the balance between caring for his human display, Joice Heth (the supposed 161-year-old enslaved African woman who his handbills claimed had once cared for George Washington, perhaps even at Ferry Farm), and maintaining her decrepitude to support the ruse, Colbert needed to keep his building in just the right limbo between treasured and abandoned in order to be convincing.[49]

All that care, neglect, and storytelling was, in total, one large, historically inflected real estate advertisement. By the time of England's visit, Colbert had already planned to sell the farm, and the Surveying Office was to be the main curb appeal. There is no doubt that England knew of what he was becoming a part. Stafford County, Virginia court documents from the 1930s reveal that the two had entered into a deal whereby the writer would use his connections and abilities to help locate backers, who would contribute to purchasing the farm from Colbert. England would get a $5,000 finder's fee for his efforts, as would Fredericksburg merchant and longtime Colbert associate John Jones. In addition to England, a group of supporters based in Washington, DC incorporated with an eye toward paying a very generous $125,000 to Colbert for his land and all the buildings thereon, including the Surveying Office. The deal they crafted allowed Colbert the full rights to the farm and all its production until the full price had been paid. From that time, he had almost a year to vacate.[50]

It was a gem of a deal, one that shows just how canny a businessman and manipulator of historical sentiment was Colbert. He began to receive checks (both valid and postdated) from the George Washington Foundation as early as 1928. The plan would have worked but for two obstacles. One was the Crash of '29 and the hard times that followed. The other was keen awareness on the part of the Wakefield Association, then involved in a similar preservation project at Washington's birthplace in Westmoreland County. Both projects focused on land devoid of much that Washington had touched, and both were competitors for dollars. That conflict reached as far as Fredericksburg, where Wakefield promoters knew a threat when they saw it.[51]

The main voice in this tussle was Wakefield Association historian Charles Arthur Hoppin, who derided Colbert's Ferry Farm project as resting on "Weemsian flotsam and jetsam which no court would admit" and which "real investigators of history have rejected." That kind of evidence would not gain one "ancestral eligibility," and it should not be the basis for creating a historical site.[52] Whereas England embraced Weems and Sawyer winked, Hoppin used Ferry Farm's most famous tree as a cudgel to batter and bruise the very notion of the site's historical merit.

Hoppin was half right. The preservation he attacked was indeed a Weemsian venture. Even though backers had managed to overlay the Cherry Tree, thinly, with the seemingly more believable Surveying Office, Hoppin never made mention of that sleight of hand. His written attacks in newspapers, pamphlets, and private letters, instead, worked to tie Ferry Farm—and, indeed, all of Fredericksburg—as closely to Weems as he could, deriding Colbert and company's claims as little more than "popular belief" or as "so-called tradition" and "cherry tree stories."[53]

But he overreached in his attack. He was on strong ground in seeing Weems behind every tree, but he also tried to deny that Ferry Farm had any claim at all to the historical Washington. He argued that the Washingtons had lived more than a mile downriver from the site. Ferry Farm, he claimed, was a fraud through and through, because Washington had not lived at—or even owned—the place "until late in the life or after the death of his mother."[54] That claim was plainly false. Ample evidence tied Washington to the land, and Fredericksburg as well, from at least 1738 until as late as 1752. Hoppin was even contradicted by George Washington himself, in his *Virginia Gazette* advertisement for the land. Amateur local historian Chester Goolrick and others were quick to make Ferry Farm's historical case in response to Hoppin's "chimerical" relocation of Washington's childhood home.[55]

But Hoppin's mistakes are themselves quite telling. It may be that he was just misreading the records, or it may be that he was playing a rough round of bare-knuckle preservation boxing. In either case, it was as if Hoppin was acting on Cabot Lodge's call to expunge Weems by extracting the historical Washington from the Cherry Tree Farm so long associated with the dreaded mythmaker. In an irony Weems would have loved, Hoppin set in motion a new set of expedient Washington childhood falsehoods, that Washington never lived at Ferry Farm—an assertion as untrue as the old Cherry Tree itself. The claim was certainly meant to disadvantage the rival Ferry Farm in favor of his own Wakefield preservation project. But Hoppin's relocation of Washington's childhood was really very much like the Surveying Office in that it deployed an artful deception to counteract the truth problems posed by Weems's Cherry Tree.[56]

The immediate effect of Hoppin's claim was to cast a shadow over Colbert's project. As the nation lurched toward the 1932 Washington bicentennial, it became clear that only one of the contending sites of Washington's youth would receive official blessing, and in the end it was the irrefutability of birth that beat out the moral, historical, and cultural value of Weems's Washington's boyhood. Wakefield became a national shrine, and Ferry Farm remained private property.

But even as the nation looked elsewhere for its commemorative Washington, the Surveying Office became Ferry Farm's centerpiece. New details and images emerged that seemed to give credibility to the new identity, and new images emerged as well.

A Fredericksburg printer named Robert A. Kishpaugh produced a colorized postcard featuring the Surveying Office as it then stood on Colbert's Washington Farm. On the back of card was a description of the land's Washington history, noting that this was the farm where Augustine Washington died in 1743 and that it sat opposite Fredericksburg—all true. The postcard also repeated the growing story that here was "the only building remaining" dating to those colonial days. But even in repeating the story, Kishpaugh's text effectively winked at its buyers. The building's identification was only that it was "*said* to have been used by Washington"[57] (italics added). The Surveying Office promoters were getting to have their cake and eat it too.

The same sleight of hand occurred a decade later when government architects came to Ferry Farm to record the office as part of the Historical America Building Survey (HABS). If anyone could tell a fraud, it was architects accustomed to the ins and outs of historical structures. The Surveying Office's wire nails, nineteenth-century bricks and sand mortar, and milled lumber were all dead giveaways to the careful observer. And indeed, the building failed to pass the most basic architectural smell tests. The team of three drafters noted problems throughout their records, but at the same time they avoided the obvious conclusion that the building was not what it claimed to be.

For example, the drafters noted that the shingles "were not original" if the structure was meant to date to the eighteenth century, but they were said to "have not been replaced within the past fifty years"; in other words, the shingles dated to right when the building had, in fact, been built. The windows were covered with what they called "new wood sheathing," and the building had a "new door." The final report, submitted by Park Service architect Stuart M. Barnette, steered clear of outright endorsing or denying. Instead, Barnette discussed which parts were old and which were newer.[58]

One page of the report marshaled the supporting evidence for the Surveying Office designation and presented it without real endorsement, however. This consisted of a historical site road marker, Sawyer's earlier writing about the building (almost all of it based on stories he probably learned at the farm), and a local business guide. It also recorded a tale from the same Chester Goolrick who had taken on Hoppin to good effect but also produced local histories that his sometime bosses at the Federal Writers' Project found to be of little use.[59] Goolrick, astoundingly, claimed that his father had been shown the office by his own parents as early as the 1840s or 1850s. The story was at best a deeply confused version of distant events if not an outright fabrication.

Barnette was employed by the Fredericksburg battlefield park and knew the area quite well.[60] He had helped oversee the 1936 excavations at Washington's birthplace down the Northern Neck and had drafted the plans of many local colonial survivals. He was as expert as any of his contemporaries. At the same time, though, he was local and would have had access to all the discussion surrounding the town's many preservation schemes. As Barnette looked over his report, he was less than impressed and noted that "it is upon such hearsay" that the building's entire Washington "tradition was based." In this way, the report was a conflicted document. On one hand, it used careful phrasing to distance the drafters from the object of their study and thus insulated them from the taint of error. On the other hand, the very fact of the HABS study suggested the historicity the wording tried to squirm away from. The HABS report laundered the building's identification, from a local story to a seemingly federally approved designation. No amount of expert distancing could stop that from happening, for those who cared to read the record that way.

The physical documents themselves even bear marks of that conflict: Where the original cover page had "Nineteenth-Century" typed into its title, someone soon after crossed that out in pencil and wrote "Eighteenth-Century" above it. The page serves as a wonderful illustration of how a story can testify against itself even as it makes its best case.

Behind all of James Cook's artful deceptions, there was a knowing agent. We have to assume that P. T. Barnum knew that Joice Heth was not really 161 years old, just as he knew that the half-fish, half-monkey Fiji Mermaid was a stitched-up phony. The reigning consensus has been, for some time, that Weems's Cherry Tree was also a conscious phony—a fiction invented by a creative imagination. It is true that there is more plausibility in a little boy chopping at a tree than there is in the same boy's Mammy having lived 161 years. Nevertheless, there is little reason to doubt the "wise historians," as George Allan England sarcastically called those who had insisted that "Weems made up the whole story out of whole cloth."[61] The survival of Weems's fiction has been due less to its truth or moral lessons than to its simple utility for those who want to believe, as well as those who want to deny. No wonder the best surviving portrait of the Parson shows him grinning like the cat who caught the mouse.

But what about the Surveying Office? There can be no doubt that it was a phony. Cameras first viewed Ferry Farm in the midst of the Civil War, and the resulting glass plates showed clearly that the building was not there to greet the soldiers. And even if it had been there, it would not have survived—no buildings did, as occupations dragged on and the army denuded the landscape of anything that could burn or make a tent drier and more comfortable.

Other photos show it popping up in the 1870s as a central part of the postwar rebuilding. Stuart M. Barnette and the New Deal's other architects were not fooled when they looked it over. They could tell that this was an 1870s building, and they made that clear in their drawings and reports. Recent site archaeology unmasks the Surveying Office even further: The eighteenth-century buildings were near, but not too near. Moreover, stones of the Surveying Office's shallow foundation were originally in the 1740s Washington home. The Surveying Office's footing rested on Washington's story as selectively as the actual building rested on reused parts of the old Washington home. A few people continued to believe the story into the 1990s as its exterior was painstakingly and lovingly "restored," but soon after that project, no one spoke the building's name, absent carefully distancing quotation marks. Today, it is Ferry Farm's respected elder statesman, housing archaeological equipment but no longer invoked as a Washington survival—not even with a Weemsian wink. If the Cherry Tree was Ferry Farm's Washington fraud of the nineteenth century, then its wooden successor, the Surveying Office, was the twentieth century's.

There is strong consensus that Weems invented the Cherry Tree. But who made up the Surveying Office? Was it J. B. Colbert? If it was, then that farmer, icemaker, dry goods merchant, and hotelier must rank with the old Parson as one of the great Washington inventors. Except for Chester Goolrick's obvious fabrication about his grandfather, there was no Surveying Office story before Colbert's day, and even Goolrick's story really dates only to the 1930s. It is unlikely that the Corsons would have made up such a tale for a building they themselves had built, and that *Frank Leslie's* did not recount it is also telling. And even if the Corsons had made it up, the story would have emerged before they sold the land and left the area (a convenient absence that created a fine space for the lie to thrive). George Allan England was a famed storyteller—a man who had, in his day, invented entire fictional worlds for his readers. But his writing about the building suggests that he was repeating what he had learned, as opposed to inventing it himself. His prose has the breathless enthusiasm of the true believer who, having found a genuine fragment of his own special true cross, cannot wait to share it with the world. Joseph Dillaway Sawyer and other chroniclers and reporters had too passing an association to be even worthy of consideration of authorship. No, all roads lead to Colbert.

He never wrote a book or an essay about Washington, but his invention was his text—a document that reveals just how deeply a specific vision of Washington had reached into people's minds. Colbert invented a Washington relic that preserved the best storytelling traditions of the Cherry Tree and the very Freudian idea that we need to know the boy in order to understand the man. He created a setting for a professional, territorial, ambitious Washington—a man Colbert and England, like many of their countrymen, wanted to resemble. And he used that object to line up a deeply remunerative land deal, one that netted him money, even though it ultimately failed to preserve the land. If they had looked down from on high, both Washington and Weems would have approved.

History landed on the Surveying Office as it became a physical stand-in for all that once stood on the land but was by then gone, an imagined enduring link to one of the most significant turns in Washington's young life and a believable object to contrast with the more mythical Cherry Tree. At the same time, though, the two were paired. Not only did they sit close to each other, but also both were objects of skepticism while still having their stories told again and again. Once the idea of historical preservation came to Ferry

Farm, the pairing of tree and office became commonplace. The same 1940s wave of enthusiasts removed the Corson house from where Colbert had placed it and restored the Surveying Office to what they imagined was its original Washington-era form. They also laid a brass plaque right behind the building to commemorate the cherry tree itself. In the 1960s, a home for troubled youth on the site of Washington's celebrated childhood set up shop in Colbert's farm house and planned to build a new facility to produce patriotic, religious, and Washington-inflected young men. Their promotional materials, the educational landscape they planned to create, and even the décor of their building all featured cherries and hatchets, and their in-house newspaper was called *The Surveyor*. They treated the Surveying Office as a sacred relic and conducted one of its many loving restorations. The Boy's Home went so far as to erect a colonial-style pyramidal roof over Colbert's icehouse, next to the Surveying Office, and declare it also a Washington relic.

In 1972, the National Register of Historical Places added Ferry Farm to its list. It cited the Surveying Office as the only significant historical survival.[62] As late as 2000, there was still some possibility that Colbert's icehouse dated to the eighteenth century as well. When Walmart came to town, the office was enlisted to represent the very real, undeniable historicity of the site, and cherry images appeared in the campaigns of both the pro- and anti-development forces. In the 1990s, the office had yet another makeover, and for a while its image adorned the new foundation's stationery along with images of the Cherry Tree. Nearly a century of telling and retelling had certainly crystallized the office into reality.

The deception of the Surveying Office worked because it seemed authorless, whereas the Cherry Tree always would be a creation of Weems. It worked because it linked one of Washington's most significant (both personally and nationally) incarnations, that of the surveyor, to a physical object right at a time when Americans were considering the limits of the frontier itself. It worked because locals wanted it to for a host of reasons ranging from local pride to increased business opportunities. But something in what Weems brought to Ferry Farm allowed for further invention. The Surveying Office, authorless as it may have seemed, was a product of multiple hands; Weems, Colbert, and Washington and his biographers were all co-authors.

6

TO CHANGE THE WORLD

Young George and Ferry Farm in the Era of Human-Induced Climate Change

I looked up from my dinner plate and saw the tree in a neighbor's yard growing a foot higher before my eyes. I'll probably never write the story that came to mind then, of how the man inside became suddenly obsessed with ridding the world of the ailanthus tree.

Alvin Aubert

Thou hast had pity on the gourd, for which thou hast not labored, neither madest it grow.

Jonah 3:10

In the summer of 2004, a team of archaeologists took a break from their usual labors to turn their hands to a new task. The team piled into the back of a pickup truck like a gang of farm laborers and bounced their way over to a far, rarely visited edge of the Ferry Farm property.

The area was the vast sunken field at the land's far southern end. In the shadow of the tall Route 3 flyover and the four-lane-wide Rappahannock Bridge sat a patch of roughly ten acres with a surface noticeably lower than the rest of the land's topsoil. This was no geological anomaly—far from it. Rather, this was land that federally employed bulldozers had graded down by as much as ten feet in order to collect its gravel and dirt to become part of Interstate 95 in the late 1960s. Stripped of its fertile topsoil and whatever archaeological evidence it had of Ferry Farm's past, and reduced to a field of substrata clay and stone, what remained was a barren ruin. Locals came to call it "the quarry."

Since then, the land has lain exposed to weather and other perils. Unable to grow grasses or be farmed, it became instead a rocky expanse, a repository for garbage and unwanted clean fill. It was an eyesore and wasteland—small wonder Walmart saw it as being an uncontroversial place to build a shopping center.

Denied its ability to be a Virginia field like any other, these acres instead became a haven for nonlocal plants, better adapted than local ones to living in a type of soil that Virginia species knew not. From gypsy moths to kudzu to snakehead fish, the ravages of recently arrived flora and fauna are well known. They are collectively termed "invasive species," and concern over their presence comes in language that ranges from the admirably ecological to the vaguely xenophobic. But in all cases, there is a certainty that there had been an order to the imagined natural world and that processes of colonization, commercial agriculture, and globalization disrupted that preexisting order.

The excavators who piled out of the truck bed in the midday heat were there to strike a blow for nativism over invasion. Their particular quarry on that day was *Ailanthus altissima*—the so-called Tree of Heaven, a quick-growing, stink-emitting tree of Chinese origin with sun-blocking, fernlike leaves. The ailanthus has the dastardly ability to rebound quickly from a cutter's wound, and it can grow at a shocking pace. But if pulled while still a sprout, the whole shallow root system can be taken from the ground without risk of return. In a matter of weeks, an ailanthus can grow as high as an adult human. Its broad spans of finger-like fern clusters rapidly block out the sun for any grasses or tiny trees unfortunate enough to be making a go at growing near the rapidly expanding colonies of these immigrants. Ailanthus will quickly take over an area and denude it of anything but itself.

That is exactly what was happening at the edge of the quarry field. Green sentinels were marking out a new territory and had to be beaten back. The archaeologists became, for the moment, the frontline troops in the home defense movement as they fanned out over the area and uprooted every ailanthus on which they could lay hands. They also became distant echoes of the little boy whose hatchet had killed the most famous Ferry Farm tree of all. Trees, invasive or otherwise, had long been part of the land's story. When John Smith and his men first visited this part of the world, a local native prisoner used the fact that the old trees still stood on the Rappahannock's banks as a way to say that the area was unsettled. As Weems's Cherry Tree took root in the American imagination, Ferry Farm owners were busily clearing the land of its actual trees. Civil War soldiers managed to find a few cherry trees still on the land and sent their fruit home as Washington-inflected souvenirs. Soon after that, though, the same soldiers sawed or chopped every tree to mere stumps. The series of hillside wartime photographs that document aspects of Ferry Farm's changing profile during the conflict show the trees going from bare autumnal health to clipped and split stumps near the ground.

The era of commemoration that began when the Corson family came down from Pennsylvania and rebuilt the war-scarred farm saw a new flowering of trees. Photos of the Corson home, and the one that J. B. Colbert later built on the same site, show tall hardwood shade trees surrounding the building and encroaching on the Surveying Office. Tourist photographs captured not only the site's new and old buildings but also featured visitors posing under large and small trees. More than a few carried handwritten notations indicating that this or that growth was understood to have been the cherry tree or possibly its descendant. By the 1940s, a bronze plaque on a stone plinth marked the spot (not too far from the Surveying Office) where the famed tree must have stood. The funds for the marker came from a group of local supporters eager to see the place receive the recognition it deserved.

More and more it was newly planted cherry trees that allowed the farm to live up to its sometime moniker, the Cherry Tree Farm. Visitors and commemorators of all stripes saw putting a tree in the ground as the most fitting way to mark the land as special and to connect in some personal way with its legacy of Washington lore. Even though the story these plantings recalled in fact dealt with the death of a tree, the drive to cover the land with new shoots was a creative arboreal endorsement and reappropriation of the story. By the 1960s, new sets of cherry trees dotted the roads in and out of the acres, the planting of those trees having becomes something of a commemorative ritual for enthusiasts and would-be preservationists. The last of those trees survived into the early 2000s, when some of the same ailanthus-killing excavators reenacted Weems's story for themselves in order to clear the area for excavation.

Ferry Farm's trees have been local and they have been imports, but they have all been part of its story. But they have only been the most visible part of a larger set of planetary changes that have been far in the background for most of the time Ferry Farm has had English-speaking residents. The intercontinental movement of trees into new areas is as old as continental drift itself but was also one part of a larger transference of plants and animals that Alfred Crosby famously labeled ecological imperialism. Following his lead and that of others, scholars have been tracing the spread of species, their many and varied impacts, change in the land itself, the differing constructions of nature, and much more.[1] This work has gone a long way toward erasing a line between the human and the natural. Ferry Farm, its trees—be they original, imported, or allegorical—its animal residents, and even its architecture have a small role to play in that mission.

It has long been a staple of Western thought that there was a meaningful and necessary distinction between so-called humanistic intellectual endeavors, such as history and the natural sciences.[2] One much-cited historian's marking of the line comes from

R. G. Collingwood, who imagined the "ordinary historian" who would hold that "all history properly so called is the story of human affairs."[3] For Collingwood, the reasons for Caesar's crossing the Rubicon were historical concerns, whereas the dynamics of the river's flow, or worse, its long processes of formation, were not historical concerns.

Dipesh Chakrabarty outlined this separation beginning with what he called the old "Viconian–Hobbsean" idea that human activity—the arena humans control, make, and occupy—is the only field of knowledge humans could truly grasp and discuss.[4] The idea became fundamental to the division of knowledges and their study in modernity. Sciences became "natural" or social. Universities and museums performed the same dividing act, with nature displayed in one hall and art in another; biology taught by one department, history by another. Scholars carved fields of inquiry into discrete disciplines while thinkers sought out the exact locations of these dividing lines they now saw as essential. The line between the human and the animal was one; the line between culture and nature was another. The distinction has been a powerful one, extending into all spheres of knowledge—even Washingtoniana. Returning for a moment to the Washington biography, the way that biographers have struggled over the question of the childhood years and asked whether Washington was a product of nature (the natural) or nurture (the human) serves as one simple example of thought lines that run from Vico to Freeman and Chernow.

The separation of the natural and the human has been the target of many challenges along the way in a wide range of fields, from philosophy to environmental history. One concern, though, has problematized the longstanding separation and given efforts to undo it an unprecedented sense of urgency. In the 1980s, biologist and ecologist Eugene Stoermer coined a term for an epoch of Earth's geological history during which humankind itself has become essentially a geological force. By the dawn of the new century, he and colleague Paul Crutzen were ready to claim that "the impacts of current human activities will continue over long periods," meaning that we are now living in that era.[5] This epoch, the Anthropocene Age, is that time in which human activity has had an effect on the climatic and environmental conditions of the planet. Volcanic activity, meteor–Earth collisions, or tectonic shifts have all played their role in shaping the conditions sustaining life. In the Anthropocene, human activities have had the same scale of effect: Humankind has moved from being one of many forms of life on the planet to being one whose actions and consequences have reconditioned the prospect of all life itself. Human activity has remade the very conditions of life on Earth and perhaps in that way—reversing Collingwood—everything is now historical.

Historians like dates, but actually putting a date on the beginning of this epoch is somewhat tricky and perhaps even something of a cruise on a ship in a bottle. The extinction of big game animals and the rise of agriculture may be one place to begin the discussion; the Columbian encounter itself is also a good starting point. However, Stoermer and Crutzen prefer to focus on the advent of technologies with lingering effects. For them, it is the steam engine that marks the uptick in human impact—the moment when production increased, tied to the consumption of fossil fuels, and set a pattern of consumption–growth–pollution that defined everything since.[6] Paul Dukes has undertaken the most ambitious attempt to perform Anthropocene history—to tell the story of the era in conjunction with so-called natural history.[7] Dukes sees the simultaneous rise of Britain as the main expansive European power and a principal manufactory, exporting the products and systems of its consumptive industrializing economy, as being the beginning of the ball; thus, Dukes begins his study with the year 1763.[8] Chakrabarty pushes the date back a bit earlier to 1750, but, following the same reasoning as this, begins with the "time when human beings switched from wood and other renewable fuels to large-scale use of fossil fuel."[9] If the question is to identify the beginning, these are logical starting points. If the question is one of reaching the point of maximum impact, better choices may be the advent of fossil fuels or perhaps the global reordering after World War I. If the question is "When did human effects become irreversible?" that is still a huge rub.

For these and other perhaps more manufactured reasons, the notion that we all now live in the Anthropocene Age is an idea still coming into its own. The academic panels empowered to mark the lines between epochs have yet to give the term their fullest backing but have been warming to the idea. In 2008, the Geological Society of America, for example, accepted the Anthropocene as a reality, noting that there is "sufficient evidence" to acknowledge that the Holocene (the previous epoch of relative warmth after the Paleolithic) has passed, and we are now citizens of new era.[10] By 2012, the idea had won enough credibility and adherents that many national geological societies had adopted it and made it part of the standard time scale.[11] Yet despite this grim recognition by the educated experts most adept at and devoted to the study of the planet and its climate, in the United States the general population is still uncertain about the conclusion. Thus, the public discussion is one of "climate change" or, worse yet, the misleading phrase "global warming"—asking questions such as, "Is it happening? At what pace? What caused it?" and, most importantly, "What can we do to stop it?" In Western Europe, governments, nongovernment organizations, scholars, and private people have moved much further along toward accepting the new reality and even acting on the assumptions of the Anthropocene.

One small but influential example comes from the British essay *Uncivilization: The Dark Mountain Manifesto*. In a pamphlet self-consciously styled after Marx's work in tone and structure, a group of artists, poets, and writers accepted their fate. "There is a fall coming," *Dark Mountain* warns us, and they do not mean an autumn of orange leaves. We face a time of great change and uncertainty as the systems and comforts of modernity collapse because of the climate change humans themselves have wrought. One can hear a tone of Marx-influenced glee in the manifesto as the authors herald modernity's collapse: "Financial wizards lose their power of levitation," and "politics as we have known it totters." In its place, they warn, "could easily arise something more elemental, with a dark heart."[12] Gripping stuff, indeed, so one can be forgiven for feeling a bit let down at *Dark Mountain*'s answer to these all-encompassing changes: better storytelling and more meaningful poetry.[13]

But *Dark Mountain* highlights something very important in the different approaches to what many are coming to realize is the gravest challenge our species has ever faced, made worse (or perhaps just more humiliating) by the fact that we brought it on ourselves. Whereas Americans are debating the reality of the situation and looking for a technological answer, others are already stocking the bomb shelters, adjusting their expectations, and relearning which mushrooms are edible.

The concept of the Anthropocene is rooted in time. Thus, whereas climate change as a phenomenon may or may not interest historians as individuals, the idea of an actual epoch—a unit of time—speaks more naturally to core historical concerns. So, here and there a few scholars have begun to explore what an Anthropocene history might look like. In his influential essay "The Climate of History: Four Theses," Chakrabarty states that although environmental history as exemplified by Alfred Crosby's Columbian Exchange opens the door to a truly new approach, it falls just short of going through the resulting opening by leaving humans essentially prisoners of the climate (a phrase in which Crosby quotes Ferdinand Braudel).

The goal, instead, is to move beyond the defined timelines and concerns and to create a history that embraces a future as well as a past—one that in some way reimplicates the human in the nonhuman and vice versa, and one that imagines a planet without humans and tries to talk about pasts in terms that did not automatically enshrine the human. In his address to the 2013 Anthropocene Project, Chakrabarty commented that this had to entail a critique of capitalism and anthropocentrism as its driving ideological force. Science, he suggested, also needs to play a key role in this new history. For example, a history of reproduction might include all manner of statistics of birth rates, and infant or maternal mortality, but would by habit exclude the evolution of the female human pelvis from its scope of inquiry.[14] This division between an assumed human scale of historical inquiry and natural history is just the one that needs to be erased.

Paul Dukes has gone further than anyone so far in trying to chart a path through the history of this unofficial epoch. As one might expect, this effort hangs to traditional markers. The rise of industrialism, Bonapartism, liberalism, Marxism, and allied movements and opponents all did their bit to spread the logic and practices of the system that fueled anthropocentric change. The result is the mess we face. That Dukes's work reads much like his other large-frame histories of the West, and of capitalism itself—or what some are coming to call "Big History"—is not so much a criticism as an echo of the fact that the Anthropocene and capitalism entwine.[15]

Mark Levene has taken this Anthropocene idea for historians and matched it with the level of passion and urgency seen in *Dark Mountain*'s manifesto. For Levene, recognition of the change or even peril that we face calls for a new ethical history, or perhaps a new ethic in the writing of history. Having lost, after 2007, any real hope that the world's leaders would take steps to address the changes we face, Levene instead embraces the *Dark Mountain* view: Troubled times are a-comin', and it is the responsibility of humanistic scholars to help pave the way to survival (cultural as much as physical) through lessons, "recovery of wisdoms," and production of art that will facilitate in some way "a reawakened sense of humanity's interconnectedness with the living planet."[16] More importantly, though, historians might be able to serve as "pathfinders and beacon carriers" in a process in which humanity creates a new "alternative, right-living space" and invests this time and space with meaning.[17]

It takes no great effort to spot the range of longstanding ideas, trends, and loyalties that are lining up behind the idea of the Anthropocene and are useful to historians—or the idea of historians as being useful to humanity by confronting the reality of the Anthropocene. Dukes's invocation of the *Bulletin of the Atomic Sciences* Doomsday Clock (recently reset to include climate-related dangers) invokes Cold War apocalyptic imagery.[18] *Dark Mountain*'s "Manifesto" self-consciously echoes Marx, and Penelope Corfield's clever essay title "Climate Reds" hints at the background of many of those now rallying to this new cause, as she calls for a more optimistic outlook to climate change reality.[19] But suggesting, as many do in the political arena, that this emerging concern is just so much older red wine in new green bottles is a foolish, dismissive read—perhaps even a species of physiological denial, as George Marshall has argued.[20]

The earth *is* really changing; the data speak with an authority that no sane person can deny and no intelligent person dare ignore.[21] It should come as no surprise that scholars and critics who have already been training their lenses on the capitalist world system are among the first nonscientists to call out in alarm at the new reality. Revolution may or may not yet come and settle a host of social problems. But while we wait, the grim and increasingly irreversible pace of climate change, on a planet that cares not whether we humans continue as a species, marches on.

If we accept the Anthropocene premise—and particularly the way that scholars have dated it—then immediately something interesting happens to the way we periodize Washington's life, his childhood, and the story of places such as Ferry Farm. Washington's life sat astride a few well-known historical epoch shifts. Politics sets one divide. Born within the British Empire, Washington died in the new independent nation he helped found. Material culture sets others. For example, Washington's father and fashionable gentrymen all over the British world ate their fine meals using two-pronged forks to spear their meat from common trenchers and bring the morsels mouthward. But in his adulthood, Washington was a master of the delicate manners of the late eighteenth century, table regimes that replaced antique two-pronged stabbers with the type of flatware we use today. Imperial fortunes set yet another divide. Washington was born into a British colonial world that always had to consider the possibility of conflict with a huge French empire at its western edge, but he lived to see that fear removed and the West become a seemingly endless source of new wealth.

Add to these familiar Washington biographical divides a new one based on climate change. Washington was born in the Holocene era but lived long enough to see the dawn of the Anthropocene. If we peg the Anthropocene to the dawn of Britain becoming the preeminent European colonial power, then Washington was a soldier in the service of the Anthropocene. Scholars of the Seven Years' War have been quick to lay its outbreak squarely on the shoulders of a "callow officer's" poor judgment and bad decisions.[22] That officer was Washington, experienced in woodscraft and leading men on the green, perhaps, but far less able when it came to the arts of four-way diplomacy between the French, the English, provincial troops, and both sides' Indian allies. The result was his mishandling of his 1754 foray to the Ohio Country and the death of French ensign Joseph Coulon de Villiers sieur de Jumonville, and many other wounded soldiers, right before Washington's eyes. Because victory in that war assured Britain—and its colonies, independent or otherwise—some measure of dominance, the man who brought it on certainly served his king well. But if that imperial moment of glory also set in motion a slow calamity that threatens to upend all we know and has left very sober minds to suggest considering a planetary future without humankind, then Washington's role in the spread of that empire takes on a more ominous tone. We are used to thinking of Washington memory as being something tied to matters of state, patriotism, national identity and politics. Are any of us ready for a time when we recall Washington for the role he played in melting the glaciers and changing the length of growing seasons? Perhaps some future generation might see him this way, but certainly not yet. If we tie the Anthropocene to the rise of fossil fuels, then Washington becomes more innocent—he certainly was there at the beginning but more along for the ride than in the driver's seat.

Augustine Washington's move to Ferry Farm was at least connected to environmental degradation, if not the conditions of the Anthropocene outright. In addition to owning the lands he eventually left to his sons, Augustine sank a large amount of time, money, and effort into establishing a set of iron mines at Accokeek, a few miles from Fredericksburg and Ferry Farm. Scholars have long argued that he moved his family to Ferry Farm so that he would have a good perch from which to keep an eye on the mine operations. That he thought them a high priority is not in doubt—he made at least two trips to England to work out the vagaries of the business, and he was very active in his partnership with Maryland's Principio mine company.[23] It may also be that part of what made Mary an attractive spouse was the fact that she already had acres near the mine site. Were that true, then in some small way Washington's very existence would have been caused by the kinds of activities that would bring on climate change.

The iron furnaces at Accokeek were a full-blown industrial mining endeavor, one of many that the early eighteenth century saw on the Rappahannock and farther west. When William Byrd II visited one site, he fairly marveled at the "rough stone" furnaces, the hundreds of feet of wooden pipe for funneling in water, the mountains of charcoal, and the "two mighty pairs of bellows" that drove the fires. Byrd also described the level of devastation the mines caused to nearby areas. He estimated that a "moderate furnace" could consume "2 Miles Square of Wood" and that the food alone for the work force would consist of no less than "1600 Barrels of Corn Yearly." Upon approaching one furnace operation he encountered "a large space of clear'd Ground, whose wood had been cut down for coaling." He claimed that a very intense heat had to be maintained to melt the ore and that near one furnace was "a House full of Charcoal holding at least 400 loads, which will be burned out in 3 months." Byrd also described the massive quantities of "West India" limestone and oyster shell used in the process and the extensive slave and animal labor going into this endeavor.[24] Every indication is that the Washington enterprise was equally extensive and was worked by dozens of enslaved Africans. Those sorts of projects were destructive, consuming massive amounts of human and material resources and dramatically changing the landscapes. The scars of that enterprise are still visible in the land, even though Accokeek did not work out quite as Augustine and his Principio Company partners may have hoped. Nevertheless, projects like it were at once Holocene age colonial resource extraction projects like many others and building blocks in the changes that led to the Anthropocene.[25]

Washington was aware of the advent of steam power, a development more directly tied to anthropocentric climate change. In 1785, Washington wrote to early steam pioneer James Rumsey and offered his "best wishes for the success" in the latter's building a boat that would move by using jets of water for propulsion.[26] In 1788, Rumsey sent Washington copies of the plans for another boat design, hoping to win presidential favor.[27] No favor came, but the blueprints remained on Mount Vernon's bookshelves. Washington also had a short correspondence with steamboat pioneer Robert Fulton, although that dealt mostly with canals, a topic close to both of their hearts. But even if Washington were out there with the workmen hammering rivets on the steam boiler, steam at that point relied on renewable wood supplies. Washington died well before nonrenewables became the prime—and epoch-changing— preferred fuel.

Washington's implication in the advent of the Anthropocene is an interesting curiosity, but it does very little to change our understanding of the man. An epochal understanding of history, though, suggests that we would want to reconsider these small junctures and divides. Indeed, if future generations choose to add this dimension to Washington memory, that will be for them to decide. I don't think those of us still living in the republic he helped found are ready to take up a framing for Washington memory that does not retain the connection so clearly stated by Jared Sparks and still very much alive. Listening to the gloomiest prognostications, it may well be that the question of climate will in time be the only historical one that matters, and thus future Washington memory may focus on things we currently care less about or see as little more than coincidence.

There is far more to discuss when it comes to landscapes such as Ferry Farm as being places straddling the line between the Holocene and Anthropocene. These landscapes are the repositories of the "big story": They have seen it all and have been made and remade with each change. Viewed through the lens of epochal history, the home that William Strother built on the land sometime in the 1720s, which Augustine Washington purchased in 1738, becomes not just another colonial Virginia building, nor is it even still another example of the early eighteenth-century house builder's craft. Instead, it becomes a piece of Holocene architecture that survived into the earliest days of the Anthropocene—a holdover from a previous epoch that lived right at the juncture of the next.

Moreover, as the building became an object of memory and commemoration, what was recalled was increasingly more than mere nostalgia. Each year, the old Washington farm became less a memory of a way of life, lost graces, or a charming past place and more of a shadow of a way of existing on the planet that was not so much tragically and lamentably disappearing (for that is the essence of nostalgia) but rather was becoming no longer possible at all for nonhuman reasons that humans helped set in motion.

Urban planners and public historians have long understood how retaining elements of a community's historical architecture, use of space, and logic can bind people to the place, restore faith in cities and towns, boost property values, and aid businesses, schools, and other institutions.[28] Recently, new concern about the renewability of building materials and the awareness that it is often cheaper and "greener" to reuse older housing stock than to build anew has enabled a convergence of discussions of sustainability and historical preservation. The Anthropocene adds a new concern to this growing list of reasons to look to older ways of doing things. As Mark Levene puts it, historians may have new value to society—to humankind, in fact—by helping to facilitate a "recovery of wisdoms, both practical and spiritual."[29] This is no mere romanticizing of the past or delighting in alternative ways of being—it is not a case of what Philip Deloria called "playing Indian," or a similar romanticization of the past or seemingly "primitive" time.[30] Instead, it is a call to reimagine the very purposes of historical (and indeed all) inquiry in the face of a species-wide shared challenge. Can we craft new lenses through which to view the past? Can we view the past not as a simple repository of better ways to do things but instead as the collected fragments of human capacity from which we can find tidbits to carry into our futures? Can we imagine new futures from these inquiries? What can an epoch-straddling place such as Ferry Farm offer to such projects? Is there a distinctive Anthropocene narrative for Ferry Farm?

Trees have played such a huge role in defining Ferry Farm as a storied place that it makes sense to build a new epochal narrative in their collective branches. Ever since the English first arrived in this corner of Virginia, they had been importing species and modifying local ones.[31] It was a cornerstone of Weems's most famous tale that the tree little George chopped at was in fact an "English" cherry tree—an obvious allusion to the Revolution, with the cherries themselves as perhaps tiny redcoats or even an anticipation of Stephen Crane's veteran Yankee's "little red badges." But imported cherry trees were only one of many alien plants English settlers planted in American soil. Grains, flowers, and vegetables of all sorts, and fruit trees (like Washington's Mount Vernon orange trees) were only the most visible on a list that included many inadvertent grasses and weeds as well. The manifold plants and animals that made the cross-Atlantic trip during the rise of the first British Empire were part of a Holocene migration. Disruptive—devastating even—as some of those species were for local varieties, they were nevertheless part of a larger global geological system that was fundamentally sustainable, or at least threatened established plant and animal orders only at a local level. Ferry Farm would have looked, smelled, and functioned differently than it might have a hundred years before the arrival of Englishmen and their nonhuman fellows, but those were just the latest manifestations of age-old changes.

The ailanthus, though, was something different. The trees the excavators pulled out of the ground, that summer in 2004, were the latest growths of the first major human-induced but nevertheless nonhuman changes Ferry Farm saw in the era of the Anthropocene. By the time the Washingtons lived at Ferry Farm, the tree had made its way from China to Europe, carefully shepherded by botanists, beginning in 1740 with a French Jesuit named Pierre D'Incarville, who sent home some seeds while on a trans-Asia jaunt.[32] Like many other species in the eighteenth century, *Ailanthus* was part of a grand movement of plants and animals (and people) as colonial people and enlightened people sought to reorder the world and make it better fit their particular needs. The need that inspired the cultivation of ailanthuses was sap for varnish, and in that case, D'Incarville picked the wrong tree. The problem was that the lovely but useless ailanthus was almost indistinguishable from its far more valuable doppelgänger, the aptly named varnish tree. As an old Chinese rhyme held, "Ailanthus planted or wild; And Lacquer Tree look alike."[33] Whether D'Incarville picked the wrong seeds himself or someone else made the error for him is unclear, but by the mid-1740s the trees were shading fashionable Parisian gardens.

In 1751, British botanist Peter Collinson and others began to plant their own ailanthuses and even gave the species their own Latin designation with the curiously foreboding name *Toxicodendron altisima*.[34] It seems that although stewards were learning that no varnish could be boiled from the tree's sap, it could nevertheless raise quite a rash. When the tree first reached Virginia is unknown, but by 1888 observers reported that it "ran wild" in the Old Dominion and in neighboring states and that it was a common sight in "old fields."[35] That phrase, "old fields," is an interesting one in the context of the war-devastated Fredericksburg area of the 1880s. Did the garden magazine letter writer who contributed the observation mean it in some sort of prosaic way, or was it a more substantive observation about the interaction between *Ailanthus*'s habits and the particular quality of the Virginia landscape?

Whichever it was, the first time we can place an ailanthus on Ferry Farm is sometime around the turn of the twentieth century, when, in an old photograph, what appears to be one is growing tall behind the 1870s Corson House. A circa-1917 photograph of the Surveying Office shows a fully grown ailanthus sitting right next to the chimney of the mid-nineteenth-century building. The scars on the lower part of the trunk show that the tree had been pruned back to keep it from harming the frame building, which was being reimagined as historical. Even so, subsequent photographs show that the tree grew to such a point that its root system was working its way under the stone and brick footer of the chimney. The tree grew right as the Corson's 1870s farm office was being reinvented as a Washington historical relic; maintaining the tree was part of that process of invention. J. B. Colbert, the farmer and the man most likely to have invented the Surveying Office story, pulled several coy tricks to create the illusion of historicity, such as not painting the clapboards and erecting a second roof over the building.[36] But the attributes of the ailanthus also worked in his favor.

As an unusually fast-growing tree, the ailanthus spread its branches at a much faster rate than local species. The effect of there being a large and seemingly venerable tree right beside the building gave the whole scene a romantic air of the past. Cutting the branches back also created the illusion that the Surveying Office was special enough to need preservation—a centerpiece of Colbert's plan to sell the land and turn the place into a Washington shrine.

By the 1950s, the tree had grown to such a point that it was positively dwarfing the building and even threatening its stone foundations. Then, by the mid-1960s, when the George Washington

Boys' Home ran the land, the tree was cut down to only a stump, and the Surveying Office was given new clapboards and paint. The shift in logics of commemoration—a change from Colbert's cultivated neglect to the Boy's Home leaders' careful "restoration"— changed the role of that particular ailanthus: Strategic pruning yielded to outright removal. For almost seventy years, the life of that one invasive tree was paired with a central part of Ferry Farm's unique invention of Washington memory. It was photographed every time a visitor snapped a shot of something associated with the land's most famous occupant. It was pruned when it seemed to threaten the building it shaded, and it was finally felled in to create a more historically sound view. For seventy years, the ailanthus lived through two overlapping changes, one being the development of Ferry Farm's Washington memory, and the other being the hardening of the use of fossil fuels that accelerated the conditions of the Anthropocene.

These two changes converged at Ferry Farm primarily by way of the automobile. By the 1920s, a new manner of visitor began to show up at the old place: the car tourist. Ferry Farm was never a major destination, to be sure, but being so close to Fredericksburg made it easy for visiting motorists to cross over the river via the bridge at the end of William Street and drive south to see the farm. The increase in snapshots of the farmstead, its buildings, and various cherry trees all point to an increased number of nonlocals seeing the sights. When J. Harry Shannon, the so-called Virginia Rambler, paid a visit sometime in the early 1920s, we know he came by car because the caption for his glass plate image of the Surveying Office and then owner J. B. Colbert noted the presence of his "driver." Likewise, visitors such as writer George Allan England and historian Joseph Dillaway Sawyer seem to have driven to the site when they came to sing its praises.[37] Those were the only ones whose visits left documentation, but by the early 1930s, Colbert was hosting visitors on the farm and even letting them sleep in the old Corson House, moved over next to the Surveying Office. Few wrote about their visits, but cars were more and more part of the story.

In the lead-up to the Washington birth bicentennial of 1932, federal planners and commemorators saw the automobile as integral to how Washington was to be remembered. Their vision included a specially constructed parkway that would tie together the three main sites of Washington's life in Virginia. Motorists could cruise from Mount Vernon down to Ferry Farm, and then on down the Northern Neck to the Pope's Creek birthplace in Westmoreland County. The project had significant local support and some enthusiasm from within the apparatus organizing the federal celebration. But as its chairman, congressman Sol Bloom, would later admit, despite all the hubbub, the strings on the nation's purse were tied tight and there was little room for a "mad squandering of the public funds" on any and all projects.[38] State monies were able to transform the old dusty run known as King's Highway back in Washington's day into State Route 3, but a single linked Washington Parkway was not to be. Yet the idea that historical memory and cars worked together became concrete in other parts of the state a decade later when federal projects put Depression-era unemployed to work creating scenic commemorative roads that fused the founders and the consumption of fossil fuels.

That road-building impulse reached its apex in President Eisenhower's 1956 legislation that began the creation of the interstate highway system. If there was a single decision that set the course for the United States' reliance on oil and hardened the course of anthropocentric climate change, it was that. The increasing prominence of the car in American life may have been part of the highway system's logic, but the increasing ability to get into one's own lead-burning Chevrolet and see the USA ensured that other, less consumptive forms of transportation would soon be eclipsed.

Cars became more than transportation—they became crucial to how life was lived and to how cities and hinterlands took shape. Cars became the very embodiment of American-style freedom.

That species of freedom came to Fredericksburg in 1967. Before that, the population of the Fredericksburg area still showed the signs of damage done during the Civil War. Emptied out, underdeveloped, and impoverished, Stafford and Spotsylvania counties were among the state's poorest—a type of Appalachia but without the mountain views and strong regional identity. Fredericksburg recovered soon enough after the war, but most of the people rebuilding were new arrivals from the surrounding countryside—such as Colbert, who came in from nearby Massaponax—or from farther afield, such as the Corsons, who came down from Pennsylvania. But even as Fredericksburg hummed back to life, the region at large remained all but forgotten.

All that changed when the Federal Highway Commission charted the path for the new four-lane ribbon that would connect Washington, DC to Richmond and points south. I-95, as it came to be called, would snake its way southward in a path through Stafford and Spotsylvania counties until it crossed Route 3 about two miles west of town. Once all linked up, that road would carry motorists all the way from New England to Florida, providing a faster alternative to the old Route 1 pathway. By the end of the 1960s, Fredericksburg's most defining attribute may well have been the exit sign carrying its celebrated name. Within a decade of its completion of the road, the region had come back to its pre–Civil War population, and that number has gotten larger and larger with each passing year. More homes, more cars, more roads, more homes, more cars.

In 1967, the group of pastors who then ran Ferry Farm as a Seventh-Day Adventist home for wayward youths were having a hard time making their monthly bills. Their project called for the erection of a large colonial-style group home to house needy boys from all over the country. The plan was pure Weems mixed with Cold War patriotism. Living on the land of Washington's childhood, amid its tales of dollar tosses and cherry trees, would help create in the boys the best values and the strength to serve the Lord and fight communism.[39] But the funds were a challenge.

The interstate itself provided the answer. As highway builders were grading their way through the counties, they desperately needed gravel for roadbeds and extra dirt and stone for embankments and overpasses. Road crews were able to offer local landowners a fair one-time deal: a handsome payment in exchange for grading a field down to the deepest subsoil. The land itself would be permanently ruined for farming, but the payment was something of a salve.[40]

That was exactly the sort of deal the pastors needed to make their dream a reality. Having divided the just over one hundred acres they owned of the original Washington six hundred into three zones (historical, farming, and pasture), they sold off the rights to the southernmost pasture parcel to the highway commission, following the logic that it was the area farthest removed from the historic core. Those were lands that were not part of Augustine Washington's original purchase but rather parcels that George later added to the core when it was Mary's home. We will never know what archaeological materials may be have been there before the graders came in and stripped it all to about ten feet down, but by the time they were done, about twenty-five acres of Ferry Farm was now a huge, clay-bottomed, infertile "quarry." What had once been topsoil and upper layers was now folded into I-95, a few miles to the west.

The quarry remained a nearly barren ruin for decades. It collected trash, a new bridge over the Rappahannock soon abutted it, the pile of brush in its center became so compacted that it began to give off smoke, scrub grasses and weeds filled in where they could, and ailanthus trees clung to its edges. When Walmart planners came to Ferry Farm with the intention of remaking the place into a shopping plaza, their vision was to place the anchor right in the midst of that wasteland, a plan that was designed to make use of the roads and to leave as much of what the pastors had called the Historical Area as intact as possible. When that plan failed, though, and all of what was left of Ferry Farm became historical and not commercial, the new vision called for the quarry to become a meadow—ideally, a haven for local species of plants and animals. That required planting of indigenous species and careful mowing to build up fertility. It also called for excavators to take a few days off from digging to pull up invasive species. In time, the grasses came back, and with them the turkeys did as well. Soon after the turkeys became a daily sight, the foxes came back, and the turkeys became rather more guarded. Then the deer came back and trampled paths through the grasses, which became ideal turkey runs.

What happened in the quarry/meadow was not a story of a rebounding landscape. In fact, there are no parts of Ferry Farm that were not powerfully shaped by life in the first two hundred years of the Anthropocene. The riverfront was widened and remade by the Army Corps of Engineers when they dredged it in the late nineteenth century. At the same time, that human-made flood-plain, with its upside-down river bottom, also saw an increase in its animal population as the land became historical. But that cannot be called recovery; the land that would have been "recovering" here was nothing more than displaced river bottom. Likewise, the quarry/meadow was not a return. It was a reinvention, something wholly new, made by many forces and impulses, among them the seemingly contrary (but in fact complementary) forces of historical memory and fossil fuel consumption, as well as a nonhuman assertion of right to the land remolded by humans. As our new epoch unfolds, the processes that took place in Ferry Farm's quarry/ meadow are exactly the ones we will see on a much larger scale: new forests springing up in the gaps of old Detroit or New Orleans streets; shifting beach fronts on Long Island, New Jersey, and the Outer Banks of North Carolina; specially built reefs in Florida and elsewhere—all planned and spontaneous compromises between the logic and drive of modernity and the realities of the changes it has brought down.

There may be lessons for more sustainable living at Ferry Farm. Excavations of the Holocene show strategies people then used to survive. It is an open question whether the conditions of the Anthropocene are such that what worked in one era will still work in another. Nevertheless, the use of local wood, locally fired bricks, and locally cut and fitted stone in building are all obvious models. The long-term plan for Ferry Farm is to see a new version of the old Washington home set on the land. This would be a familiar act of historical commemoration. Regional historical sites, large and small, boast these sorts of reconstructions, or new constructions in a historical vein—many dating from the years around the Washington bicentennial. In the 1930s, the colonial revival represented a confluence of historical memory and contemporary styling. Revivalist decorators and builders sought to emulate an imagined feel of the colonial past, albeit one filtered through a thick, lingering Victorian lens.[41] The result was a middle-class housing taste that aped Georgian symmetry in window layout and room shape but filled those rooms with themed knicknackery and larded the windows with acres of drapes. Colonial revival connected historical memory and then-current living spaces through the magic of consumerism; it was therefore a project for only those who could afford to buy in.

But rebuilding at Ferry Farm could be something very different. New construction has been a regional theme ever since the highway came through. From the GI bill, to rampant suburbanization in the 1980s, to the present fueled by artificially cheapened gasoline, the landscape has sprouted new homes the way it once grew tobacco and corn. Most of these new homes have been built in the same manner and to the same standards. They are all products of the far-reaching supply lines made possible by the Anthropocene's use of fossil fuels. Wood is harvested, pulped and molded elsewhere, and driven in. Sheets of insulation and wind-blocking Tyvek are woven far from the site and driven in. Latex paint—a petroleum product—covers most walls, themselves made of gypsum and paper whose sources are too remote to be knowable. In the eighteenth century when builders used imported materials, they worked hard to highlight the fact. Now, distance and importation are so common that they are silenced by uniformity.

In this built environment, a single new home at Ferry Farm, built in the Holocene style, would be swallowed up by the sheer numbers of Anthropocene homes filling old fields as ailanthuses once did. At the same time, there is something remarkable in reconstruction. The work that went into the building's proposed design was historical in nature; that is, at no time was discussion driven by concerns of convenience of layout, sustainability of materials, or curb appeal of design. But historical concerns themselves set very strict limitations on what would and would not work. Builders set the template in the 1720s, and what will emerge at the beginning of a much later century will follow their lead. Local stone will go into the foundation footers and cellars, locally fired bricks will make up parts of the chimneys, and it is even possible that locally felled timber will go into the framing. It is certainly true that locally appropriate wood will be used; this will not be a frame made up of ailanthus beams. The shapes of rooms, flow of air, and views will all be set without regard for virtually anything learned about house design in the Anthropocene.

The building will serve as a platform for to interpret Washington's childhood to the museum-visiting public, a place for retelling the many stories of the place in the many voices that have been heard over the centuries. The building will also be a vibrant, three-dimensional presentation of findings, which will allow visitors to receive the latest version of Washington's childhood in an immersive setting.

Ever since Ferry Farm's excavation began in earnest in 2001 there has been a growing program of historical interpretation on the site. The Kenmore Association, which became the George Washington Foundation soon after it purchased the land, walked through a few different programs before settling on the current interpretive vision. Initial efforts carried on the existing narratives, making much of the Surveyor's Office, which still had a few believers left as the twenty-first century dawned. Work crews carefully re-sided the building, once again, in well-cut cedar clapboards. Regimes had changed so much from Colbert's day, when decay was the marker of venerability; by the 1990s, it was loving restoration that most conveyed a sense of value and historicity. On top of that, after the litany of failed preservation efforts that culminated in the thwarted Walmart sale, visible shows of able stewardship were valuable in and of themselves. And given that the 1870s building was the only thing on the land that could sustain a Washington designation (even though few believed it by then), a high-profile restorative act was a signal that care was being taken. In time, though, the archaeology itself conveyed that message, and the foundation began an extensive and truly remarkable restoration of Betty Washington Lewis and Fielding Lewis's 1770s home in Fredericksburg that set the standard for similar efforts. The new foundation may have needed to initially show its abilities, but very soon it had far outstripped other local efforts.

The farm's other inherited interpretive element was the Cherry Tree itself. Initially, the foundation held the story at arm's length, falling into the same trap as did Joseph Dillaway Sawyer back in 1927: that of mocking the Cherry Tree while elevating the Surveying Office. Early foundation letterhead used a seal bearing a small 1930s image of young George and his axe and ringed with the phrase "A Few Truths," a clever choice that allowed it to both invoke the famous story and distance itself from the tale. What was clear was that Washington's childhood would, in one way or another, be the main focus. Programs teaching school children the games popular with their eighteenth-century predecessors, and using familiar lessons about family and farm, became set pieces in how the site functioned as a historical museum.

As the site's archaeology became the center of the interpretation by the middle the new century's first decade, it served as the main exhibit while also beginning to establish just what the site's Washington story would be. I have already discussed the main outline of that narrative, and it easy to see how a newly reconstructed Washington farmscape will serve that goal and will bolster educational programs dealing with young Washington and eighteenth-century life in general. But the landscape as interpretive object deserves somewhat more discussion in light of the Holocene/Anthropocene divide.

Local nature preservation activists, such as the Friends of Rappahannock, were among the parties that stepped up in 1996 to help buy the land from Walmart. Their interest was different from that of the private donors and federal funders, who saw in the site's Washington connection a value worth paying for. Naturalists, both in the community and in the foundation itself, saw a unique opportunity in the more than three miles of uninterrupted Rappahannock River frontage created by making Ferry Farm a preserved site. That frontage was far from pristine. It had been used in various ways since the English first settled in the area and built homes and wharves along its length. It had been radically reshaped by the Army Corps of Engineers, who in the 1880s dredged the river bottom and deposited the resulting silt along the northern bank. A singularly dramatic flood in 1942 washed away oil tanks and buildings along the river. The result was that people pulled activity back from the water line and left the floodplain to fill with trees, many of which were the invasive ailanthus. The roots of those trees nestle with an extended gas pipeline that runs the length of the land, marked by occasional orange poles. Nevertheless, this stretch served the needs of the many turkeys, foxes, deer, and birds that returned in quantity.

The farm's other area of interest to naturalists was the old quarry. The idea there was to establish a meadow of indigenous grasses, and it was in aid of that project that the truckload of ailanthus killers set out to pull up trees. This meadow was severely hampered by the lack of topsoil, and it will be a long time before there has been enough planting and dieoff to create a fertile bed. Nevertheless, removed from the regimes of pesticide-heavy agriculture and the constant threat of development, and gradually being freed of many of its invasive species, Ferry Farm stands out in the landscape for reasons well beyond its tie to Washington. The addition of locally sourced, reconstructed buildings will only enhance that uniqueness. Locals and tourists will have a resource on hand, as we head into uncertain times, that speaks of many pasts, in many voices.

Historical landscapes conceptualized this way represent a projection of Holocene logic into the Anthropocene. Their historical nature makes the buildings and landscape less dependent on the networks and comforts that are most threatened by the massive climate-related changes imagined by the likes of *Dark Mountain* than the thousands of other homes all over the area. Just as Washington memory brought back the turkeys, Washington memory is now enabling a redo of what a house and environs can be and in so doing is revealing an alternative way to build, and perhaps to live. The colonial revival of the early twentieth century was a consumer event. Might a new, Anthropocene colonial revival that is anticonsumerist come into being? It might be that the next era of Washington memory will be less concerned with what he was and did and more with the places his memory inspired and the lifeways they reimagined.

Every February I am invited to give talks about Washington. Usually, I have lots to say about Ferry Farm, the Cherry Tree, and the man whose name overarches both of them. I am happy to give an ever-evolving version of that talk and keep people current on where the work stands. A challenge from a rabbi in Tampa, though, led me to think about the Cherry Tree in a new light, and in time I came to realize that there was perhaps a lesson in this line of thought for how we historians can gather many threads together and address the issue of human-induced climate change in ways beyond charting how we got here.

The challenge was simple: What specifically Jewish content is there in this work? What could I bring to a synagogue audience that was more than just American history, or at least tied American history and archaeology to the concerns of my religion?

My focus turned to the central act in Parson Weems's fable: the killing of the cherry tree. The evidence we have makes clear that Weems did, indeed, have formal religious training. Although that training focused on the Christian scriptures, there certainly would have been a grounding in the Christian readings of the Jewish texts as well. Although the contexts, interpretations, and outcomes are very different between different faiths, it is hard to imagine that, in his studies, Weems never ran across a single verse in what he would have called the Book of Deuteronomy, which Jews know as *Devarim*, or "Words." The verse comes in a section in which Moses—then aged, dying, and offering his last lessons in the texts he brought to Earth—discusses the proper way to wage war. Amid guidelines for establishing positions and the disposition of troops, the text describes the appropriate behavior towards trees—fruit trees in particular.

Verse 20:19 states that, when besieging a town for a long time with an intention of taking the town, you should not use an axe on the fruit trees, because soon enough you will want to eat their fruit. The next verse states that it is fine to cut down the other trees, but one should leave the fruit trees unharmed. It is true that in Weems's story Washington was not involved (yet) in a siege, but it is nevertheless an uncomfortably unavoidable conclusion that on at least one level, Weems's story—one designed to teach morals and values—has at its center a biblical sin.

Certainly Weems would respond to my charge by arguing that his faith itself represents a new covenant, one that negates the need for the Torah's many rules like this one; that is the entire point of his faith's idea of a new covenant. Likewise, rabbinic voices would quickly point out that the injunction against killing fruit trees is, at its most elemental level, one of the 613 biblical rules for Jews. Washington, not being a Jew, was not expected to follow those rules (although some rules are understood as being more widely applicable). In fact, Washington is one historical figure whom no one has ever claimed was a Jew—unlike Christopher Columbus, Benjamin Franklin, Abraham Lincoln, Franklin Roosevelt, and many others erroneously labeled as Jews by either conspiracy-minded anti-Semites or by Jews eagerly looking to bring their own ethnic story to other historical narratives.

The verse itself has been the subject of much discussion over centuries of rabbinic commentary. The reason is that the Hebrew in one part of the verse is oddly phrased. A central tenet of traditional Jewish exegesis is that odd phrasing, reversed word order, juxtapositions, seeming contradictions, and narrative disjuncture in the Bible are there to teach more about what the text means. Each little incongruity is itself a treasure trove of meaning. One need not be a believer to see and appreciate that this simple premise has been the wellspring of a vast flow of creative thinking and meaning making, as over three thousand years, great minds struggled to make sense of the complicated text and do so in dialogue with many other thinkers, contemporary and long gone.

The complicated phrase in question reads this way in transliterated Hebrew: *ki ha'adam eytz ha'sadeh lavo mipanecha bamatzor.* English translations have varied. Weems would have read the verse in King James's version as meaning that one should not kill a fruit tree, but one may eat of it, "for the tree of the field is man's life, to employ them in the siege." In other words, such trees provide sustenance and therefore should not be killed wantonly.

The actual Hebrew, though, is far from this translation and much more confusing. The simplest way to say this part of the verse is "because a man is the tree of the field, to go before you in siege?" although most commentators have read the crucial word *ki* ("because" in Modern Hebrew) as being used in a questioning form that Hebrew allows. The result is in effect a sentence with the word "why" implied before it—as if to say, "Why? Because 'the man' (i.e., the tree of the field) would siege before you?" The complexity of the sentence itself accounts for the many varied translations. Most modern Jewish translators render the sentence as, "Is the tree of the field a man, to go into the siege before you?"[42]

But the odd phrasing set in motion an interesting and meaningful rabbinic discussion. At the center sits the great eleventh-century French scholar Rabbi Shlomo Yitzhaki—or Rashi, as he is acronymically known—who defined the canonical meaning that is behind current translations, Jewish or otherwise. Rashi wrote, "The word *ki* here means 'perhaps': Is the tree of the field *perhaps* a man who is to go into the siege by you, that it should be punished by the suffering of hunger and thirst like the people of the city? Why should you destroy it?" But Rashi's Spanish-born near-contemporary, Rabbi Abraham ben Meir Ibn Ezra, saw it differently and argued that the phrasing—particularly the tricky pairing of "man, tree of the field"—was to be read as meaning that the tree is the *life* of a man, and therefore that is the reason it is to be spared. Fifteenth-century Portuguese authority Rabbi Isaac Abarabanel balanced these two reasons to spare fruit trees and added his own insight that the Torah was hiding *both* reasons in the verse. This would make the phrase a double prohibition: Do not kill the tree, because it is a source of life and because it cannot harm you in war as your enemies can. That the act required a double prohibition only highlights how meaningful it was.

At the same time, there developed a thriving discussion using the verse to suggest that a man and a tree are comparable in important ways. The Second Temple Era through fifth-century sages of the Talmud recalled the verse and saw in it a lesson about the character of a teacher. Rabbi Yochanan noted that, just as some trees bear fruit and others do not, so too there are good teachers and poor ones; do not cut down the good ones, but have at the poor ones. The Medieval Talmudic commentators known collectively as the Tosafot tempered this third-century lesson to make "cut down" merely meaning a call to cut oneself off from poor teachings. Sixteenth-century Polish Rabbi Jacob ben Isaac Ashkenazi wrote that just as a tree produces fruit, man produces children. Thus, when man is cut down, that pain is felt widely (through his offspring); so too the cries of chopped-down fruit tree are heard all over the world. Bohemian Rabbi Judah Loew ben Bezalel used the verse in the 1500s to argue that a man was like a tree in that his arms and head were rooted in heaven as he was tied to the earth below.

But it was Moshe ben Maimon (Maimonides), the great Spanish-born twelfth-century sage, who saw in the verse a large overarching moral principle. In his Mishneh Torah he taught that the lesson here was a simple one: Do not destroy wantonly.[43] Indeed, anyone who kills a fruit tree or destroys a building, or stops up a well or even wastes food violates the probation against wasteful destruction.[44] Thus, the verse is speaking not only about war practices but also about the nature of man and the ethics of how to relate to the material world. It speaks of an ethical worldview that calls for moderation in action, as opposed to one that privileges acquisition at all costs. Maimonides calls on us to look critically at the conditions that brought on the Anthropocene—changes he no doubt would have seen as the fulfillment of the biblical warning that not acting in the correct way will cause the earth itself to turn against us. He also helps form a new voice for telling the Cherry Tree fable.

No doubt Weems never knew any of this rabbinic commentary. Indeed, if he had, he might have picked a less charged act for his character to commit. But one wonders about the legions of Jewish immigrant school children at the end of the nineteenth century, learning the language and icons of American political culture through texts such as the Cherry Tree fable while also learning their own religious tradition that offered such a complicated view of tree killing.

Maimonides linked the tree killing verse to a larger ethics of restraint and respect. This puts a different spin on the site of the most famous tree killing in American history and literature. It also provides a new way to think of this tale—to give it new meaning as we, as a species, move into uncertain times of our own making. Mark Levene has written that one thing historians can do to meet our new future is to look at past beliefs and practices to see what we can dust off. He specifically invokes the Jewish idea of Tikkun Olam—fixing the world.[45] This idea has moved to the center of American contemporary Progressive Jewish practice and thought. Various reform movements in the nineteenth and twentieth centuries sought to create a Judaism enacted less through traditional ritual and more focused on the religion as a broadly applicable ethical code. The results of that experiment are still being tallied, but by foregrounding the idea of Tikkun Olam as a theme for restraint and conservation, it has obvious environmental application.

The Cherry Tree is of use here as well. Weems wanted readers to focus on the moment when the son confesses and receives absolution from a loving father—a logical narrative for a minister of the church. But as the rabbi first asked of me, is there a Jewish read in this? Yes. Like a biblical patriarch, our American patriarch does something of dubious moral standing, but in his misdeed we are reminded of how we all must act and the ethics we need to bring to bear—in this case, more than two thousand years of discussion of why we must not be wasteful and how we are ourselves like trees. Chakrabarty called for a collapsing of the categories of the human and the natural as we face life and scholarship in the Anthropocene. Man, the Tree of the Field, was there first.

We can likewise reimagine Ferry Farm and its Cherry Tree, and the moral of the Cabbage Seed story, in light of Maimonides's ethics. Given the land's long association with this story, it is perfectly poised—simultaneously as a historical site, a museum, and a preserved landscape—to tease out of Weems's much loved and much maligned stories a new moral meaning that the old Parson could never have imagined at the dawn of the Anthropocene, when he thought the worst thing about killing a tree was angering a father. We know better now, and we need to create histories to pass that knowledge along while we can.

As long as we revere Washington in our civil polity, we will have his childhood to contend with. It is unlikely that one day we will achieve the sort of tidy, simple historical understanding of that part of his famous life sought by so many biographers. It is equally unlikely that we will fall back into the sort of romantic moralistic view presented by the fabulists. Instead, we are stuck with something that is essentially a river made of many streams—and like a body of water, it is a mirror when viewed at the right angles.

NOTES

"THE MOST STORIED GROUND IN AMERICA": AN INTRODUCTION

1 Michael Zitz, "For 4½ Years, Bob Siegrist Was Ferry Farm," *Freelance Star* (June 29, 1993), D1.

2 M. L. Weems, *The Life of Washington*, ed. Peter Onuf (Armonk, NY: M. E. Sharp Press, 1996), 11, hereafter cited as *LoW*.

3 *LoW*, 11.

4 *LoW*, 11–12.

5 The most thorough study of the Cherry Tree as image remains Karal Ann Marling's *George Washington Slept Here: Colonial Revivals and American Culture, 1876–1986* (Cambridge, MA: Harvard University Press, 1988).

6 Psalm 24:1 KJV.

7 According to Washington historian Jack Warren, it was the only farmable piece of Virginia he ever sold off: "The Childhood of George Washington," *Northern Neck of Virginia Historical Magazine* 49, no. 1 (1999), 5791.

8 The best work on Washington's vision for Mount Vernon and its environs is Joseph Manca's *George Washington's Eye: Landscape, Architecture, and Design at Mount Vernon* (Baltimore, MD: Johns Hopkins University Press, 2012).

9 See Patricia West, "Inventing a House Undivided: Antebellum Cultural Politics and the Enshrinement of Mount Vernon," in *Domesticating History: The Political Origins of America's House Museums* (Washington, DC: Smithsonian Institution, 1999), 1–37; see also Scott Casper, *Sarah Johnson's Mount Vernon: The Forgotten History of an American Shrine* (New York: Hill and Wang, 2008) for later meanings from Mount Vernon.

10 The curious and still somewhat unresolved dispute over the exact

location of the Washington birthplace home has been taken on in a few essays and books. Most notable among these are Joy Beasley, "The Birthplace of a Chief: Archaeology and Meaning at George Washington's Birthplace National Monument," in Paul A. Shackel, ed., *Myth, Memory, and the Making of the America Landscape* (Gainesville: University Press of Florida, 2001); Seth Bruggeman, *Here, George Washington Was Born: Memory, Material Culture, and the Public History of a National Monument* (Athens: University of Georgia Press, 2008). See also Seth Bruggeman, *National Park Service, George Washington Birthplace National Monument: Administrative History, 1930–2000* Westmoreland, VA: GWBNM, 2006).

11 *George Washington Birthplace National Monument, Virginia* (Washington, DC: U.S. Department of the Interior, 1941); Bruggeman, *Here, George Washington Was Born.*

12 Michael Kammen, *A Season of Youth: The American Revolution and the Historical Imagination* (New York: Alfred Knopf, 1978), 38–43.

13 Patricia West, *Domesticating History: The Political Origins of America's House Museums* (Washington, DC: Smithsonian Press, 1999).

14 I outlined this process in an essay in *The Virginia Magazine of History and Biography*. The preceding paragraphs come from that essay. "'Crystallized into Solid Reality': How Mason Locke 'Parson' Weems Shaped George Washington's Boyhood Home," *Virginia Magazine of History and Biography* 120, no. 1 (April 2013), 107–45.

15 Almost all biographies make some comment on this issue. For one sample statement well rooted in both documentation and the flow of the discussion, see Dorothy Towhig, "The Making of George Washington," in Warren Hofstra, ed., *George Washington and the Virginia Backcountry* (Madison, WI: Madison House, 1998), 6.

16 John Bodnar, *Remaking America: Public Memory, Commemoration, and Patriotism in the Twentieth Century* (Princeton, NJ: Princeton University Press, 1992). In his influential book, Bodnar sees "public memory" emerging for an intersection of "official memory"—that deployed by governments, institutions, and the powerful—as opposed to "vernacular memory" or "vernacular culture." This he defines as landing more often on concerns of experience of the past and located more in family lineages and experiences. "Ordinary people" (a term

Bodnar used with acknowledged caution) are, as he wrote, "more likely to honor pioneer ancestors rather than founding fathers" (16). One need only look at Jill Lepore's *The Whites of Their Eyes: The Tea Party's Revolution and the Battle over American History* (Princeton, NJ: Princeton University Press, 2010) to see just how much the content of Bodnar's dichotomy has shifted since its writing. Indeed, even Lepore's book is seeming a timepiece only three years after its publication. Bodnar's Gramscian distinction, though, concerns itself mainly in the working of state hegemony, which is to say, the function of state power in ways that are simultaneously effective, hidden, and internalized by subalterns. See T. J. Jackson Lears, "The Concept of Cultural Hegemony: Problems and Possibilities," *The American Historical Review* 90, no. 3 (June 1985), 567–93; Thomas R. Bates, "Gramsci and the Theory of Hegemony," *Journal of the History of Ideas* 36, no. 2 (April–June 1975), 351–66. I do not share this orientation and therefore eschew this otherwise useful distinction that rests on concerns stemming from class distinction and the workings of the state. Nevertheless, memory is a vital historical theme influencing this work. See Michael Kammen, *Mystic Chords of Memory: The Transformation of Tradition in American Culture* (New York: Alfred Knopf, 1991); Kirk Savage, *Standing Soldiers, Kneeling Slaves: Race, War, and Monument in Nineteenth-Century America* (Princeton, NJ: Princeton University Press, 1997); David Glassberg, *Sense of History: The Place of the Past in the American Life* (Amherst: University of Massachusetts Press, 2001).

17 Michael Kammen, *The Machine That Would Go of Itself: The Constitution in American Culture* (New York: Alfred Knopf, 1986).

18 1976 is only now beginning to be treated historically. See Tammy Gordon, *The Spirit of 1976: Commerce, Opportunity, and the Politics of Commemoration* (Amherst: University Press of Massachusetts, 2013).

19 Barry Schwartz, *George Washington: The Making of an American Symbol* (New York: The Free Press, 1987), 9.

20 François Furstenberg, *In the Name of the Father: Washington's Legacy, Slavery, and the Making of a Nation* (New York: Penguin, 2006), 98–99.

21 Karal Ann Marling, *George Washington Slept Here: Colonial Revivals*

and American Culture (Cambridge, MA: Harvard University Press, 1988).

22 Edward Lengel, *Inventing George Washington: America's Founder in Myth and Memory* (New York: Harper Collins, 2011).

23 Lepore, *The Whites of Their Eyes.*

24 Scott Casper has crafted a wonderful alternative history of Mount Vernon, in *Sarah Johnson's Mount Vernon: The Forgotten History of an American Shrine* (New York: Hill and Wang, 2009). Although Washington is not a major factor in the book, it is nevertheless a wonderful example of what the Washington memory theme can produce.

25 Cornelius Holtoft and Howard Williams claim that landscape is "the inhabited or perceived environments of human communities in the past and present incorporating both natural and artificial elements," in Dan Hicks and Mary Beaudry, eds., "Landscape and Memories," in *The Cambridge Companion to Historical Archaeology* (New York: Cambridge University Press, 2006), 235–54. This is a useful, if somewhat all-encompassing, definition of landscape coming from archaeology. See also Denis E. Cosgrove, *Social Formation and Symbolic Landscape* (Madison: University of Wisconsin Press, 1988), 13. Definitions of landscape intersect with discussions of "place" and "space," the former being more the purview of historians and the latter more often a language of anthropologists. All told, though, these related concerns seek to develop subtle understandings of human mediations, interactions, shaping, valuation, and discussion of the settings of their lives. Carl Sauer has had considerable influence laying out foundational frameworks for all these geography and historical geography discussions. See "The Problem of Land Classification" *Annals of the Association of American Geographers* 11 (1921), 3–16; and "Landscape," in Robert Larkin and Gary Peters, eds., *Dictionary of Concepts in Human Geography* (Westport, CT: Greenwood Press, 1983), 139–44. David Lowenthaul also played a formative role in part through his essay "The American Scene," *Geographic Review* 58, no. 1 (January 1968), 61–88. D. W. Meinig has had a far-reaching transfield influence via his ten-part typology for understanding the fact that a landscape is made up of "not only what lies before our

eyes, but what lies within our heads," in "The Beholding Eye: Ten Versions of the Same Scene," *Landscape Architecture* (January 1976), 34. Meinig and Lowenthaul both emphasized the multiple voices with which landscapes can speak. Environmental historians have devoted attention to the concept of "nature," early on in the field's development, as an object used and acted upon, and more recently as a problematic and sometimes confounding construction. In this discussion, though, "landscape" has survived somewhat as being a term of physical reality, as opposed to a product of cognition. Richard White provides an excellent example of this by contrasting "hybrid landscapes," meaning those whose physical reality is shaped by a variety of human and nonhuman forces, with the romantic notion of a "pure" or untouched "natural" landscape. Richard White, "From Wilderness to Hybrid Landscapes," *The Historian* 66 (2004), 557–64. Historical archaeology has gone down a somewhat different path, informed in no small part by the archaeologist's actual involvement in the physical landscape as part of the process of reconstructing past ones. This relationship led W. G. Hoskins to declare landscapes to be the "richest historical record that we possess," in *The Making of the English Landscape* (London: Hodder and Stoughton, 1955), 14. Christopher Tilley identified that landscape is "both medium *for* and outcome *of* action and previous histories of action," in *A Phenomenology of Landscape: Places, Paths, and Monuments* (Oxford: Berg, 1994), 23. Archaeologist Matthew Johnson has written that reading has been the dominant shared metaphor for how to engage with the landscape. Indeed, the reading metaphor is one of the most influential in landscape studies. Matthew Johnson, *Ideas of Landscape* (New York: Blackwell Publishing, 2007), 44.

26 Barry Schwartz, "Social Change and Collective Memory: The Democratization of George Washington," *American Sociological Review* 56, no. 2 (April 1991), 221–36. Schwartz's essay was part of a body of work that was coping with the concept Michel Foucault called "discourse," just before that idea became common in the Anglophonic world. Schwartz assembled a wide array of Anglophonic theorists and argued essentially that Washington's image functioned as a discourse, applicable in many settings to many people and discussions but free

of an obligation to be consistent or permanently linked to any single context.

27 Schwartz, "Social Change and Collective Memory."

28 Julia A. King, *Archaeology, Narrative, and the Politics of the Past: The View from the Southern Maryland* (Knoxville: University of Tennessee Press, 2012), I think represents the best of new approach to place, memory, archaeology, and narrative to be seen in current historical archaeological scholarship. I see this work as following in her footsteps. For a broader range of historical archaeology work, see James Deetz, *In Small Things Forgotten: An Archaeology of Early American Life* (New York: Anchor Press/Double Day, 1977); James Deetz, *Flowerdew Hundred: The Archaeology of a Virginia Plantation, 1619–1864* (Charlottesville: University of Virginia, 1993); Mary C. Beaudry, *Findings: The Material Culture of Needlework and Sewing* (New Haven, CT: Yale University Press, 2007); Stephen A Mrozowski, Grace H. Ziesing, and Mary C. Beaudry, *Living on the Boott: Historical Archaeology at the Boott Mills Boardinghouses, Lowell, Massachusetts* (Amherst: University of Massachusetts Press, 1996); Anne Elizabeth Yentsch, *A Chesapeake Family and Their Slaves: A Study in Historical Archaeology* (Cambridge, England: Cambridge University Press, 1994); Rebecca Yamin and Karen Beschere Metheny, *Landscape Archaeology: Reading and Interpreting American Historical Landscapes* (Knoxville: University of Tennessee Press, 1996); Matthew Johnson, *An Archaeology of Capitalism* (Hoboken, NJ: Wiley-Blackwell, 1996); Barbara J. Little, *Historical Archaeology: Why the Past Matters* (Walnut Creek, CA: Left Coast Press, 2007); Barbara J. Heath and Jack Gary, *Jefferson's Popular Forest: Unearthing a Virginia Plantation* (Gainesville: University of Florida Press, 2012); Rebecca Yamin, *Digging in the City of Brotherly Love: Stories from Philadelphia Archaeology* (New Haven, CT: Yale University Press, 2008); Stephen A. Mrozowski, *The Archaeology of Class in Urban America* (Cambridge, England: Cambridge University Press, 2012); Susan Kern, *The Jeffersons at Shadwell* (New Haven, CT: Yale University Press, 2012).

29 Jack Warren, "The Childhood of George Washington," *The Northern Neck of Virginia Historical Magazine* 49, no. 1 (1999), 5790–91.

30 Jessica Brunelle, "The Youth of George Washington," *A Companion to George Washington* (Oxford: Wiley Press, 2012).

31 Edward Lengel, *Inventing George Washington: America's Founder in Myth and Memory* (New York: Hill and Wang, 2011), 19, 22, 24.

32 I have told this story as a narrative in *Where the Cherry Tree Grew: The Story of Ferry Farm, George Washington's Boyhood Home* (New York: St. Martin's Press, 2013).

I. "SOMEWHERE THIS HAD BEGINNINGS"

1 Worthington Chauncey Ford, *George Washington* (Boston: Small, Maynard, and Co., 1910), 4.

2 Sparks quoted in Marcus Cunliffe, *George Washington: Man and Monument* (Boston: Little Brown and Co., 1958), 14.

3 J. Frost, *Pictorial Life of George Washington* (Philadelphia: Charles Gillis, 1847), 14.

4 Ibid., 16.

5 James T. Flexner, *George Washington: The Forge of Experience (1732– 1775)* (New York: Little Brown and Co., 1965), 3.

6 Norwood Young, *George Washington: Soul of the Revolution* (New York: Robert McBride, 1932), xi.

7 C. M. Stevens, *The Wonderful Story of Washington* (New York: Cupples and Leon Co., 1914), 2.

8 One count estimates as many as 400 Washington biographies, broadly defined. I make no claim to have read anywhere near that quantity. My study rests on a selective reading of about one hundred biographies spread out over time. There are about fifteen core works that make up the cannon, but I have added to these a number of lesser works that range from the obscure to the bizarre. I have defined the childhood years as encompassing everything from birth and ancestry until the late 1740s or early 1750s, when Washington settled into his surveying career. At that point, most of the stories settle out and level off, as the body of documentation becomes large enough to sustain what we might call a more historical discussion. Before that, though, is a period in which other devices sustain and support the narrative. The lengths of these biography sections vary from the few hundred words written by John Marshall to sections as long as seventy pages. In all cases, however, the same themes and approaches emerge.

9 Wayne Whipple, *The Story-Life of Washington* (Philadelphia: Winston Co., 1911), xiv.

10 "George Washington to Sir Isaac Heard," May 2, 1792, *The Writings of George Washington* 32:32–33. See also Jack Warren Jr., "George Washington and the Genealogist," *National Geological Society Quarterly* 87 (December 1999), 261–71.

11 Ibid.

12 Ibid.

13 See "The English Cleric and the Virginia Adventurer: The Washingtons, Father and Son," in Don Higginbotham, ed., *George Washington Reconsidered* (Charlottesville: University of Virginia Press, 2001), 15–37, for a more current handling.

14 John Marshall, *The Life of George Washington,* Vol. II (London: Richard Phillips, 1804), 2.

15 Aaron Bancroft, *The Life of George Washington,* Reprint (Boston: Phillips, Sampson, and Co., 1855), 1.

16 Mason Locke Weems, *The Life of Washington,* ed. Peter Onuf (Armonk, NY: M. E. Sharp Press, 1996), 1.

17 Jared Sparks, *The Life of Washington* (Boston: Little, Brown and Company, 1853), 1–2.

18 Ibid., 2.

19 Ibid., 2.

20 Washington Irving, *The Life of George Washington* (New York: G. P. Putnam and Co., 1856), 1.

21 Barry Schwartz, "Social Change and Collective Memory: The Democratization of George Washington," *American Sociological Review* 56:2 (April 1991), 221–36. Schwartz revealed this process as taking place in the years around the Civil War. However, his work did not look at this issue of race and ancestry in that process.

22 Caroline Matilda Kirkland, *Memoirs of Washington* (New York: D. Appleton and Co., 1857), 37; See also "The Death of Mrs. Kirkland," *The New York Times* (April 10, 1864).

23 Kirkland, *Memoirs of Washington,* 37.

24 Edward Everett, *Life of George Washington* (New York: Sheldon and Company, 1860), 25.

25 Bradley T. Johnson, *General Washington* (New York: D. Appleton and Co., 1894), 6–7.

26 Ibid., 8.

27 Edward M. Taylor, *George Washington, The Ideal Patriot* (New York: Eaton and Mains, 1897), 49.

28 Stanley Weintraub, *General Washington's Christmas Farewell: A Mount Vernon Homecoming, 1783* (New York: Free Press, 2003), 66.

29 David Humphreys, *Life of General Washington with George Washington's Remarks*, ed. Rosemarie Zagarri (Athens: University of Georgia Press, 1991), 7.

30 Ibid.

31 Scott Casper, *Constructing American Lives: Biography and Culture in Nineteenth-Century America* (Chapel Hill: University of North Carolina Press, 1999), 96.

32 Sparks, *The Life of Washington* (Boston: Little, Brown and Company, 1853), 3.

33 Weems, *The Life of Washington*, 19.

34 Edward Everett Hale, *The Life of George Washington: Studied Anew* (New York: G.P. Putman's Sons, 1883), 1; Taylor, *George Washington, The Ideal Patriot*, 54.

35 S. G. Arnold, *The Life of George Washington, First President of the United States* (New York: T. Mason, 1840), 9; Kirkland, *Memoirs of Washington*, 42.

36 Irving, *The Life of George Washington*, 16.

37 William M. Thayer, *George Washington: His Boyhood and Manhood* (London: Hodder and Stoughton, 1883), 8.

38 Stevens, *The Wonderful Story of Washington*, 6, 8.

39 Charles Arthur Hoppin, "The House in Which George Washington Was Born," *Tyler's Quarterly* 8, no. 2 (October 1926), 88.

40 Normal Hapgood, *George Washington* (London: Macmillan, 1901), 4.

41 John Adams quoted in Flexner, *George Washington*, 12.

42 Paul Longmore, *The Invention of George Washington* (Charlottesville: University Press of Virginia, 1999), 213; Francois Furstenburg, "Atlantic Slavery, Atlantic Freedom: George Washington's Library, Slavery, and Trans-Atlantic Abolitionist Networks," *William and Mary Quarterly* 3rd ser., 68 (April 2011), 247–86.

43 Marshall, *The Life of George Washington*, 2.

44 John Corry, *The Life of George Washington* (New York: M'Carty and White, 1809), 7; Anna C. Reed, *The Life of George Washington* (1829),

19; Stephen Simpson, *The Lives of George Washington and Thomas Jefferson* (Philadelphia: Henry Young, 1833), 2.

45 James Trumbull, *Life of George Washington, First President of the United States* (New York: D and S Forbes, 1829), 3.

46 Trevor Frederick Hill, *On the Trail of Washington* (New York: D. Appleton and Co. 1921), 15.

47 Whipple, *The Story-Life of George Washington*, 47.

48 Samuel Smucker, *Life and Times of George Washington* (Philadelphia: J. W. Bradley, 1860), 19; E. Cecil, *Life of George Washington: Written for Children* (Boston: Crosby and Nichols, 1962), 2.

49 Arnold, *The Life of George Washington*, 19.

50 Sparks, *The Life of Washington*, 5.

51 Louis Martin Sears, *George Washington* (New York: Thomas Y. Crowell Co., 1932), 2.

52 James O'Boyle, *Life of George Washington* (New York: Longmans Green and Co., 1915), 5.

53 S. G. Arnold, *George Washington, President of the United States* (New York: T. Mason and G. Lane, 1840), 16.

54 J. T. Headley, *Life of George Washington* (New York: Charles Scribner, 1856), 18.

55 Hill, *On the Trail of Washington*, 6.

56 Whipple, *The Story-Life of George Washington*, 31.

57 Hill, *On the Trail of Washington*, 8, 6.

58 Rupert Hughes, *George Washington: The Human Being and the Hero* (New York: William Morrow Co., 1926), 22.

59 Ibid., 21.

60 John C. Fitzpatrick, *George Washington Himself* (Indianapolis, IN: Bobbs-Merrill, 1933), 20.

61 Charles W. Stetson, *Washington and His Neighbors* (Richmond, VA: Garrett and Massie, 1956), 9.

62 George Washington Parke Custis, *Recollection and Private Memoirs of Washington* (Washington, DC: William H. More, 1859), 92.

63 Hill, *On the Trail of Washington*, 7; Horace Scudder, *George Washington: A Historical Biography* (New York: Houghton Mifflin, 1889), 28; Taylor, *George Washington, the Ideal Patriot*, 73; Whipple, *The Story-Life of George Washington*, 32.

64 William Thayer, *The Farmer Boy and How He Became Commander in Chief* (Boston: Walker, Wise, and Co., 1864), 37.

65 Johnson, *General Washington*, 14.

66 Silas Weir Mitchell, *The Youth of Washington* (New York: The Century Co., 1904), 30.

67 Ibid.

68 William E. Woodward, *George Washington: The Image and the Man* (New York: Boni and Liverlight, 1926), 23.

69 Hill, *On the Trail of Washington*, 7; Joseph Dillaway Sawyer, *Washington* (New York: Macmillan, 1927), 82.

70 Jack Warren has advocated for Marye's school and even suggested that Washington may have learned some French there. Jack Warren, "The Childhood of George Washington," *Northern Neck of Virginia Historical Magazine* 49, no. 1 (1999), 5803. Nevertheless, apart from Douglas Freeman, Warren has provided perhaps the closest read of the childhood evidence.

71 Whipple, *The Story-Life of George Washington*, 48; O'Boyle, *Life of George Washington*, 5.

72 Corry, *The Life of George Washington*, 8; Sparks, *The Life of Washington*, 3.

73 Elbridge Brooks, *The True Story of George Washington* (Boston: Lothrop, 1897), 16; Woodrow Wilson, *George Washington* (New York: Harper and Brothers, 1903), 46.

74 Stevens, *The Wonderful Story of George Washington*, 8.

75 Bancroft, *The Life of George Washington*, 2.

76 Sparks, *The Life of Washington*, 9.

77 Irving, *The Life of George Washington*, 19; Smucker, *The Life and Times of George Washington*, 21; Hale, *The Life of George Washington*, 4.

78 Irving, *The Life of George Washington*, 25; Everett, *Life of George Washington*, 38; Ford, *George Washington*, 5; Smucker, *The Life and Times of George Washington*, 21.

79 Woodward, *George Washington*, 18.

80 Flexner, *George Washington*, 13; Woodward, *George Washington*, 33.

81 Horace Edwin Hayden, *Virginia Genealogies: A Genealogy of the Glassell Family* (Wilkes Barre, Pennsylvania, 1891), 77; Moncure Daniel

Conway, *Barons of the Potomac and the Rappahannock* (New York: The Grolier Club, 1892), 240.

82 Marshall, *The Life of George Washington,* 2; William Roscoe Thayer, *George Washington* (Boston: Houghton Mifflin, 1922), 9; S. G. Arnold, *The Life of George Washington* (New York: T. Mason and G. Lane, 1840), 18.

83 Sawyer, *Washington,* 95.

84 Hayden, *Virginia Genealogies,* 77.

85 Marshall, *The Life of George Washington,* 2; William Roscoe Thayer, *George Washington,* 9.

86 John Bodnar, *Remaking America: Public Memory, Commemoration, and Patriotism in the Twentieth Century* (Princeton, NJ: Princeton University Press, 1992).

87 Sparks, *The Life of Washington,* 4.

88 Simpson, *Lives of George Washington and Thomas Jefferson,* 2; Sparks, *The Life of Washington,* 4.

89 Arnold, *The Life of George Washington,* 10; Smucker, *Life and Times of George Washington,* 18; Anna Hyde, *Life of Washington* (New York: James Miller, 1868), 33; Arnold, *The Life of George Washington,* 11.

90 Kirkland, *Memoirs of Washington* (New York: D. Appleton, 1857), 46.

91 Ibid., 46; Everett, *Life of George Washington,* 35; Hyde, *Life of Washington,* 33.

92 Lawrence of Chotank's quotation appears in many places; in this case I used the one in Benson Lossing, *Mary and Martha, the Mother and Wife of Washington* (New York: Harper and Brothers, 1886), 33.

93 Smucker, *Life and Times of George Washington,* 18.

94 Henry Cabot Lodge, *George Washington, in Two Volumes* (Boston: Houghton Mifflin, 1889), 1:10–11.

95 The most influential study of that process remains Peter Novick, *That Noble Dream: The Objectivity Question and the Historical Profession* (New York: Cambridge University Press, 1988). See also Joyce Appleby, Lynn Hunt, and Margaret Jacob, *Telling the Truth About History* (New York: W. W. Norton, 1995); Georg G. Iggers, *Historiography in the Twentieth Century: From Scientific Objectivity to the Postmodern Challenge* (Middleton, CT: Wesleyan University Press, 2005).

96 Paul Leicester Ford, *The True Washington* (Philadelphia: J. B. Lippincott, 1896), 17.

97 Gail Bederman, *Manliness and Civilization: A Cultural History of Gender and Race in the United States, 1880–1917* (Chicago: University of Chicago Press, 1996).

98 Irving, *The Life of George Washington,* 23.

99 O'Boyle, *Life of George Washington,* 4.

100 United States George Washington Bicentennial Commission, *Life of George Washington* (Washington, DC: United States Government, 1932), 3; Sawyer, *Washington,* 74, 81–82.

101 Young, *George Washington,* 30; Nathaniel Wright Stevenson, *George Washington* (New York: Oxford University Press, 1940), 31; Stevens, *The Wonderful Story of Washington,* 4.

102 Woodward, *George Washington,* 15.

103 Shelby Little, *George Washington* (New York: Minton, Balach and Co., 1929), 2.

104 Samuel Eliot Morison, *The Young Man Washington* (Cambridge, MA: Harvard University Press, 1932), 10–11.

105 Douglas Southall Freeman, *George Washington: A Biography,* Vol. 1 (New York: Charles Scribner's Sons, 1948), 192–93.

106 Alan Nevins, "Washington Minus His Pedestal," *New York Times* (October 17, 1948), BR1.

107 Flexner, *George Washington,* 19.

108 Ibid., 19.

109 Ron Chernow, *Washington: A Life* (New York: Penguin Press, 2010), 10–11. Chernow sees in Mary the formidable foe what he called the "first formidable general" Washington would face. He gives to Mary horsemanship skills, a love of dancing, and a few other more engaging traits. But the overall impression is the single most negative view since Morison. Others have been content to follow the Morison–Freeman lead with very little consideration. See also Hargow Giles Unger, *The Unexpected George Washington: His Private Life* (New York: Wiley, 2006).

110 Nevins, "Washington Minus His Pedestal," BR1.

111 Hughes, *George Washington,* 15.

112 Ibid., 15.

113 United States George Washington Bicentennial Commission, *The Mother of George Washington*, 3; Sawyer, *Washington*, 74, 81–82.

114 Susan Riviere Hetzel, *The Building of a Monument* (Lancaster, PA: Wickersham Company, 1903), 37.

115 I discussed the details of the struggle around the first and second Mary Washington monuments in *Where the Cherry Tree Grew* (New York: St. Martin's Press, 2013).

116 Mrs. Roger A. Pryor, *The Mother of Washington and Her Times* (New York: Macmillan, 1903), 96.

117 See Paula Felder, *Fielding Lewis and the Washington Family: A Chronicle of 18th Century Fredericksburg* (Fredericksburg, VA: The American History Company, 1998) and *Forgotten Companions: The First Settlers of Spotsylvania County and Fredericksburgh Town* (Fredericksburg, VA: The American History Company, 2000).

118 Joseph Ellis, *His Excellency George Washington* (New York: Alfred Knopf, 2004), 3.

2. COMPLETING THE CIRCUIT OF MEMORY

1 That phrase comes from Albert Bushnell Hart, describing Washington as a "business man" on the eve of the Washington birth bicentennial. "George Washington as a Business Man, *Bulletin of the Business Historical Society* 5, no. 1 (January 1931), 15.

2 Douglas Southall Freeman, *George Washington: A Biography*, Vol. 1 (New York: Scribner and Sons, 1948), 197 and footnote 30.

3 Joseph Ellis, *His Excellency George Washington* (New York: Alfred Knopf, 2004), 10.

4 Ibid., 12.

5 Paul Longmore, *The Invention of George Washington* (Charlottesville: University of Virginia Press, 1999), 13.

6 Refer to Philander Chase, "A Stake in the West: George Washington as a Backcountry Surveyor and Landholder," in Warren Hofstra, ed., *George Washington and the Virginia Backcountry* (Madison, WI: Madison House, 1998), 159–94, for a very good review of Washington's surveying career. The reigning, most through study of the role of the surveyor in colonial Virginia remains Sarah Hughes, *Surveyors*

and Statesmen: Land Measuring in Colonial Virginia (Richmond: The Virginia Surveyors Foundation, and the Virginia Association of Surveyors, 1979).

7 George Washington, "Gen. Washington's Memorandum Cash Account," LWS Collection, Morristown National Historical Park, Morristown, NJ, September 20, 1747.

8 H. de Luzancy, A Panegyrick to the Memory of His Grace Frederick Late Duke of Schonberg (London: R. Bentley, 1690). Washington later wrote to Jonathan Boucher about buying this book. See "George Washington to Jonathan Boucher, July 9, 1771," in Theodore J. Crackel, ed., The Papers of George Washington Digital Edition (Charlottesville: University of Virginia Press, 2008).

9 Laura Galke, "American Ethnogenesis, c. 1680–1760: Commemorating William and Mary," unpublished paper presented at the Mid Atlantic Archaeology Conference, Ocean City MD, March 2015.

10 Jason Farr, "The Unlikely Success of a Provincial Surveyor: George Washington Finds Fame in the American Frontier, 1749–1754," in Edward Lengel, ed., A Companion to George Washington (New York: Wiley-Blackwell, 2012), 19–20.

11 Charles Henry Ambler, Washington and the West (Chapel Hill: University of North Carolina Press, 1936), 28.

12 Barnet Schecter, George Washington's America: A Biography Through His Maps (New York: Walker and Company, 2010).

13 Ambler, Washington and the West, 28; Edward Lengel, for example, notes the significance of Washington's mapping skills and Western knowledge in connection to Braddock's campaign, in General George Washington: A Military Life (New York: Random House, 2006), 50.

14 Ambler, Washington and the West, 28.

15 These books were almost always pitched at childhood audiences, and many took considerable liberty, even inventing complicated imagined dialogue. For examples, see Augusta Stevenson, George Washington, Boy Leader (New York: Bobbs-Merrill, 1942); Ida C. Mirriam, Washington's Boyhood (New York: Albert Whitman, 1933); and Gilchrist Waring, Ferry Farm: A Story of George Washington's Boyhood (Petersburg, VA: Dietz Press, 1978).

16 I am indebted to George Washington Foundation researcher Travis Walker for this tip.

17 George Washington, *The Diaries of George Washington,* Vol. III, ed. Donald Jackson (Charlottesville: University of Virginia Press, 1978), 52–53, hereafter cited as *Diaries.*

18 Ibid., 52–53.

19 Ibid., 53.

20 Ibid.

21 The whole trip is covered in *Diaries,* 52–53.

22 Kenneth Lockridge, *On the Sources of Patriarchal Rage: The Commonplace Books of William Byrd and Thomas Jefferson and the Gendering of Power in the Eighteenth Century* (New York: NYU Press, 1993).

23 Jack Warren makes the same case in one sentence of his essay in Washington's childhood. See "The Childhood of George Washington," *Northern Neck of Virginia Historical Magazine* 49, no. 1 (1999), 5793.

24 *Diaries,* 52.

25 Douglas Southall Freeman, *George Washington, A Biography, Volume Three, Planter and Patriot* (New York: Scribner and Sons, 1951), 280–81.

26 John Ferling, *The Ascent of George Washington* (New York: Bloomsbury Press, 2010), 10.

27 Freeman, *George Washington, A Biography, Volume Three,* 280–81. Ron Chernow also mentions the 1771 trip, but briefly and mostly as a chance swipe at Mary, in *Washington: A Life* (New York: Penguin Press, 2010), 158.

28 Catlett not only patented the land, he also was killed in the Indian war leadup to Bacon's Rebellion. See Nell Marion Nugent, *Cavaliers and Pioneers: Abstracts of Virginia Land Patents and Grants, 1623–1666* (Baltimore, MD: Genealogical Publishing Company, 1963).

29 Willie Graham, Carter L. Hudgins, Carl Lounsbury, Fraser D. Neiman, and James P. Whittenburg, "Adaptation and Innovation: Archeological and Architectural Perspectives on the Seventeenth-Century Chesapeake," *William and Mary Quarterly, Third Series* 64, no. 3 (July 2007), 451–522; Cary Carson, Norman F. Barka, William M. Kelso, Gary Wheeler Stone, and Dell Upton, "Impermanent Architecture in the Southern American Colonies," *Winterthur Portfolio* 16 (1981),

135–96; Matthew Johnson, *Housing Culture: Traditional English Architecture in an English Landscape* (Washington, DC: Smithsonian Institution Press, 1993); Matthew Johnson, *English Houses 1300–1800: Vernacular Architecture, Social Life* (New York: Longman, 2010).

30 "Washington to Benjamin Harrison," March 21, 1781.

31 Ibid.

32 "George Washington to John Augustine Washington, January 16, 1783," *The Writings of George Washington* (Washington, DC: Government Printing Office, 1931), 26:41.

33 Ibid.

34 "George Washington to Mary Washington, February 15, 1787," in Theodore J. Crackel, ed., *The Papers of George Washington Digital Edition* (Charlottesville: University of Virginia Press, 2008).

35 Ibid.

36 "George Washington to the Mayor and Commonality of Fredericksburg, February 4, 1784," *The Writings of George Washington* (Washington, DC: Government Printing Office, 1931), 27:332.

37 See Dorothy Twohig, "The Making of George Washington," in Warren Hofstra, ed., *George Washington and the Virginia Backcountry* (Madison, WI: Madison House, 1998), 6–8.

38 *Diaries,* 52.

39 George Washington, *The Papers of George Washington, Colonial Series,* ed. W. W. Abbot (Charlottesville: University of Virginia Press, 1983–1995), 1:6, hereafter cited as *PGW.*

40 "George Washington to James Craik," in Dorothy Twohig et al., eds., *The Papers of George Washington, Confederation Series* (Charlottesville, University of Virginia Press, 1992), 6:423.

41 I will discuss this fire in detail later. Jack Warren was the scholar who made the first argument for the house fire, based mostly on documentary evidence, all discussed later. The error was the assumption that it was a total conflagration and not the more limited fire the site revealed. Warren, "The Childhood of George Washington."

42 Laura Galke, "The Mother of the Father of Our Country: Mary Ball Washington's Genteel Domestic Habits," *Northeast Historical Archaeology* 39 (2009), 29–43.

43 Chase, "A Stake in the West," 159–94.

44 Warren, "The Childhood of George Washington," 5793.

45 Lawrence Martin, ed., *The George Washington Atlas* (Washington, DC: The Washington Bicentennial Commission, 1932), Plate 9.

46 *PGW,* 10:2.

47 Ibid., 2.

48 Ibid., 10.

49 Ibid., 9.

50 There are other examples of Washington being involved in secret surveys. During the same year of 1771, Washington asked William Crawford to conduct a private survey of Ohio Valley lands. See Patrick Griffin, *American Leviathan: Empire, Nation, and Revolutionary Frontier* (New York: Hill and Wang, 2007), 122.

51 1771 Survey Notes.

52 Dale Brown, "Report on Preliminary Ground Survey on the Grave Yard Area of Ferry Farm," George Washington Foundation, Fredericksburg, VA, 2011.

53 1771 Survey Notes.

54 George Washington, 1771 Survey of Ferry Farm.

55 The name comes from Robert "King" Carter, whose estate, Nomini Hall, sat at the end of the road. It served as the main commercial and administrative highway down the Northern Neck proprietary.

56 *PGW,* 1:6.

57 See Freeman, *George Washington: A Biography,* Vol. 1 (New York: Charles Scribner's Sons, 1948).

58 Washington, 1771 Survey.

59 Martin, *The George Washington Atlas,* Preface. Questions about the location of Washington's childhood home were invented largely in the 1920s by Charles Arthur Hoppin, the project historian for the Wakefield Association, which was then fundraising to turn the Westmoreland County birthplace site into a shrine. See Charles Arthur Hoppin, "The House in Which George Washington Was Born," *Tyler's Quarterly Historical and Genealogical Magazine* 8, no. 2 (October 1926), 75.

60 *Virginia Gazette* ad quoted in George H. S. King, "Washington's Boyhood Home," *William and Mary Quarterly* Second Series 17, no. 2 (April 1937), 275.

61 Ferling, *The Ascent of George Washington*, 10.

62 See Joseph Manca, *George Washington's Eye: Landscape, Architecture, and Design at Mount Vernon* (Baltimore, MD: Johns Hopkins University Press, 2012), 14–55.

63 James Thomas Flexner, *Washington: The Indispensable Man* (New York: Little Brown, 1969), 58–59.

3. THE SUBTERRANEAN YOUNG WASHINGTON

1 This quotation was broken in segments and appears to represent parts of Governor Kaine's comments to reporters after his speech at Ferry Farm on July 3, 2008. See Theresa Vargas, "Remains of George Washington's Boyhood Home Finally Unearthed," *The Washington Post* (July 3, 2008), http://www.bendbulletin.com/csp/mediapool/sites/BendBulletin/News/story.csp?cid=1465082&sid=497&fid=151.

2 I traced out details of this conflict in *Where the Cherry Tree Grew*, chapter 8. See also Jim Hall, "Protecting the Past," *Free Lance Star*, April 1, 1995, B5; *The Washington Post*, February 25, 1995, F18; "History of Wal-Mart Ferry Farm Deal Traced," *Stafford County Sun*, August 28/29, 1996, A13; Michael Janofsky, "Protesters Fight a Plan for Washington's Home," *The New York Times*, March 13, 1996, A12; "What's Buried at Ferry Farm," *Free Lance Star*, March 2, 1996, A10; "Is Ferry Farm a 'Pipe Dream'?" *Free Lance Star*, March 4, 1996, A6; Maryann Haggerty, "First in War, First in Peace—Next in Wal-Mart," *The Washington Post*, March 7, 1996, A1; Christine Neuberger, "Wal-Mart Sticking to Plan as Decision Is Delayed," *Richmond Times-Dispatch*, March 12, 1996, B3; and Rusty Dennen, "Wal-Mart Battle over Ferry Farm Site Recalled," *Free Lance Star*, July 5, 2008 (digital article reposted online at Fredericksburg.com).

3 "What's Buried at Ferry Farm," A10.

4 David Zax, "George Washington's Boyhood Home," *Smithsonian Magazine*, September 2008, available at Smithsonianmag.com.

5 For examples, see Julia King and Douglas Ubelacker, "Living and Dying at Patuxent Point," in Julia King and Douglas Ubelacker, eds., *Living and Dying on the 17th Century Patuxent Frontier* (Crownsville, MD: Maryland Historical Trust, 1996), 105–20; Thao Phung, Julia

King, and Douglas Ubelacker, "Alcohol, Tobacco, and Excessive Animal Protein: The Question of Adequate Diet in the Seventeenth-Century Chesapeake," *Historical Archaeology* 43, no. 2 (2009), 61–82; Douglas Ubelaker, "Pipe Wear: Dental Impact of Colonial Culture," *Anthropologie* 34, no. 3 (1996), 321–27; and Douglas Owsley and Douglas Ubelaker, "Isotopic Evidence for Diet in the Seventeenth-Century Colonial Chesapeake," *American Antiquity* 68, no. 1 (2003), 129–39.

6 Julia King, "Household Archaeology, Identities, and Biographies," in Dan Hicks and Mary Beaudry, eds., *The Cambridge Companion to Historical Archaeology* (New York: Cambridge University Press, 2006), 293–313.

7 Several reports support my discussion of the site's archaeology. See David Muraca, Paul Nasca, and Philip Levy, *Report on the Excavation of the Washington Farm: The 2002 and 2003 Field Seasons,* The George Washington Foundation, Fredericksburg, VA State Site No. 44ST174, 2011; David Muraca, Paul Nasca, and Philip Levy, *Report on the Excavation of the Washington Farm: The 2004 and 2005 Field Seasons,* The George Washington Foundation, Fredericksburg, VA State Site No. 44ST174, 2010; David Muraca, Paul Nasca, and Philip Levy, *Report on the Excavations at the Washington Farm: The 2006 and 2007 Field Seasons,* The George Washington Foundation, Fredericksburg, VA State Site No. 44ST174, 2010; William L. Leigh, "Phase 1 Archaeological Survey of 4 Acres in Parcel B at Ferry Farm, Stafford County, Virginia," James River Institute for Archaeology, Inc., Jamestown, VA, December 1989; James G. Harrison and Robert M. Adams, "Archaeological Survey, Testing, and Monitoring of a Sewer and Water Corridor at Ferry Farm, Stafford County, Virginia," Harrison and Associates, Fredericksburg, VA, May 7, 1990; James G. Harrison and Robert M. Adams, "Ferry Farm II: A Phase I Archaeological Survey of a 30 Acre Tract at Ferry Farm, Stafford County, Virginia," Harrison and Associates, Fredericksburg, VA, August 27, 1990; Alain Outlaw et al., "A Study of the Architecture, the History, and the Archaeology of George Washington's Ferry Farm, Stafford County, Virginia," Espey, Huston & Associates, Williamsburg, VA, January 1993; Dennis Pogue, "George Washington's Boyhood Home: An Assessment of Archaeological Findings," Mount Vernon, VA,

1996; Gary Norman, "Archaeology at George Washington's Ferry Farm: Prepared for the George Washington's Ferry Farm Steering Committee," Fredericksburg, VA, 1997; Gary Norman, "The 'George Washington Survey Office' at Ferry Farm," Kenmore Association, Inc., Fredericksburg, VA, 1997; and Paul Schuster, "A Preliminary Report on Archaeological Investigations at George Washington's Ferry Farm: 44ST174—1997 and 1998 Seasons," Kenmore Association, Fredericksburg, VA, 1998.

8 John Ferling, *The Ascent of George Washington* (New York: Bloomsbury Press, 2010), 10.

9 Joseph Ellis, *His Excellency George Washington* (New York: Alfred Knopf, 2004), 9.

10 Paul Johnson, *George Washington: The Founding Father* (New York: Harper Collins e-books, 2009), 32. Additionally, a trend toward targeted biographies, as opposed to full-scale "life and times" biographies, has made it even easier to change over to selected significant moments. These works include those of Richard Brookhiser, *Founding Father: Rediscovering George Washington* (New York: The Free Press, 1997); Peter Henriques, *Realistic Visionary: A Portrait of George Washington* (Charlottesville: University Press of Virginia, 2006); and Edward Lengel, *General George Washington: A Military Life* (New York: Random House, 2007). Some of the highest-profile Washington writing of late eschews biography altogether. Needless to say, Ferry Farm plays no role in well-received books like those by Francois Furstenburg and Henry Wiencek.

11 Douglas Southall Freeman, *George Washington: A Biography* (New York: Charles Scribner, 1948), 77.

12 Samuel Eliot Morison, "The Young Man Washington," in James Morton Smith, ed., *George Washington: A Profile* (New York: Hill and Wang, 1969), 42–43.

13 James Flexner, *Washington the Indispensable Man* (New York: Little Brown Co., 1974), 4.

14 Paul Longmore, *The Invention of George Washington* (Charlottesville: University Press of Virginia, 1999), 6.

15 Jack Warren, "The Childhood of George Washington," *Northern Neck of Virginia Historical Magazine* 49, no. 1 (1999), 5791. Warren was

probably mistaken, in part, about the move, as he tied it to an erroneous assumption that the Washingtons had to rebuild the Strother
home at Ferry Farm.

16 Charles Arthur Hoppin, "The House in Which George Washington
Was Born," *Tyler's Quarterly Historical and Genealogical Magazine* 8,
no. 2 (October 1926), 75.

17 Harrison Clark, *All Cloudless Glory: The Life of George Washington,*
2 vols. (Washington, DC: Regnery Press, 1996).

18 George Washington, *The Papers of George Washington, Colonial Series,* W. W. Abbot, ed. (Charlottesville: University of Virginia Press,
1983–1995), 1:6.

19 Thena Jones, "Reconstructing the Washington Farm and Catlett
Patents," Report on File, George Washington Foundation, Fredericksburg, VA, 1993.

20 This issue of confirming assumptions in the written record has
dogged historical archaeology ever since Ivor Noel Hume called it
the "'handmaiden of history," a term he meant as praise, not con-
demnation. See Philip Levy, "Always a Handmaiden, Never a Bride:
The Relationship Between Historians and Historical Archaeologists,"
Archaeology Magazine (March 2000), published online at Archaeol-
ogy.Org; and Alan Mayne, "On the Edges of History: Reflections
on Historical Archaeology," *American Historical Review* 113, no. 1
(2008), 93–118. The best work I think has moved beyond this worry
and blended approaches to make contributions that are at once
theoretical, methodological, and historical. For some of my favorite
examples, see Julia A. King, *Archaeology, Narrative, and the Politics of
the Past: The View from the Southern Maryland* (Knoxville: University
of Tennessee Press, 2012); Mary C. Beaudry, *Findings: The Material
Culture of Needlework and Sewing* (New Haven, CT: Yale University
Press, 2007); Stephen A. Mrozowski, Grace H. Ziesing, and Mary C.
Beaudry, *Living on the Boott: Historical Archaeology at the Boott Mills
Boardinghouses, Lowell, Massachusetts* (Amherst: University of Massa-
chusetts Press, 1996); Matthew Johnson, *An Archaeology of Capitalism*
(Hoboken, NJ: Wiley-Blackwell, 1996); Barbara J. Little, *Historical
Archaeology: What the Past Matters* (Walnut Creek, CA: Left Coast
Press, 2007); and Barbara J. Heath and Jack Gary, *Jefferson's Popular*

Forest: Unearthing a Virginia Plantation (Gainesville: University of Florida Press, 2012).

21 The George Washington Foundation's Laura Galke has brought a careful eye to some of the site's unique finds and reads in them the actions of Mary. Galke argues that Mary became masterful at doing much with little. See "The Mother of the Father of Our Country: Mary Ball Washington's Genteel Domestic Habits," *Northeast Historical Archaeology* 38 (2009), 29–48.

22 Ibid.

23 Richard Bushman, *The Refinement of America: Persons, Houses, Cities* (New York: Vintage Books, 1993); Cary Carson, Ronald Hoffman, and Peter J. Albert, eds., *Of Consuming Interests: The Style of Life in the Eighteenth Century* (Charlottesville: University of Virginia Press, 1994).

24 T. H. Breen, *The Marketplace of Revolution: How Consumer Politics Shaped American Independence* (New York: Oxford University Press, 2005); John Coombs and Douglas Bradburn, eds., *Early Modern Virginia: Reconsidering the Old Dominion* (Charlottesville: University of Virginia Press, 2011).

25 See Galke, "The Mother of the Father of Our Country."

26 Albert Tillson, *Accommodating Revolutions: Virginia's Northern Neck in an Era of Transformations, 1760–1810* (Charlottesville: University of Virginia Press, 2010); Alan Kulikoff, *Tobacco and Slaves: The Development of Southern Cultures in the Chesapeake, 1680–1800* (Chapel Hill: University of North Carolina Press, 1986); T. H. Breen, *Tobacco Culture: The Mentality of the Great Tidewater Planters on the Eve of Revolution* (Princeton, NJ: Princeton University Press, Reprint 2010).

27 Augustine Washington's Will, 1743, King George County Wills, King George County, Virginia, Book 1, 138, hereafter cited as AW Will.

28 Moncure Daniel Conway, *Barons of the Potomac and the Rappahannock* (New York: The Grolier Club, 1892), 240.

29 King George County Order Book, King George County Wills, King George County, Virginia, Book 1, 670.

30 M. L. Weems, *The Life of Washington,* ed. Peter Onuf (Armonk, NY: M. E. Sharp Press, 1996), 6–7.

31 Carl Lounsbury, "Beaux-Arts Ideals and Colonial Reality: The Recon-
    struction of Williamsburg's Capitol, 1928–1934," *Journal of the Society
    of Architectural Historians* 49, no. 4 (December 1990), 373–89; William
    B. Rhoads, "The Colonial Revival and American Nationalism," *Journal
    of the Society of Architectural Historians* 35, no. 4 (December 1976),
    239–54; Bridget May, "Progressivism and the Colonial Revival: The
    Modern Colonial House, 1900–1920," *Winterthur Portfolio* 26, no. 2
    (Summer–Autumn 1991), 107–22; Barksdale Maynard, "The Early
    Nineteenth-Century Rediscovery of American Colonial Architecture,"
    Journal of the Society of Architectural Historians 59, no. 3 (September
    2000), 338–57; Seth Bruggeman, "Costumed Ladies and Federal
    Agents," in *Here, George Washington Was Born: Memory, Material
    Culture, and the Public History of a National Monument* (Athens: Uni-
    versity of Georgia Press, 2008), 51–85; Karal Ann Marling, "The Colo-
    nial Revival: Heroic Imagery for the American Home, 1893–1924," in
    *George Washington Slept Here: Colonial Revivals and American Culture,
    1876–1986* (Cambridge, MA: Harvard University Press, 1988), 151–84.

32 Mary Beaudry, "Household Structure and the Archaeological Record:
    Examples from New World Historical Sites," in *The Written and the
    Wrought: Complimentary Sources in Historical Archaeology, Essays in
    Honor of James Deetz* (Berkeley, CA: Kroeber Anthropological Society
    Papers, 1995), 1–16; Mary Beaudry, "House and Household: The
    Archaeology of Domestic Life," in Geof Egan and Robert Michael,
    eds., *Old and New Worlds* (Oxford: Oxbow Books, 1999), 117–26.
    The conclusions about Mary Washington's consumption patterns risk
    falling into a problem Beaudry outlined—specifically, that such stud-
    ies tend to confirm insights from documents ("Household Structure
    and the Archaeological Record," 119). The solution to this risk is to
    follow Beaudry's advice to not treat the household as a reflection of
    single homeowner's will and purchasing power and instead to see it
    as a matrix with multiple players making differing contributions to
    its makeup. See also, King, "Household Archaeology, Identities, and
    Biographies," 293–313.

33 I rely here on King's definition in "Household Archaeology, Identities,
    and Biographies."

34 Archaeologist Jerome Handler has found the only other carnelian

beads in the Americas. See his online newsletter for "An African-Type Healer/Diviner and His Grave Goods: A Burial from a Plantation Slave Cemetery in Barbados, West Indies," 1995, http://www.diaspora.uiuc.edu/newsletter.html; Jerome Handler, "An African-Type Healer/Diviner and His Grave Goods: A Burial from the Plantation Slave Cemetery in Barbados, West Indies," *International Journal of Historical Archaeology* 1, no. 2 (1997). See also Laura Wilkie, "Secret and Sacred: Contextualizing the Artifacts of African American Magic and Religion," *Historical Archaeology* 31 (1997): 81–106; Christopher Fennell, "Conjuring Boundaries: Inferring Past Identities from Religious Artifacts," *International Journal of Historical Archaeology* 4, no. 4 (2000); Yvonne Chireau, *Black Magic: Religion and the African American Conjuring Tradition* (Los Angeles: University of California Press, 2003); and Laura Galke, "Ritual Caches and Ethnicity: How Do We Recognize Them and Who Is Responsible for Their Creation?" *Journal of Middle Atlantic Archaeology* 19 (2003), 59–71.

35 David Muraca, "Murder and Magic at Ferry Farm," *Journal of Fredericksburg History* (2009), 11.

36 D. Brad Hatch, "A Report on the Analysis of Faunal Remains from the Washington Root Cellar and Slave Quarter (44ST174)," Department of Anthropology, University of Tennessee, Knoxville, June 2014. See also Steven Mrozowki, "Environments of History: Biological Dimensions of Historical Archaeology," in Martin Hall and Stephen Silliman, eds., *Historical Archaeology,* Blackwell Studies in Global Archaeology (Oxford: Blackwell Publishing, 2006), 23–41; and David Landon, "Zooarchaeology and Historical Archaeology Progress and Prospects," *Journal of Archaeological Method and Theory* 12, no. 1 (March 2005), 1–36.

37 Philip Levy, David Muraca, and Brad Hatch, "Two Meals for Two Tables: Faunal Data from Washington Home Site Cellars," Society for Historical Archaeology Annual Meetings, Seattle, Washington, January 2015.

38 Laura Galke, David Muraca, Philip Levy, John Coombs, and Amy Muraca, "Small Finds, Space, and Social Context: Exploring Agency in Historical Archaeology," *Northeastern Historical Archaeology* 40 (June 2011), 1–18.

39 Cary Carson, "The Consumer Revolution in Colonial British America: Why Demand?," in Cary Carson, Ronald Hoffman, and Peter J. Albert, eds., *Of Consuming Interests: The Style of Life in the Eighteenth Century* (Charlottesville: University Press of Virginia, 1994), 483–697.

40 Breen, *Marketplace of Revolution*.

41 Michael Rozbicki Byrd, *The Complete Colonial Gentleman: Cultural Legitimacy in Plantation America* (Charlottesville: University of Virginia Press, 2003).

42 Mary-Cate Garden, Philip Levy, Nicole M. Hayes, Lisa Fischer, Joanne Bowen, Donna Sawyers, and David Muraca, "Life at Richard Charlton's Coffeehouse: A Story of Archaeology, History, and Hot Drinks in Eighteenth-Century Williamsburg," Archaeological Report (Colonial Williamsburg Foundation, Williamsburg, VA, 2000).

43 Arthur Waugh, ed., *The Pamphlet Library* (London: Kegan Paul, Trench, Trubner, 1898), 367.

44 Nicholas Noyes, "An Essay Against Periwigs," 1702, in Myra Jehlen and Michael Warner, eds., *English Literatures of America 1500–1800* (London: Routledge, 1996), 410.

45 Ibid., 411.

46 Galke et al., "Small Finds, Space, and Social Context," 1–18; Thomas Bullock, Maurice B. Tonkin, and Raymond R. Townsend, *Wigmaking in Colonial America* (Williamsburg, VA: Colonial Williamsburg Foundation, 1957); Karin Calvert, "The Function of Fashion in 18th-Century America," in Cary Carson, Ronald Hoffman, and Peter J. Albert, eds., *Of Consuming Interests: The Style of Life in the Eighteenth Century* (Charlottesville: University Press of Virginia, 1994), 252–306; Stevens J. Cox, *The Wigmaker's Art in the 18th Century* (Philadelphia: George S. MacManus Company, 1965); Lynn Festa, "Personal Effects: Wigs and Possessive Individualism in the Long Eighteenth Century" *Eighteenth Century Life* 29, no. 2 (2005), 47–90; Richard Le Cheminant, "The Development of the Pipeclay Hair Curler: A Preliminary Study," in Peter Davey, ed., *The Archaeology of the Clay Tobacco Pipe. VII, More Pipes and Kilns from England,* British Archaeology Report 1982 Brit. ser. 100, 345–54.

47 George Washington, Account Book, May 16, 1752.

48 Edward A. Chappell, "Housing a Nation: The Transformation of Liv-

ing Standards in Early America," in Cary Carson, Ronald Hoffman, and Peter J. Albert, eds., *Of Consuming Interests: The Style of Life in the Eighteenth Century* (Charlottesville: University Press of Virginia, 1994). See also Denis Pogue, "The Transformation of America: Georgian Sensibility, Capitalist Conspiracy, or Consumer Revolution?" *Historical Archaeology* 35, no. 2 (2001), 41–57.

49 Fraser Neiman, "Temporal Patterning in House Plans from the 17th Century Chesapeake," in Theodore Reinhart and Dennis Pogue, eds., *The Archaeology of 17th Century Virginia* (Richmond: Archaeology Society of Virginia, 1993); Cary Carson et al., "Impermanent Architecture in the Southern Colonies," *Winterthur Portfolio* 16 (1981), 135–96; Willie Graham et al., "Archaeological Perspectives on the Seventeenth-Century Chesapeake," *William and Mary Quarterly* Third Series 64, no. 3 (July 2007), 451–522.

50 Howard Colvin and John Newman, eds., *Of Building: Roger North's Writings on Architecture* (Oxford: Clarendon Press, 1981), 68. See also John Coombs, *Building the Machine: The Development of Slavery and Slave Society in Early America,* PhD dissertation, The College of William and Mary, Williamsburg, VA, 2003, Chapter 6, 180–210.

51 Donald Lienbaugh, "All the Annoyances and Inconveniences of the Country," *Winterthur Portfolio* 29 (1994), 1–18.

52 Moncure Conway, *Barons of the Potomack and Rappahannock* (New York: The Grolier Club, 1892), 68–69.

53 Ibid. See also Warren, "The Childhood of George Washington," 5790–91; "Robert Douglas to George Washington," May 25, 1795, George Washington Papers, Library of Congress; Conway, *Barons of the Potomac and Rappahannock,* 68–69; David Humphreys, *Life of General Washington,* ed. Rosemarie Zagarri (Athens: University of Georgia Press, 2006).

54 Humphreys, *Life of General Washington.*

55 Wayne Whipple, *The Story-Life of George Washington* (Philadelphia: Lindsay and Banks, 1911), 30–31; William Thayer, *The Farmer Boy and How He Became Commander in Chief* (Boston: Walker, Wise, and Co., 1864), 6.

56 Whipple, *The Story-Life of George Washington,* 41.

57 Hoppin, "The House in Which George Washington Was Born."

58 Rupert Hughes, *George Washington: The Human Being and the Hero* (New York: William Morrow Co., 1926), 17.

59 Weems, *The Life of Washington*, 46.

60 Pope's Creek Fire Materials, Charles Hatch, *Chapters in the History of Pope's Creek Plantation,* 100–101.

61 "Robert Douglas to George Washington," May 25, 1795, George Washington Papers, Library of Congress; Conway, *Barons of the Potomac and Rappahannock,* 68–69.

62 Warren, "The Childhood of George Washington," 5785–5809.

63 This conclusion is based on a 2013 reexamination of George Washington Birthplace National Monument's full archaeological record and collection. The 1930s archaeology of the site was far less conclusive than later interpretations have held. See "Draft Report," Philip Levy and Amy Muraca, *2013 George Washington Birthplace National Monument Archaeological Reassessment Report of Findings,* Westmoreland, VA, 2014.

4. FRUITS OF MORALITY AND FRUITS OF THE MARKET

1 Mason Locke Weems, *Mason Locke Weems: His Works and Ways in Three Volumes,* ed. Emily Ellsworth Ford Skeel (New York: n.p., 1929), Vol. 2, 126, hereafter cited as Skeel. This three-volume set also contains a wealth of information about Weems and his publication history.

2 Weems has had an array of scholars over the centuries. See Peter Onuf's introductory essay in M. L. Weems, *The Life of Washington* ed. Peter Onuf (Armonk, NY: M. E. Sharp Press, 1996), hereafter cited as *LoW*; Garry Wills, *Cincinnatus: George Washington and the Enlightenment* (Garden City, NJ: Doubleday, 1984), 27–53; Edward Lengal echoes the current consensus on Weems in *Inventing George Washington: America's Founder, in Myth and Memory* (New York: Harper Collins, 2011), 18–26. The most enduring and thorough biography of Weems remains Lewis Leary, *The Book-Peddling Parson* (Chapel Hill, NC: Algonquin Press, 1984). See also Skeel, *Mason Locke Weems.*

3 Weems, *The Life of Washington.*

4   Most of the writing about Weems has been interested in questions of the veracity of his work. There have been some exceptions to discussing only Weems as truth teller or a liar. Catherine Clinton, "'Wallowing in a Swamp of Sin': Parson Weems, Sex, and Murder in Early South Carolina," in Catherine Clinton and Michele Gillespie, eds., *The Devil's Lane: Sex and Race in the Early South* (New York: Oxford University Press, 1997), 24–38; Francois Furstenberg, "Mason Locke Weems: Spreading the American Gospel," in *In the Name of the Father: Washington's Legacy, Slavery, and the Making of a Nation* (New York: Penguin Press, 2006), 105–45. See also Scott Casper, *Constructing American Lives: Biography and Culture in Nineteenth-Century America* (Chapel Hill: University of North Carolina Press, 1999), 19–77.

5   David Glassberg, *Sense of History: The Place of the Past in American Life* (Amherst: University of Massachusetts Press, 2001), 19.

6   Skeel, 2:xix; Harrold Kellock, *Parson Weems of the Cherry Tree* (New York: The Century, 1928), 12.

7   Skeel, 3:388.

8   Ibid., 394.

9   Ibid.

10   Ibid., 395.

11   Ibid., 398–99.

12   Ibid., 397.

13   Leary, *The Book Peddling Parson,* 10.

14   Ibid., 12.

15   Bishop Mead, *Old Churches, Ministers and Families of Virginia* (Philadelphia: J.B. Lippincott, 1897), 232–37. Also see Lawrence Wroth, *Parson Weems: A Biographical and Critical Study* (Baltimore, MD: Lord Baltimore Press, 1911), 15.

16   Kellock, *Parson Weems of the Cherry Tree,* 36.

17   Wroth, *Parson Weems,* 17.

18   Kellock, *Parson Weems of the Cherry Tree,* 21–23.

19   Ibid., 22–23.

20   Leary, *The Book-Selling Parson,* 14.

21   Jennifer Hughes, *Telling Laughter: Hilarity and Democracy in the Nineteenth-Century United States,* dissertation, Emory University,

Athens, GA, 2009, 74–75. Hughes references David Reynolds, *Beneath the American Renaissance: The Subversive Imagination in the Age of Emerson and Melville* (Cambridge, MA: Harvard University Press, 1989).

22 Wroth, *Parson Weems,* 43.

23 Leary, *The Book-Peddling Parson,* 13.

24 Dixon Wecter, *The Hero in America: A Chronicle of Hero Worship* (New York: Charles Scribner and Sons, 1941), 133.

25 Francois Furstenburg, *In the Name of the Father: Washington's Legacy, Slavery, and the Making of a Nation* (New York: Penguin, 2006), 137.

26 Leary, *The Book-Peddling Parson,* 27.

27 Francois Furstenburg argues that portions of Washington's library may have been stocked by Weems specifically for the favor of the inevitable thank you letter and the seeming approval it afforded. See *In the Name of the Father,* 110, 116.

28 Cathy N. Davidson, *Revolution and the Word: The Rise of the Novel in America* (New York: Oxford University Press, 2004), 83.

29 Casper, *Constructing American Lives,* 72.

30 Furstenburg, *In the Name of the Father,* 145.

31 Skeel, 2:127.

32 Ibid., 127.

33 Ibid., 136.

34 Ibid., 152.

35 Ibid., 387.

36 Ibid.

37 Ebenezer Hazard, "The Journal of Ebenezer Hazard in Virginia 1777," ed. Fred Shelley, *Virginia Magazine of History and Biography* 62, no. 4 (October 1954), 419.

38 *LoW,* 6–7.

39 Ibid.

40 Furstenburg, *In the Name of the Father,* 107.

41 *LoW,* 8, 12.

42 Ibid., 12.

43 Ibid., 11.

44 Ibid., 8.

45 Ibid. Weems sets this story in 1737. That would be before the family

actually had moved to Ferry Farm. But he also set it amid a suite of childhood tales that focused on this land specifically. Because these are fictional tales—and I would argue meant to be read as parables and not history—there is no need to worry too much about the specifics of actual dates. Weems associated these tales in their entirety with Ferry Farm, and all subsequent lore has followed his lead.

46 Dolores P. Sullivan, *William Holmes McGuffey: Schoolmaster to the Nation* (Cranbury, NJ: Associated University Press, 1994), 46–62.

47 William Thayer, *The Farmer Boy and How He Became Commander in Chief* (Boston: Walker, Wise, and Co., 1864), 45.

48 Harold Mahan, *Benson J. Lossing, and Historical Writing in the United States, 1830–1890* (Westport, CT: Greenwood, 1996).

49 Benson Lossing, *Pictoral Field-Book of the American Revolution* (New York: Harper Brothers, 1852), 2:214, hereafter cited as *PFBAR*.

50 *LoW*, 9.

51 *PFBAR*, 2:220.

52 Ibid.

53 Ibid., 2:219.

54 Ralph Waldo Emerson, "The American Scholar," *The Collected Works*, Vol. 1 (Cambridge, MA: Harvard University Press, 1971), 69.

55 John Gadsby Chapman, *The American Drawing-Book: A Manual for the Amateur* (New York: J.S. Redfield Clinton Hall, 1847), 2.

56 Robert Chaianese, "Avoidance of the Sublime in Nineteenth-Century American Landscape Art: An Environmental Reading of Depicted Land," *Amerikastudien/American Studies* 43, no. 3 (1998), 437–61.

57 "Memoranda of an Agreement, October 29, 1839," Mann and Teasdale Collected Cases, transcribed by Jill Ficarrotta, Ferry Farm Archives, Fredericksburg, VA, 7, 11, hereafter cited as "Mann and Teasdale."

58 "Mann and Teasdale," 15.

59 Early Fredericksburg has not had the study it should, its larger history having been somewhat overshadowed by the battle and the effects of the war. One excellent and enduring study is Oscar Darter, *Colonial Fredericksburg and Neighborhood in Perspective* (New York: Twayne Publishers, 1957).

60 The scale of this enterprise is still visible in the form a deep railroad cut, now a footpath, in Alum Springs Park just off of Route 3 in town.

61 Jane Hollenbeck Conner, *Lincoln in Stafford* (Stafford, VA: Parker Publishing, 2006), 13.

62 Mason Locke Weems, *The Life of Washington,* ed. Marcus Cunliffe (Cambridge, MA: Harvard University Press, 1962), 3.

63 William Draper, *Recollections of a Varied Career* (Boston: Little, Brown, and Co., 1908), 97.

64 Correspondence of the Herald, May 13, 1862, Quiner Collection, State Historical Society of Wisconsin copies in Ferry Farm Collection, File 2 "Civil War Letters." Hereafter cited as FFCWL. Horace Currier, Letter, May 18, 1862, File 2, FFCWL.

65 John H. W. Stuckenberg, *"I'm Surrounded by Methodists: The Diary of John H. W. Stuckenberg Chaplain of the 145th Pennsylvania Volunteer Infantry,"* ed. David Hedrick and Gordon Barry Davis Jr. (Gettysburg, PA: Thomas Publications, 1995), 55.

66 Correspondence of the Herald, May 13, 1862, Letters of the Seventh Wisconsin, May 15, 1862, FFCWL. George Brayton, Sunday May 11, 1862, *1862 Diary,* Manassas National Battlefield Files.

67 S. Millett Thompson, *A Diary Covering Three Years and a Day* (Boston: Houghton Mifflin and Co., 1888), 39.

68 Ibid., 94. Weems's original claims not that George chopped down the tree but rather that he chopped *at* it, and Weems opined that he "doubts the tree ever got the better of it." Weems, *LoW.*

69 Thompson, *A Diary Covering Three Years and a Day,* 68.

70 FFCWL File 4 P 7.

71 Lisa Brady, *War upon the Land: Military Strategy and the Transformation of Southern Landscapes During the American Civil War* (Athens: University of Georgia Press, 2012), 20. Brady shows how this perception of the South as being alternately a wilderness or poorly used by its inadequate stewards served as a justification for the widespread destruction the Northern soldiers wrought during the course of the war.

72 James Sterling, in Alan Gallay, ed., *Voice of the Old South* (Athens: University of Georgia Press, 1994), 245–46; Charles Dickens, *American Notes for General Circulation* (London: Chapman and Hall, 1842), 15–16.

73 In two papers presented at the Society for Historical Archaeology Annual Meetings, Paul Nasca described the fate of Ferry Farm's build-

ings between 1862 and 1865. I rely on his excellent, but unfortunately unpublished, work here, as I did in *Where the Cherry Tree Grew*.

74 James Deetz, "Landscapes as Cultural Statements," in William Kelso and Rachel Most, eds., *Landscape Archaeology* (Charlottesville: University Press of Virginia, 1990), 1.

75 "A Home for Neglected Boys," published by Lifeline, Youth for Christ, Wheaton, IL: Archives of the Billy Graham Center.

5. "THE LOCAL APPELLATION BASED ON TRADITION ONLY"

1 Dixon Wecter, *The Hero in America: A Chronicle of Hero Worship* (New York: Scribner's, 1941), 135.

2 *Fredericksburg Daily Star,* Fredericksburg, VA, September 7, 1903, 3.

3 "Colbert Farm Stationery," *Colbert vs. Gressitt,* Stafford County Court House, Stafford, VA.

4 George Allan England, "Washington's Old Home Farm," *Daughters of the American Revolution Magazine* 59, no. 12 (December 1925), 738.

5 The history of Virginia historical preservation breaks down into a few camps. One camp situates the narrative within local, state, and national politics. See David James Kiracofe, "The Jamestown Jubilees: 'State Patriotism' and Virginia Identity in the Early Nineteenth Century," *Virginia Magazine of History and Biography* 110, no. 1 (2002), 35–68; and Anders Greenspan, *Creating Colonial Williamsburg: The Restoration of Virginia's Eighteenth-Century Capital* (Chapel Hill: University of North Carolina Press, 2002). Colonial Williamsburg, in particular, lends itself to this approach as well as being a unique object of fascination. George Yetter, *Williamsburg Before and After: The Rebirth of Virginia's Colonial Capital* (Williamsburg, VA: Colonial Williamsburg Foundation, 1988), is at once overview and celebration. The museum as preserved landscape and living object was at the center of an important and deeply divisive discussion; see Eric and Richard Handler, "After Authenticity at an American Heritage Site," *American Anthropologist* 98, no. 3 (September 1996), 568–78; Eric Gable, Richard Handler, and Anna Lawson, "On the Uses of Relativism: Fact, Conjecture, and Black and White Histories at Colonial Williamsburg,"

American Ethnologist 19, no. 4 (November 1992), 791–805; and Cary Carson, "Lost in the Fun House: A Commentary on Anthropologists' First Contact with History Museums," *Journal of American History* 81, no. 1 (June 1994), 137–50. See also Richard Handler and Eric Gable, *The New History in an Old Museum: Creating the Past at Colonial Williamsburg* (Durham, NC: Duke University Press, 1997). Other scholars explore the various and often competing interests that shaped preservation movements and the histories they created and offered. Most notable among these are Charles Hosmer, *Preservation Comes of Age: From Williamsburg to the National Trust, 1926–1949* (Charlottesville: University Press of Virginia, 1981); James Lindgren, *Preserving the Old Dominion: Historic Preservation and Virginia Traditionalism* (Charlottesville: University Press of Virginia, 1993); and Seth Bruggeman, *Here, George Washington Was Born: Memory, Material Culture, and the Public History of a National Monument* (Athens: University of Georgia Press, 2008). Virginia preservationists play a large role in the literature on the colonial revival. See Carl Lounsbury, "Beaux-Arts Ideals and Colonial Reality: The Reconstruction of Williamsburg's Capitol, 1928–1934," *Journal of the Society of Architectural Historians* 49, no. 4 (December 1990), 373–89; and Karal Ann Marling, *George Washington Slept Here: Colonial Revivals and American Culture, 1876–1986* (Cambridge, MA: Harvard University Press, 1988).

6 James Lindgren, "'Virginia Needs Heroes': Historic Preservation on the Progressive Era," *The Public Historian* 13, no. 1 (Winter 1991), 22–23.

7 Lindgren, *Preserving the Old Dominion*.

8 Bruggeman, *Here, George Washington Was Born*.

9 Hugh Trevor-Roper, "The Highland Tradition of Scotland," in Eric Hobsbawm and Terrence Ranger, eds., *The Invention of Tradition* (New York: Cambridge University Press, 1983), 15–41; Yael Zerubavel, "The Historic, the Legendary, and the Incredible: Invented Tradition and Collective Memory," in John R. Gillis, ed., *Commemorations: The National Politics of Identity* (Princeton, NJ: Princeton University Press, 1994), 105–123.

10 Andrea Stulman Dennett, *Weird and Wonderful: The Dime Museum in America* (New York: New York University Press, 1997), 30.

11 See Susan Riviere Hetzel, *The Building of a Monument* (Lancaster, PA: Wickersham Co., 1903).

12 *Gressitt v Colbert,* Stafford County Courthouse, Stafford, VA.

13 Ibid.

14 John W. Burgess, "Political Science and History," *The American Historical Review* 2, no. 3 (April 1897), 407.

15 There has only been one major study of Lossing, and that is Harold Mahan's *Benson J. Lossing, and Historical Writing in the United States, 1830–1890* (Westport, CT: Greenwood, 1996). However, Lossing was a significant milestone on the road to a professionalized historical craft.

16 David Muraca, Paul Nasca, and Philip Levy, *Report on the Excavation of the Washington Farm: The 2002 and 2003 Field Seasons,* The George Washington Foundation, Fredericksburg, VA State Site No. 44ST174, 2011; David Muraca, Paul Nasca, and Philip Levy, *Report on the Excavation of the Washington Farm: The 2004 and 2005 Field Seasons,* The George Washington Foundation, Fredericksburg, VA State Site No. 44ST174, 2010; David Muraca, Paul Nasca, and Philip Levy, *Report on the Excavations at the Washington Farm: The 2006 and 2007 Field Seasons,* The George Washington Foundation, Fredericksburg, VA State Site No. 44ST174, 2010.

17 England, "Washington's Old Home Farm," 737.

18 Lindgren, *Preserving the Old Dominion.*

19 "Colonial Days Reenacted at Dedication of Kenmore," *Washington Post* (May 10, 1925), 4.

20 England, "Washington's Old Home Farm," 742.

21 M. L. Weems, *The Life of Washington* ed. Peter Onuf (Armonk, NY: M. E. Sharp Press, 1996), 19, hereafter cited as *LoW.*

22 John Marshall, *The Life of George Washington* (New York: Walton Books, 1930), 2.

23 Washington Irving, "Life of George Washington," in Herbert L. Kleinfeld, ed., *The Complete Works of Washington Irving* (Boston: Twayne Publishers, 1982), 24–28.

24 Henry Cabot Lodge, *George Washington* (New York: Houghton Mifflin, 1898), 60.

25 Rupert Hughes, *George Washington: The Human Being and the Hero* (New York: William Morrow and Co., 1926), 43; W. E. Woodward,

George Washington: The Image and the Man (New York: Boni and Liverlight, 1926), 43.

26 George Allan England, "Washington's Home," *New York Times*, January 2, 1926, 12.

27 Frederick Jackson Turner, "The Significance of the Frontier in American History," in Martin Ridge, ed., *Frederick Jackson Turner: Wisconsin's Historian of the Frontier* (Madison: State Historical Society of Wisconsin, 1986).

28 There are only two published essays dedicated solely to England. One is Mark Pittinger's study of the racial and genocidal dimensions of England's best-known book, *Darkness and Dawn* (1914), "Imagining Genocide in the Progressive Era: The Socialist Science Fiction of George Allan England," *American Studies* 35, no. 1 (1994), 91–108. The other is my own essay dealing with England and his travel writing about Key West, Florida and other Caribbean places. "'The Most Exotic of Our Cities': Race, Place, Writing, and George Allan England's Key West," *The Florida Historical Quarterly* (April 2011), 431–61. See also "George Allan England: Writer, Linguist, and Sportsman," September 16, 1981, Collections of the Woodstock Historical Society Museum, Woodstock, ME. For a sample of England's writings on socialism, the future, and travel, see George Allan England, "International Socialism as a Political Force," *Wayland's Monthly* 99 (July 1908), 12. See also England, "Socialism and the Law: The Basis and Practice of Modern Legal Procedure and Its Relation to the Working Class," Fort Scott, KS: Legal Department Appeal to Reason, 1913; England, "Fiat Pax," New York: American Association for International Conciliation, 1914; England, "America's Island of Felicity," *Travel* (1928), 43; and England, *Darkness and Dawn*, Reprint ed. (Westport, CT: Hyperion Press Inc., 1974).

29 George Allan England, *Vikings of the Ice* (London: Hurst and Blackett, 1924).

30 England, "Washington's Old Home Farm," 742.

31 *LoW*, 8.

32 Ibid., 6.

33 Ibid., 6–7.

34 Ibid., 7.

35 Joseph Dillaway Sawyer, *Washington*, Vol. 1 (New York: Macmillan, 1927), 78–79.

36 The colonial revival had helped condition this as an era of interest in Washington preservation projects in Williamsburg, the George Washington Birthplace site, and other "nostalgia" efforts such as Henry Ford's Greenfield Village; all were part of the larger backdrop. See Lindgren, *Preserving the Old Dominion*; Bruggeman, *Here, George Washington Was Born*; and Marling, *George Washington Slept Here*; Patricia West, *Domesticating History: The Political Origins of America's House Museums* (Washington, DC: Smithsonian Books, 1999).

37 Harold Brackman, "'Yanked Down Out of Olympus'": Beard, Woodward, and Debunking Biography," *Pacific Historical Review* 52, no. 4 (November 1983), 416; Lengel, *Inventing George Washington*.

38 Henry Cabot Lodge, *The Life of George Washington*, Vol. 1 (New York: Houghton Mifflin, 1920), 43.

39 Lengel, *Inventing George Washington*, Chapter 6, 140–58.

40 Hughes, *George Washington*, 16, 23.

41 Woodward, *George Washington*, 16.

42 Sawyer, *Washington*, 79. He also confused his farm titles a bit later, calling the farm Pine Tree Farm (122), a name never used for the land.

43 Claude Bowers, "A Shelf of Recent Books," *The Bookman; A Review of Books and Life* 64, no. 4 (December 1926), 502.

44 Ibid.

45 Sawyer, *Washington*, 87–88.

46 Ibid., 78–79.

47 "Fredericksburg, The Home of Washington's Boyhood, and the Burial Place of His Mother," *Frank Leslie's Popular Monthly* 19, no. 2 (February 1885), 2. I refer to the copy available through the American Periodicals Database, and thus my pagination reflects theirs.

48 Ibid., 3.

49 The Joice Heth story has made a few recent appearances. The best and most thorough is Benjamin Reiss, *The Showman and the Slave: Race, Death, and Memory in Barnum's America* (Cambridge, MA: Harvard University Press, 2001).

50 *Colbert vs. Gressitt*, Stafford County Courthouse, Stafford, Virginia.

51 I covered this in narrative form in *Where the Cherry Tree Grew: The*

Story of Ferry Farm, George Washington' Boyhood Home (New York: St. Martin's Press, 2013).

52 "Charles Arthur Hoppin to Mrs. H. L. Rust," April 5, 1928, Correspondence, Hoppin, Box 1 Folder 3, GWA Papers, George Washington Birthplace National Monument, Westmoreland, VA.

53 Ibid.

54 Charles Arthur Hoppin, "The House in Which George Washington Was Born," *Tyler's Quarterly* 8, no. 2 (October 1926), 75.

55 Chester Goolrick, "Washington's Boyhood Home," *The New York Times* (January 2, 1927), XX12.

56 Hoppin's creative errors survived at least as late as 1998, when they reappeared in biographer Harrison Clark's *All Cloudless Glory: The Life of George Washington* (Washington, DC: Regnery Press, 1998). Clark cited Hoppin as his authority in making the same long-disproven argument. Clark was an enthusiast, and Regnery Press specializes in topics of special interest to Republican party members and movement conservatives. The book was their offering on a favorite topic and not in and of itself of any great consequence. During his research, Clark had a brief exchange with local Fredericksburg historian Paula Felder, in which she alerted him to the failings of Hoppin's argument. Clark's reply was that he found Hoppin's writing during his research at Mount Vernon, and that was good enough for him to believe it. "Harrison Clark to Paula Felder," Ferry Farm Files, Fredericksburg, VA.

57 Kishpaugh Postcard, Ferry Farm Archives, George Washington Foundation, Fredericksburg, VA.

58 HABS Report, "George Washington's Surveying Office," Architectural Drawing and Text Report. LOC, HABS Files. HABS no. VA-90. The entire archive of HABS drawings and reports is available online through the Library of Congress website.

59 "Eudora Ramsey Richardson to Henry Alaberg," March 31, 1939, WPA, Federal Writers' Project, Virginia Correspondence, 1938–June 1939, National Archives Annex, College Park, MD.

60 Joan Zenzen, *At the Crossroads of Preservation and Development: A History of Fredericksburg and Spotsylvania National Military Park* (Fredericksburg, VA: National Park Service, 2011).

61 George Allan England, *The Youth's Companion* 100, no. 7 (February 18, 1926), 136.

62 "Washington, George, Boyhood Home Site, National Historic Landmark Nomination," OMB No. 1024-0018, Washington, DC: United States Department of the Interior, National Park Service, 1999; Charles R. Marshall et al., "Proposed George Washington Boyhood Home, Ferry Farm: Suitability–Feasibility Report," Richmond: NPS, Virginia State Office, June 1972.

6. TO CHANGE THE WORLD

1 Peter Coates, "Emerging from the Wilderness (or, from Redwoods to Bananas): Recent Environmental History in the United States and the Rest of the Americas," *Environment and History* 10, no. 4 (November 2004), 407–38.

2 David Christian, "Bridging Two Cultures: History, Big History, and Science," *Historically Speaking* (May/June 2005), 21–26.

3 R. G. Collingwood, *The Idea of History* (New York: Oxford University Press, 1956), 212.

4 Dipesh Chakrabarty, "The Climate of History: Four Theses," *Critical Inquiry* 35, no. 2 (Winter 2009), 201.

5 Paul Crutzen and Eugene Stoermer, "The 'Anthropocene,'" *Global Change Newsletter* 41 (2000), 17.

6 Ibid.

7 Paul Dukes, *Minutes to Midnight: History and the Anthropocene Era from 1763* (London: Anthem Press, 2011), 127.

8 Ibid., 7–13.

9 Chakrabarty, "The Climate of History," 208.

10 Quoted in Chakrabarty, "The Climate of History," 210.

11 F. Gradstein, J. G. Ogg, M. D. Schmitz, G. M. Ogg, *The Geological Time Scale 2012*, 2 vols. (Amsterdam: Elsevier BV, 2012).

12 Paul Kingsnorth and Dougald Hine, *Uncivilization: The Dark Mountain Manifesto,* the Dark Mountain Project, http://dark-mountain.net.

13 In an interesting and somewhat earlier work, George Meyerson argued that environmental crisis and collapse heralded the end of postmodernism as the environment proved itself to be the very sort of metanarrative of which postmodern thought denied the existence. See George Meyerson, *Ecology and the End of Postmodernism* (London: Totem Books, 1997).

14 Dipesh Chakrabarty, "Keynote," The Anthropocene Project Conference, 2013; video recordings of the various presentations are available at http://www.hkw.de/anthropocene.

15 See Giovanni Arrighi, *The Long Twentieth Century: Money, Power, and the Origins of Our Times* (New York: Verso, 1994); and Joyce Appleby, *The Restless Revolution: A History of Capitalism* (New York: W. W. Norton, 2011).

16 Mark Levene, "Climate Blues: Of How Awareness of the Human End Might Re-instill Ethical Purpose to the Writing of History," *Environmental Humanities* 2 (2013), 159. See also David Cromwell and Mark Levene, eds., *Surviving Climate Change: The Struggle to Avert Global Catastrophe* (London: Pluto Press, 2007). See also David Glassberg, "Place, Memory, and Climate Change," *The Public Historian* 36, no. 3 (August 2014), 17–30.

17 Levene, "Climate Blues," 222.

18 *Bulletin of the Atomic Sciences,* http://thebulletin.org/overview.

19 Penelope Corfield, "Climate Reds: Responding to Global Warming with Relative Optimism," September 2011, http://rescue-history-from-climate-change.org/publications_articles.php. This paper was part of a Web-based discussion and was not meant as a detailed research presentation.

20 George Marshall, "Why We Find It So Hard to Act Against Climate Change" (December 1, 2009), http://www.yesmagazine.org. I thank Mark Levene for calling my attention to Marshall's work on the mindset of climate change denial.

21 Popular works on the topic include Mark Maslin, *Global Warming: A Very Short Introduction* (New York: Oxford University Press, 2004); Tim Flannery, *The Weather Makers: The History and Future Impact of Climate Change* (New York: Atlantic Monthly Press, 2006); Mark Lynas, *Six Degrees: Our Future on a Hotter Planet* (Washington, DC: National Geographic Society, 2008); William Calvin, *Global Fever: How to Treat Climate Change* (Chicago: University of Chicago Press, 2008); and David Archer and Stefan Rahmstorf, *The Climate Crisis: An Introductory Guide to Climate Change* (New York: Cambridge University Press, 2010).

22 Fred Anderson, *Crucible of War: The Seven Years' War and the Fate*

of Empire in British America, 1754–1766 (New York: Alfred Knopf, 2000), 7. Anderson not only begins his authoritative study of the war with this incident but ends the book at Mount Vernon as well, thus effectively bracketing this important conflict with images of Washington. An even grimmer assessment of Washington can be found in J. Frederick Fausz, "'Engaging in Enterprises Pregnant with Terror': George Washington's Formative Years Among the Indians," in Warren Hofstra, ed., *George Washington and the Virginia Backcountry* (Madison, WI: Madison House, 1998), 115–55.

23 The most detailed discussion of this enterprise is in Douglas Southall Freeman, *George Washington: A Biography*, Vol. 1 (New York: Charles Scribner's Sons, 1948).

24 William Byrd, *The Writings of Colonel William Byrd of Westover in Virginia, Esqr.*, ed. John Spencer Bassett (New York: Doubleday, Page, 1901), 345, 348–49, 350. See also Otis Young, "Origins of the American Copper Industry," *Journal of the Early Republic* 3, no. 2 (Summer 1983), 117–37.

25 See Bryan Ward-Perkins, "We'll Cope, Mankind Always Has: The Fall of Rome and the Cost of Crisis," in Mark Levene, Rob Johnson, and Penny Roberts, eds., *History at the End of the World?* (Penrith, England: Humanities E-Books, 2010), 46–52, for an essay dealing with similar issues of Holocene environmental degradation in the context of Anthropocene realities. See also John Brooke, *Climate Change and the Course of Global History: A Rough Journey* (New York: Cambridge University Press, 2014); "Forum: Climate and Early American History," *William and Mary Quarterly* 3rd Series, 72, no. 1 (January 2015).

26 "George Washington to James Rumsey, June 5, 1785," in John C. Fitzpatrick, ed., *The Writings of George Washington* (Washington, DC: Government Printing Office, 1931–1944), 28:159–60.

27 Frank Grizzard, *George Washington: A Biographical Companion* (Santa Barbara, CA: ABC-CLIO, 2002), 278.

28 Delores Hayden, *The Power of Place: Urban Landscapes as Public History* (Boston: MIT Press, 1997).

29 Levene, "Climate Blues," 159.

30 See Philip Deloria, *Playing Indian* (New Haven, CT: Yale University Press, 1999).

31 Some major works dealing with this issue include Alfred Crosby Jr., *The Columbian Exchange: Biological and Cultural Consequences of 1492, 30th Anniversary Edition* (Westport, CT: Praeger, 2003); Crosby, *Ecological Imperialism: The Biological Expansion of Europe, 900–1900,* 2nd ed. (New York: Cambridge University Press, 2004); William Cronon, *Changes in the Land: Indians, Colonists, and the Ecology of New England,* 2nd ed. (New York: Hill and Wang, 2003); Timothy Silver, *A New Face on the Countryside: Indians, Colonists, and Slaves in South Atlantic Forests, 1500–1800,* Studies in Environment and History (New York: Cambridge University Press, 1990); and Mark Fiege, *The Republic of Nature: An Environmental History of the United States* (Seattle: University of Washington Press, 2013).

32 Shiu Ying Hu, "Ailanthus," *Arnoldia* 39, no. 2 (1979), 29–50.

33 Ibid., 33.

34 William J. Bean, *Trees and Shrubs Hardy in the British Isles,* Vol. 1 (London: John Murray, 1919), 175; Shiu Ying Hu, "Ailanthus," 33.

35 A. H. Curtiss, "To the Editor," *Garden and Forest* (1888), 239.

36 "George Washington Surveying Office" Report, Drafting, and Photographs, 1935, Historic American Building Survey, Library of Congress Prints and Photographs Division, Washington, DC.

37 George Allan England, "Plea for Preservation," *Washington Post,* November 1, 1925, E2; Joseph Dillaway Sawyer, *Washington,* Vol. 1 (New York: Macmillan, 1927), 78–79.

38 Sol Bloom, *The Autobiography of Sol Bloom* (New York: G. P. Putnam and Sons, 1948), 217. See also Philip Levy, "The Farmer and the Bicentennial," in *Where the Cherry Tree Grew: The Story of Ferry Farm, George Washington's Boyhood Home* (New York: St. Martin's Press, 2013).

39 "Information and Work Plan for the George Washington Boys' Home (GWBH)," Archives of the Billy Graham Center, Wheaton, Illinois (ABGC), George Washington Boys' Home Files, unpaginated report; "Home Family Has Grown to 10," *Free Lance Star,* February 16, 1968, 7; William Lakeman, "Rezoning Sought for GWBH," *Free Lance Star,* May 23, 1969, 12; Paige Williams, "Stafford County Trying to Buy Washington's Boyhood Home, *The Washington Post,* August 11, 1988.

40 My account derives heavily from oral interviews conducted at Ferry Farm with Miliken now stored in the archives of the George Washington Foundation, Fredericksburg, VA. I offered a brief narrative of this project in *Where the Cherry Tree Grew*.

41 Carl Lounsbury, "Beaux-Arts Ideals and Colonial Reality: The Reconstruction of Williamsburg's Capitol, 1928–1934," *Journal of the Society of Architectural Historians* 49, no. 4 (December 1990), 373–89; William B. Rhoads, "The Colonial Revival and American Nationalism," *Journal of the Society of Architectural Historians* 35, no. 4 (December 1976), 239–54; Bridget May, "Progressivism and the Colonial Revival: The Modern Colonial House, 1900–1920," *Winterthur Portfolio* 26, no. 2 (Summer–Autumn 1991), 107–22; Barksdale Maynard, "The Early Nineteenth-Century Rediscovery of American Colonial Architecture," *Journal of the Society of Architectural Historians* 59, no. 3 (September 2000), 338–57; Seth Bruggeman, "Costumed Ladies and Federal Agents," in *Here, George Washington Was Born: Memory, Material Culture, and the Public History of a National Monument* (Athens: University of Georgia Press, 2008), 51–85; Karal Ann Marling, "The Colonial Revival: Heroic Imagery for the American Home, 1893–1924," in *George Washington Slept Here: Colonial Revivals and American Culture, 1876–1986* (Cambridge, MA: Harvard University Press, 1988), 151–84.

42 In working with this verse I referred primarily to biblical texts in the Chumash (the canonical printing of what is commonly called the Five Books of Moses) published by Artscroll, the main Orthodox Jewish publisher of biblical texts and commentary materials. *The Chumash: The Stone Edition* (New York: Mesorah Publications Ltd., 1993); *Sapierstien Edition Rashi* (New York: Mesorah Publications Ltd., 1999); *Baal Haturim Chumash* (New York: Mesorah Publications Ltd., 2003); *Ramban Chumash* (New York: Mesorah Publications Ltd., 2010).

43 Philip Birnbaum, ed., *Maimonides' Mishneh Torah* (New York: Hebrew Publishing Company, 1967), 321.

44 Ibid. A useful translation of this verse can be found online at http://www.on1foot.org/text/maimonides-mishneh-torah-laws-kings-610.

45 Levene, "Climate Blues," 222.

INDEX

Abarabanel, Isaac, 232
Accokeek Iron Furnace, 13, 109, 189; activities of, 213; and environment, 212–13
Adam, 150
Adams, John, 39, 140, 141; death of, 6
Ailanthus altissima, 202; history, of 216; removed from Ferry Farm, 228; and Surveying Office, 218
Ambler, Charles Henry, 64
American Historical Association, 177
American Revolution, memory of, 9
Anglican Church, 140
Anglican ministry, 140
Anglo-Saxons, 34–35
animals eaten at Ferry Farm, 117–18
Annapolis, Maryland, 140
Anne Arundel County, Maryland, 139, 141
Anthropocene age, 23, 207, 228; concept of, 206–7, 211; and fossil fuels, 219, 220, 225; history of, 209; and housing design 225; inspiring new colonial revival, 229; Weems and, 234
Appleby School, 50, 46, 127
Aquia sandstone, 123
archaeology: and biographies,

114; and Civil War, 163; and descriptions of the Washington home lot, 115; and diet, 117 and evidence of education, 114; and evidence of house fire, 73; and faunal remains, 116–17; and George Washington, 132; and George Washington's birthplace, 131, 195; and table wares, 73
architecture: and Holocene and Anthropocene, 215
Army Corps of Engineers, 223, 227
Arnold, S. G., 41
Atlantic World, 123, 132, 149
Aubert, Alvin, 201
automobiles, 220–21

ball clay pipes, 103
ball clay wig curlers, 119
Ball, Joseph, 15, 48, 110
Bancroft, Aaron, 31, 47, 49
Barnette, Stuart M., 195, 197
Barnum, P. T., 174, 190
Battle of Tel Chai, 174
Battle of the Boyne, 63
Belvoir Plantation, 79
Bezalel, Jacob Loew ben, 232
Bicentennial Celebration of 1976, 9
biography and archaeology, 113
Bloom, Sol, 220
Boy Scouts of America, 182

279

31901056889076

CPSIA information can be obtained at www.ICGtesting.com
Printed in the USA
LVOW08s0139050216

473690LV00003B/7/P

9 781940 425900